The Tokyo Trial and War Crimes in Asia

Mei Ju-ao

The Tokyo Trial and War Crimes in Asia

Second Edition

palgrave
macmillan

Mei Ju-ao
Shanghai, China

ISBN 978-981-15-9815-9   ISBN 978-981-15-9813-5 (eBook)
https://doi.org/10.1007/978-981-15-9813-5

Jointly published with Shanghai Jiao Tong University Press
The edition is not for sale in China Mainland. Customers from China Mainland please order the print book from: Shanghai Jiao Tong University Press.
ISBN of the China Mainland edition: 9787313183620

Translation from the Chinese language edition: 东京审判亲历记 by Ju-ao Mei, © Shanghai Jiao Tong University Press 2016. Published by Shanghai Jiao Tong University Press. All Rights Reserved.
1st edition: © Shanghai Jiao Tong University Press, All Rights Reserved 2018
2nd edition: © Shanghai Jiao Tong University Press 2020
This work is subject to copyright. All rights are solely and exclusively licensed by the Publisher, whether the whole or part of the material is concerned, specifically the rights of translation, reprinting, reuse of illustrations, recitation, broadcasting, reproduction on microfilms or in any other physical way, and transmission or information storage and retrieval, electronic adaptation, computer software, or by similar or dissimilar methodology now known or hereafter developed.
The use of general descriptive names, registered names, trademarks, service marks, etc. in this publication does not imply, even in the absence of a specific statement, that such names are exempt from the relevant protective laws and regulations and therefore free for general use.
The publishers, the authors, and the editors are safe to assume that the advice and information in this book are believed to be true and accurate at the date of publication. Neither the publishers nor the authors or the editors give a warranty, express or implied, with respect to the material contained herein or for any errors or omissions that may have been made. The publishers remain neutral with regard to jurisdictional claims in published maps and institutional affiliations.

Cover credit: The National Archives and Records Administration

This Palgrave Macmillan imprint is published by the registered company Springer Nature Singapore Pte Ltd.
The registered company address is: 152 Beach Road, #21-01/04 Gateway East, Singapore 189721, Singapore

An Old Foreword To The International Military Tribunal For The Far East (I)

Dr. Mei Ju-ao passed away years ago. However, my memories of him were triggered when Mei Xiao'ao, his son, came to me with his book, '*The International Military Tribunal for the Far East*' (unfinished), and asked me to write a prologue for it. I was pleased to do so, for both the reading public and my own pleasure. Although this book remains unfinished, it is of great significance because it introduces the establishment and development of war crime strategies after World War II. Implementation of these strategies, throughout the Tokyo Trial, further clarified the condemnation of aggressive war crimes. Like the Nuremberg Trial, the Tokyo Trial not only prosecuted conventional war crimes that went against the laws and customs of war as prescribed by international law, but also defined crimes against peace and crimes against humanity, and elaborated the concept of 'conspiracy' in aggression. While all the four chapters written by Dr. Mei elaborate upon the facts and procedures of the Tokyo Trial, Chapter 1 also explains the legal basis for punishing the Japanese Class-A war criminals. A general explanation cannot replace an in-depth legal analysis, but it still helps the readers understand the initiation and development of the Tokyo Trial; to further their understanding, they can also refer the Tribunal's final judgement text.

Furthermore, Dr. Mei's book reveals many details about the Tokyo Trial that outsiders to the Trial do not have access to, such as: the process of organizing the Tribunal, and the coordination between its various departments; listing of Class-A war criminals, and their arrest and interrogation; the seating arrangement of the bench, and its internal working system; the organization, duties and working procedures of the prosecution and the defence; and the participation of American defence lawyers, and its significance. However, it is a pity that the final stage of the Trial, that is, the process of convicting and sentencing the defendants (especially, the war criminals responsible for Chinese invasion), is not reflected in these four chapters. Dr. Mei may have planned to cover this interesting section in his subsequent chapters; it is regrettable that he could not. At the time of the Trial, the KMT ('Kuomintang', the Nationalist Party) government lacked sound judgement; they thought that since Japan had invaded China, the Trial must only be a formality, and the war criminals ought to be punished indiscriminately, without burdening native victims with evidence. However, to their great surprise, the United States sent a troop of lawyers to defend the accused; also, seven of the eleven judges came from common law countries. The imbalance between the prosecution and defence, favoured the accused. Although the Tokyo Charter stipulated that 'The Tribunal shall not be bound by technical rules of evidence', the Tribunal adopted common law procedures. Under pressure, China had to object to the mechanical application of highly technical rules of evidence, and also speedily obtain relevant evidences such as telegrams archived in Japan's Ministry of War, to produce at the final stage of cross-examination of the defendants and their witnesses; these evidences substantiated the allegations made against the accused. Consequently, the main aggressors against China, such as Kenji Doihara, Seishiro Itagaki, Iwane Matsui, Akira Muto and Koki Hirota, were duly convicted and sentenced to death, and their crimes were made known to the world.

China has adopted an 'opening-up' policy since the third plenary session of the Eleventh Central Committee of the Communist Party of China. Therefore, there has been a dramatic rise in the number of foreign-related cases, most of which are conducted abroad. 'To know both yourself and your enemy', we need to learn more about litigation procedures of other countries, especially those of common law countries, for which we currently lack sufficient material. In Chapter 4 of this book, Dr. Mei explains the trial procedures under the common law system and their practical applications. Despite differences, if any, between the Tokyo Trial as an international criminal trial, and foreign-related civil and commercial cases, many procedural rules (especially rules of evidence) are equally applicable for both. Dr. Mei's book not only contributes to research on procedural law, but provides much-needed references for dealing with foreign-related cases today.

Dr. Mei and I met in Chongqing during the War of Resistance against Japan. In early 1946, I visited the United States and Britain, and conducted a field survey on their judicial systems and practices. I was happy to learn that Dr. Mei would be a judge in the Tokyo Tribunal. I was invited to join the Chinese prosecution team in Tokyo in early 1947. While serving different roles, we both went through the tortuous process of the Tokyo Trial. It has been thirteen years since Dr. Mei passed away, and the rest of the Chinese personnel who worked for the Trial are now scattered in various places, excepting professors E Lvgong and Wu Xueyi who have also passed away. Mr. Xiang Zhejun (Che-chun Hsiang), the then Chinese prosecutor, is now 95 years old and confined to bed. Mr. Liu Zijian teaches at Princeton University, Mr. Gui Gongchuo at Taiwan University, and Messrs. Qiu Shaoheng, Yang Shoulin, Gao Wenbin, Zhou Xiqing and Zhang Peiji, at different universities in Beijing and Shanghai. Part of Mr. Qiu's work is associated with China's legal system. Mei Xiao'ao's visit has reminded me of events that happened over forty years ago, which I still vividly remember. I write this prologue with the hope that these former colleagues remain healthy, and continue to contribute to China's prosperity, world peace and human progress till their last breath.

I wish that I could meet my former colleagues again and recollect the past, and supplement this unfinished writing for Dr. Mei.

Beijing, China　　　　　　　　　　　　　　　　　　　　　　　Ni Zhengyu
August 1986

Ni Zhengyu (Judson T. Y. Nyi, 1906—2003), joined the Tokyo Trial in 1947–1948 and prosecuted Kenji Doihara, Seishiro Itagaki, Iwane Matsui and other Class-A Japanese war criminals. He was appointed as an associate fellow with the Institut de Droit International in 1991. He passed away in 2003 at the age of 97.

An Old Foreword To The International Military Tribunal For The Far East (II)

Dr. Mei Ju-ao, my dear friend, passed away more than ten years ago. His posthumous work, '*The International Military Tribunal for the Far East*' (unfinished), which has been published and circulated, is a blessing for the legal fraternity in China.

Dr. Mei dedicated his whole life to law. He studied law in his early years, and at the age of twenty-four, earned his J. D. (Juris Doctorate) from the University of Chicago. After returning to China, he involved himself in legal education and legislative work. In 1946, as the Chinese judge, he participated in the trial of major Japanese war criminals in the International Military Tribunal for the Far East in Tokyo, which lasted for nearly three years. On the eve of the founding of new China, the KMT government appointed him as the Minister of Justice; however, he refused to assume office and at his personal risk, returned to Beijing from Hong Kong. He then served as a legal adviser to the Ministry of Foreign Affairs—an office he held until his death. During this period, he attended many international conferences as an expert in law and diplomacy. Dr. Mei immensely contributed to law in his lifetime, and his work in the International Military Tribunal for the Far East is highly esteemed.

The trial of war criminals, as pointed out by Dr. Mei, 'was an extraordinary event in the international community after World War II, and was also a pioneering undertaking in the history of mankind'. Having failed in their objectives in World War I and hoping to succeed this time, the major allies of World War II reaffirmed the principle of punishing war criminals, in several agreements. Thus, two international military tribunals, in Nuremberg and Tokyo, were set up after the war for the trial of war criminals. The two tribunals successfully completed their functions in one year and two and a half years, respectively.

From the perspective of international law, war crimes and war criminals are new terminologies established during the Nuremberg and Tokyo trials. Their establishment demonstrates a new development in international laws, especially in those concerning war. There has always been a distinction between just and unjust wars in international law, but in modern times this is equivalent to the difference between wars of, and against aggression. Although we still do not have well-formed rules of international law governing such a distinction, wars of aggression have always been condemned. The punishment for war crimes is derived from the principles of differentiating wars of and against aggression, and condemning wars of aggression; this helps reinforce these principles in international law. Two trials of war criminals following World War II, i.e. the trials held in Nuremberg and Tokyo, mark a milestone in the history of international law.

Before his death in 1973, Dr. Mei documented his experience of the trial of war criminals in the International Military Tribunal for the Far East in 1962. Unfortunately, once the 'Cultural Revolution' broke out, his writing abruptly came to a halt and he could not resume it again in his lifetime. Therefore, this book is an unfinished draft of four chapters. However, despite being incomplete, the four chapters of the book have addressed many important problems such as the establishment of the Tribunal and its jurisdiction, the Charter and organization of the Tribunal, arrest and prosecution of major Japanese war criminals and trial procedures of the Tribunal. This book is rich in content and profound in its analysis. It is a valuable book that can serve as a reference for the study of international law and politics. Books on the International Military Tribunal for the Far East and trials of war criminals such as this, are rare and are of great significance.

As a jurist, it was a glorious and arduous task for Dr. Mei to participate in the trial of international war criminals. After overcoming setbacks such as insufficient support from the KMT government, and hindrance and delay by the international reactionary forces, he finally persuaded the International Military Tribunal for the Far East to pass a judgement against certain major Japanese war criminals—an action consistent with the requirements of justice.

Dr. Mei Ju-ao and I became friends in 1949. A few days after he returned to Beijing, we attended the inaugural meeting of the Chinese People's Institute of Foreign Affairs together. At the meeting, Premier Zhou Enlai praised Dr. Mei's work and remarked 'he has done a great thing for the people and won honour for the country', which was the best appraisal Dr. Mei had received for his work.

Beijing, China   Wang Tieya
May 1986

Wang Tieya (1913–2003), outstanding jurist of international law in modern China, professor at Peking University, and at Beijing Institute of Politics and Law. He also served as director of the Institute of International Law at Peking University. In 1987, he was elected Academician of the Academy of International Law. He died in Beijing in 2003 at the age of 90.

IN MEMORY OF OUR FATHER (FOREWORD)

Thanks to the efforts of the Tokyo Trial Research Center and Shanghai Jiao Tong University, this book of our father's is to be published, which is of great significance not only to our family but also to the country. It will undoubtedly facilitate an in-depth study of the Tokyo Trial, while being a record of our lingering memory of our beloved father, Dr. Mei Ju-ao.

I

Our late father, Mei Ju-ao, was born on 7 November 1904 in Zhuguqiao Mei Village in Nanchang, Jiangxi Province. Compared with provinces like Hunan, Guangdong, Jiangsu and Zhejiang, Jiangxi was slow to accept new trends. However, our grandfather, a well-informed, clear-minded and knowledgeable gentleman, decided to send his eldest son, our father, to the Exemplary Primary School of Jiangxi Province, a modern school which was at that time rarely known or praised. Under the steady support of our grandfather, our father, who was only twelve years old, was admitted to Tsinghua School in Beijing in 1916. Having no connections, being far away from home and unable to even speak the official language (Mandarin) well, he encountered many difficulties while studying at Tsinghua. Students had to strictly follow a semi-military timetable and actively participate in Western-styled physical exercises. No subject could be treated carelessly; if they did, they could be expelled from school or prevented from being promoted to the next grade. Many foreign teachers taught in English and most students had a good command over the language. However, father knew little English and so could hardly understand the lectures. He had no choice but to learn the language and be on par with the rest.

Every day, at the break of dawn, there would be two young students by the lotus pond on Tsinghua campus. Sometimes they mumbled to themselves or recited texts aloud, and other times they asked each other questions and answered them. As time progressed, they became fluent and sophisticated in their communication. The two students were our father and our grand-uncle, Mei Yangchun, studying English together. Mei Yangchun was only four years older than father, and was admitted to Tsinghua School from Jiangxi Province in the same year. Their relentless efforts paid off and they could now progress in other subjects. Their teachers and schoolmates took notice of their excellent academic records during their eight years at Tsinghua School. Later, Mei Yangchun became a famous engineer who managed the design and construction of important bridges such as the Nanjing Yangtze River Bridge.

Our father became ambitious and developed varied interests in his later years at Tsinghua. He served as chief editor of the Tsinghua School Magazine, and organized a progressive group named 'Chao Tao' together with some other students including Shi Huang, Ji Chaoding and Xu Yongying, who were early members of the Communist Party of China. Shi Huang died young as a martyr. Ji Chaoding and Xu Yongying engaged in revolutionary work and were prominent leaders in the 1950s and 60s.

In 1924, our father went to study in the United States. He studied at Stanford University and University of Chicago Law School, where he received his J.D. degree at the end of 1928. While staying abroad, he had been worried about the destiny of his own country. In response to the call for the Northern Expedition to 'overthrow the governance of the Northern warlords' by the National Revolutionary Army, he joined Shi Huang, Ji Chaoding, Xu Yongying and some other Chinese students in the United States, and established a research institute to study Dr. Sun Yat-sen's ideology, and to actively promote revolutionary ideas among Chinese students studying abroad.

In 1929, after visiting European cities such as Paris, Berlin, London and Moscow, he returned to China after an absence of nearly five years.

II

In the sixteen years spanning from his graduation to assuming the position of judge in the international court, father taught courses in civil law, criminal law, common law, international law and politics at Shanxi University, Nankai University and Wuhan University, successively. He also served as a part-time professor at Fudan University, Central School of Politics, and the Judge Training Institute of the Ministry of Justice. From 1934 onwards, he became a member of the Legislative Council of the KMT government, participated in its legislative work and served as acting chairman of its foreign affairs committee. At the same time, he worked as deputy director of Sun Yat-sen Institute for the Advancement of Culture and Education, and as chief editor of Collection of Current Affairs (a semi-monthly journal). As an editor, he wrote, translated and edited volumes of articles on law, foreign affairs and international politics.

His writings in this period centred around common law, civil law, Chinese and Western legal ideology and China's constitution and criminal law; some of his writings are: *A Research on the Anglo-Saxon System of Law*; *The Napoleonic Code and Its Influence*; *The History and Organization of Soviet Revolutionary Courts*; *The History, Schools and Trends of Modern Law*; *The Rule of Law in China's Old Legal System*; *Criticism of the Constitutional Guarantee Section of the Draft Constitution*; and *Comments on the Amendment to the Criminal Code*. His academic career represented his knowledge scope, theoretical and practical proficiency and rich research findings. His long experience in lecturing, investigating, reading and writing, laid a solid foundation for his legal theory and practice, which in turn prepared him for the position of an international court judge in Tokyo.

As a scholar of law, he had observed that under the political system of KMT's 'one-party dictatorship', 'the party is above all else. Each government act is based on the party's principles and assumes responsibility for the party alone. It does not make any contract with its people and has no obligation towards them. In other words, the party only has rights over the people, not obligations' (*Political Tutelage and Provisional Constitution*). Based on his observation that the law was used as a tool for the powerful and the rule of law could not be implemented, he posed a poignant question, 'What is destroying people's liberty and trampling on people's rights? Is it not the extralegal forces of government and the military through violence?' (*Comments on the Revised Initial Draft of the Constitution*)

Moreover, he was critical of the legal education at that time, an idea that may have arisen out of his teaching experience. Legal science and law should be taken seriously, 'however, law in China has become the most shallow and boring subject', and increasingly, teaching of law was just 'fiddling around'. The teacher taught for money, and the students learned for a diploma; therefore, 'the society often considers legal education as a means to earn a livelihood or manipulate people, and not as a science or an academic subject. The reasons why China's rule of law is not established, and its law is despised may vary, but the corruption of legal education is one of the leading causes' (*A Discussion on the Textbooks and References for Common Law Courses*).

The above examples are fragments of his thoughts on the science of law, which may continue to be significant today. (For the quoted articles, please refer to *A Collection of Mei Ju-ao's Essays on Law*, China University of Political Science and Law Press, 2007.)

In our father's time, land was seized and plundered, and people lived in grief. When father thought of his parents, relatives and friends being displaced because of the Japanese invasion, Chinese troops fighting in a bloody war, his fellow countrymen struggling under Japan's occupation, and some government officials profiteering from our nation's calamity, his mood was melancholy. One could say that he was as gloomy as the fog surrounding the wartime capital Chongqing (a mountain city known for its thick fog, where he lived during the war). However, he was impressed by Mr. Ma Yinchu's brilliant analysis of China's wartime economy, and his insightful comments in *Xinhua Daily* and *Ta Kung Pao*. Although the reality was grim, our father's ideals and faith in justice never waned. He only needed an opportunity to express them.

III

The Chinese, along with other peace-loving people of the world, have finally triumphed in the anti-fascist war after immense struggles and sacrifices. After the war, the international community established military tribunals in Nuremberg and Tokyo, where key offenders in Germany and Japan were respectively tried. In February 1946, the GHQ (General Headquarters) appointed nine judges (later increased to eleven) of the International Military Tribunal for the Far East (the 'Tokyo Trial'), on the nomination of the Allied Powers. As recommended by the concerned people, our father was appointed to the solemn trial seat on behalf of China.

Some of the popular captions used to describe the exploits of our father as a judge of the Tokyo Trial in the period between March 1946 and the end of 1948, were 'a sword given by compatriots as a present', 'a dispute over seating arrangements', 'insistence on the death penalty' and 'making an oath by the sea'. In the second chapter of *'The International Military Tribunal for the Far East'* (unfinished) enclosed in this book, father has meticulously presented the dispute over seating arrangements prior to the trial, and revealed its relevance to the nation's interests and dignity. He divulged details about heated debates on the measurement of penalty in *The Tokyo Trial Correspondence*, originally articulated in *The Tokyo Trial Manuscripts of Mei Ju-ao*—'after a long discussion, a heated argument ... and the complex and odd process, it is hard to explain everything in just a few words. Besides, it is also improper for me to make any disclosure here'. It is a pity that our father could not complete his writing of *'The International Military Tribunal for the Far East'* because of the 'Cultural Revolution'. Consequently, future generations will be unaware of the details of the discussion on the measurement of penalty, which were kept confidential by the then concerned judges.

Diary entries of about fifty days were also included in *The Tokyo Trial Manuscripts of Mei Ju-ao*, which traced our father's journey to Tokyo through the first few days of his court career. At the end of his personal diary, was the note: 'from [14 May 1946], to see in another notebook'. However, the 'other notebook' vanished without a trace during the 'Cultural Revolution'. From the brief notes in his diary, we can infer his feelings at that time.

Having received systematic legal training, he clearly distinguished between the function of the judges and prosecutors in the common law system. He was familiar with the judicial principles of presumed innocence, equality between defence and prosecution, neutrality of the judges, and benefit of doubt for the defendants. Being aware that the Chinese prosecutor Hsiang Che-chun was strenuously collecting evidence and drafting the indictment, father could not assist him because he had to uphold his judicial impartiality. It was also hard to explain to his fellow countrymen the relationship between a judge and a prosecutor, which made his situation complex.

In fact, the Tokyo Trial was both a legal arena, and a political and diplomatic occasion. It could not be equated with an ordinary court because the interests of different countries varied as world trends changed, and affected the Tokyo Trial. At the same time, disputes such as between 'substantive' and 'procedural' justice, problems of 'bias of the judge' or arguments on 'abolition of death penalty', could not be resolved by general principles in textbooks and opinions gathered from academic discussions. Therefore, they could not be the basis on which the Tokyo Trial, an exclusive trial for special circumstances, was appraised.

When serving as a judge in Tokyo, father continued to observe and reflect upon the Japanese society. He was worried about the destiny of his motherland and keenly aware that the post-war Japanese economy was not as bad as it was contrived to be, that is, they may have 'made a poor mouth' of the situation. In terms of national outlook and health, the Japanese were stronger than the Chinese. He wrote in his diary: 'I wonder why Gen. MacArthur's GHQ was so considerate of Japanese people for a presumed food scarcity, and why he made meticulous plans for them. Such a defeated country should really be regarded as "God's favoured one" as compared to my victorious country in great difficulty and misery; I cannot but sigh for our inferiority' (2 May 1946). 'However, we should be vigilant while being lenient ... What I am most concerned about is whether his (MacArthur's) policy is detrimental to the national interests or hindering the development of my country—this problem has been hovering in my mind all day today' (12 April 1946).

Although our father was Western educated, his affection for his country and homeland as a traditional Chinese intellectual was deeply rooted. 'Those who are in foreign countries are pained at their own country's failure to live up to their expectations' (9 April 1946), 'There is no better way to stop rumours than by self-cultivation, China has to win credit for herself' (26 April 1946), 'All my colleagues, sent by different countries are experienced and prestigious senior judges, so I have to work extremely conscientiously and sincerely, and never be sloppy' (10 April 1946), and 'I shall be vigilant! I shall be solemn! For, the opportunity of sitting at the bench today to punish these culprits was built on the flesh and blood of millions and millions of my compatriots' (3 May 1946). From an overview of father's diary, one notices the recurring phrases, 'to win credit for' and 'to be solemn'. In his telegram to the Minister of Foreign Affairs on 24 April 1948, he wrote: 'It is my duty to strive with all my might to win the victory of this unprecedented international war of law and justice.' Our father's sense of mission, and his vision of the overall situation was vividly depicted. Therefore, it is obvious that our father contributed immensely to the fairly satisfactory results of the Tokyo Trial.

IV

When the Tokyo Trial ended, the Chinese regime was in the process of being changed. Our father refused to accept the position of 'State Councillor and Minister of Justice' and move to Taiwan. He instead left for Beijing via Hong Kong. In Beijing, he served as an adviser to the Ministry of Foreign Affairs of the People's Republic of China (PRC), with a commission document signed by Zhou Enlai, premier and then foreign minister of the PRC.

Upon returning to the mainland, our father lived peacefully with liberal wages and benefits, and was highly esteemed for his professional work. He had a joyful time humming Peking opera music in the spacious courtyard, and sketching cartoons on the frosted windows. He taught his daughter nursery rhymes in his hometown dialect, and bought toy swords for his son. However, he could not help being nervous, as it was inevitable that he faced continuous political campaigns, reported ideologies, changed perspectives, and learnt Russian. Fortunately, the 'local climate' at the Ministry of Foreign Affairs, under the supervision of Zhou Enlai, Chen Yi and other senior leaders, was a little better than at other government institutions. Although the subjects of sociology and political science were abolished, and the Soviet Union legal theory was fully adopted in China, the senior experts of the Ministry of Foreign Affairs were still able to research on certain aspects of international law and politics; they could refer academic theories even as they attended to the immediate needs of the situation. By the time the 'Cultural Revolution' happened, Zhou Gengsheng, Liu Zerong and other seniors had published academic treatises; our father's work, '*The International Military Tribunal for the Far East*' was half-complete, and his papers, '*New Concept of War Crimes*' and '*On Tani Hisao, Matsui Iwane and the Nanking Massacre*' had been issued. Despite the unfair treatment that father had received from the Anti-Rightist Campaign, from 1957 to 1958, he continued to be introspective and patriotic, and contributed to research work.

However, when the 'Cultural Revolution' broke out, the relatively pleasant atmosphere of the Ministry of Foreign Affairs changed into a turbulent one. Our father was labelled as a 'reactionary academic authority' and his writing materials, such as notes, cards, clippings and diaries were confiscated. It was now impossible for him to continue writing '*The International Military Tribunal for the Far East*'. Apart from being forced to do manual labour under surveillance as a reformative measure, he also had to waste his time and energy writing 'investigation materials' and 'self-critical reports'. His health deteriorated as he heard the horrific accounts of deaths; the news of some old acquaintance committing suicide, or beaten to death was always being circulated. Sadly, he did not live to see the end of the 'Cultural Revolution', but passed away on 23 April 1973, at the age of 68.

Like many intellectuals who assume social responsibility, father continued to worry about the nation even in his difficult, later years. Our father submitted written resolutions against 'revolutionary rebels' who engaged in riotous behaviour such as setting fire to the British Office of the Chargé d' Affaires, and seizing power of the ministry, thus hurting public sentiments and damaging the nation's reputation. Without fearing for his own safety, he advised investigating, and preventing the actions of the transgressors. In response to the charges that he was a 'reactionary academic authority', 'opposer of Sino-Japanese friendship', 'supporter of US-Japanese reactionaries' and 'believer in the restoration of the old regime', he defended himself by saying 'I am nothing but a little, broken outdated dictionary', 'I have no special skills, not even a decent work that I've written…', 'As is known to all, I was the most earnest person to reveal the ambitious collusion of the US and Japan to resurrect militarism', and 'I was a principal offender wanted by the Kuomintang government. On a lighter note, should the restoration of the old regime take place, I am afraid that I would be killed by them earlier than you, young comrades!'

Today, of all our father's remarks which were full of significance, the one most frequently quoted is from the paper '*On Tani Hisao, Matsui Iwane and the Nanking Massacre*': 'I am not a revanchist. Neither do I intend to ascribe the debt of blood owed to us by the Japanese imperialists to the Japanese people. I believe, however, that to forget the suffering of the past is to be vulnerable to tragedy in the future.' Who would have thought that the words 'to forget the suffering of the past is to be vulnerable to tragedy in the future' would be rebuked for 'slandering our party's forgetfulness'? In fact, a few years before he made that remark, he made some other observations that were equally thought-provoking: 'Some problems shall be ascribed to the system rather than to certain people. For instance, Liu Qingshan grafted several billions (old denomination), which would have been impossible even in the KMT days. So, we should initiate reform at the institutional level.' 'We are facing serious problems by craving greatness and success, being subjective and doing things beyond our means in order to be impressive (in economic construction).' 'It is dogmatism to worship and fawn on the Soviet Union as if they were a deity, and to follow the words of the "Soviet experts" like golden rules.'

A line from an ancient poem: 'The sound lingers when the vermilion string is flicked, as it comes from a lonely heart in the past', best describes our father's later years and his resonating impact upon our lives.

It has been forty years since our beloved father left us. The things he left behind remain unaltered, and the trees by his graveyard have grown tall. We are grateful that the nation's rule of law has begun to change for the better, and an in-depth study of the Tokyo Trial has finally been carried out. We hope that our profound regret regarding our father's lost work could be satiated by the focussed efforts of our youngsters today. This would be such a blessing for both our late father and the country.

Beijing, China
September 2013

Mei Xiaokan
Mei Xiao'ao

About This Book

This is an unfinished manuscript which is written in the period between 1962 and 1965. In Mei's original plan, there were to be seven chapters, out of which only the first four were completed, and are presented in this book. The 'Cultural Revolution' disrupted his writing, during which all his manuscripts were confiscated, and Mei was politically persecuted. In his later years, he managed to recover the handwritten manuscript of the four completed chapters. Fifteen years after his death in 1973, these four chapters were first published by China's Law Press, under the title of '*The International Military Tribunal for the Far East*', and republished as a newer edition in 2005. It is evident that these chapters bear historical significance. Unfortunately, Mei's synopsis, un-transcribed writings and reference materials for the remainder of the book are nowhere to be found—a sad loss for historians and legal scholarship. Ni Zhengyu and Wang Tieya, two prominent figures in international law who enthusiastically supported Mei's publications, passed away after the manuscript was first published, and their prefaces are included in this book. Xiaokan and Xiao'ao, Mei's daughter and son, not only edited his initial publication in the 1980s, but also immensely contributed to each of the subsequent editions and collections. Their preface, 'In Memory of Our Father' beautifully summarizes Mei's life. Finally, please note that Chinese names in this book largely follow the standard Chinese Pinyin system, and the Chinese convention of placing the family name before the first name; whereas,

Japanese names follow the Western convention, wherein the first name precedes the family name.

Contents

1 **Establishment and Jurisdiction of the International Military Tribunal for the Far East**   1
  1.1 *International Trials of Major War Criminals: A Pioneering Undertaking After World War II*   1
  1.2 *Lessons Learned from the Failure of International Trials After World War I*   2
  1.3 *Preparatory Work During World War II*   4
  1.4 *Process of Establishing the Two Tribunals*   5
  1.5 *Jurisdiction of the Two Tribunals*   10
  1.6 *Class-A War Criminals and International Trials*   35

2 **Charter and Organization of the International Military Tribunal for the Far East**   39
  2.1 *Introduction to the Tokyo Charter*   39
  2.2 *Location and Layout of the Tokyo Tribunal*   45
  2.3 *Members of the Tribunal: Judges and President*   53
  2.4 *International Prosecution Section*   76
  2.5 *The Defence: Japanese and American Counsel*   87
  2.6 *Administrative and Personnel Arrangements*   100

3 **Arrest and Prosecution of Japanese Major War Criminals**   119
  3.1 *Four Arrest Warrants from the General Headquarters*   119

3.2	Investigation and Preparation for Prosecution by the IPS	138
3.3	Selection and Bibliographic Information of the 28 Defendants	149
3.4	Eleven Countries' Indictment Against Japanese Major War Criminals	184
3.5	Characteristics and Defects of the Indictment	208

4 Trial Proceedings of the International Military Tribunal for the Far East 219

4.1	Basic Provisions on Trial Proceedings in the Tokyo Charter	219
4.2	Procedures for the Presentation and Admission of Evidentiary Documents	222
4.3	Procedures for the Attendance and Testifying of Witnesses	233
4.4	Affidavits from Non-attending Witnesses and the Defendants' Confessions	253
4.5	Criticism of the Trial Proceedings	261

Index 269

About the Author

Mei Ju-ao was born in Nanchang, Jiangxi Province in 1904. He graduated from Tsinghua School (predecessor of Tsinghua University) in 1924 and then travelled to the United States to study at Stanford University and University of Chicago Law School, where he received his J.D. degree. After returning to China in 1929, Mr. Mei worked successively or simultaneously, as a professor at Shanxi University, Nankai University, Wuhan University, Fudan University and the Central Political School. During that time, he taught courses such as political science, civil law, criminal law, introduction to the common law, and international law. From 1934 onwards, he served as a member of the Legislative Council of the KMT government, and an acting chairman of its Foreign Affairs Committee. After the victory of the 'War of Resistance' against Japan, he was designated to be the judge of the International Military Tribunal for the Far East representing China, by the government, in 1946. In about three years of trial work, he made great efforts to safeguard national dignity and maintain international justice; he always strived to pass a just sentence. At the end of 1948, the KMT government appointed him as Councillor of the Executive Council and Minister of Justice, but he refused to assume office and fled to Hong Kong. He arrived in Beijing under the arrangements made by the representatives of the Communist Party of China, in early December 1949. From 1950 onwards, he served as an adviser to the Ministry of Foreign Affairs, a representative to the National People's Congress and member of its Bills Committee, a member of the Chinese People's Political Consultative Conference and World Peace Council, the Executive Director of the Chinese People's Institute of Foreign Affairs, and Director of the Chinese Society of Political Science and Law. Mr. Mei suffered injustice in the 'Anti-Rightist Movement' and the 'Cultural Revolution' and passed away in Beijing in 1973, at the age of 68.

LIST OF FIGURES

Fig. 2.1	Courtroom of the International Military Tribunal for the Far East	49
Fig. 2.2	Diagram of the courtroom	52
Fig. 2.3	The judges	54
Fig. 2.4	The prosecutors	82
Fig. 3.1	The Class-A war criminals	155
Fig. 4.1	Prosecution and defence	223
Fig. 4.2	Puyi's testimony	254

CHAPTER 1

Establishment and Jurisdiction of the International Military Tribunal for the Far East

1.1 INTERNATIONAL TRIALS OF MAJOR WAR CRIMINALS: A PIONEERING UNDERTAKING AFTER WORLD WAR II

World War II was a fiasco for the Axis Powers; Germany surrendered on 8 May 1945, and Japan, on 2 September 1945.

Following Germany's and Japan's surrender, the Allied Powers established two international tribunals in Nuremberg (Germany) and Tokyo (Japan) called the International Military Tribunal (also known as the 'Nuremberg Tribunal' or the 'Nuremberg Trial'), and the International Military Tribunal for the Far East (also known as the 'Tokyo Tribunal' or the 'Tokyo Trial'), respectively.

Despite the minor differences in the organization of the two tribunals (refer Chapter 2), they shared common objectives—to arrest, investigate, prosecute, try and sentence some of the key leaders of the Axis Powers as primary major war criminals.[1] These major war criminals or 'Class-A war criminals', of Nazi Germany and fascist Japan, were fundamentally responsible for the planning, preparation, initiation or waging

---

[1] Article 1 of *Charter of the International Military Tribunal*: 'In pursuance of…, there shall be established an International Military Tribunal for the just and prompt trial and punishment of the major war criminals of the European Axis.' Article 1 of *Charter of the International Military Tribunal for the Far East*: 'The International Military Tribunal for the Far East is hereby established for the just and prompt trial and punishment of the major war criminals in the Far East.'

© Shanghai Jiao Tong University Press 2020
M. Ju-ao, *The Tokyo Trial and War Crimes in Asia*,
https://doi.org/10.1007/978-981-15-9813-5_1

of wars of aggression. They played a crucial role in the formulation and implementation of state policies pertaining to wars of aggression.

The trial of the Class-A war criminals by officially organized international courts through legal procedures, was a commendable feat by the international community after World War II, and a pioneering undertaking in human history. Prior to that, the leaders of a defeated country, even if they were the instigators of wars of aggression, were beyond the reach of law and could not be subject to court trials or legal sanctions.

Historically, it was not uncommon for the head of state or a government official to be killed or imprisoned by the enemy during war. A well-known example is that of Napoleon I, who was exiled for life on the island of St. Helena after being defeated by Britain, Russia, Austria and Prussia in 1815; but his exile was not a decision adjudicated by any international tribunal or domestic court. To impose legal sanctions on the leaders of defeated countries was indeed a creative action after World War II.

1.2 Lessons Learned from the Failure of International Trials After World War I

At the end of World War I, the Allies had wished to subject the German head of state and senior officials to international trials; however, they could not, and their failure was a farcical situation in history.

During and after World War I, the slogan 'hang the Kaiser' was rampant among the Allied and Associated Powers. Since the War was of unprecedented magnitude, and resulted in huge losses and widespread human suffering, the victims loathed Kaiser Wilhelm II and the German leaders who initiated the War. They desired to avenge their suffering by inflicting swift and severe punishment upon the German leaders.

At the Paris Peace Conference in 1919, there was a proposal to legally punish the Kaiser and other important war criminals in accordance with the four articles (Articles 227–230) of Chapter 7, under the subtitle, 'Penalties' of the Treaty of Versailles.

According to Article 227, 'a special tribunal will be constituted to try' Kaiser Wilhelm II, 'for a supreme offence against international morality and the sanctity of treaties'. Additionally, Article 228 stipulates that 'the German Government recognizes the right of the Allied and Associated Powers to bring before military tribunals' the main instigators and perpetrators of the war under the Kaiser.

In accordance with these provisions of the Treaty of Versailles, the Peace Conference appointed an international commission to research on individual responsibilities towards the war, list the names of the guilty and draft a charter for the tribunal; these functions were duly accomplished by the commission.

However, the attempts of the Allied and Associated Powers to conduct trials on major German war criminals went in vain because of the following reasons:

1. The victory of the Russian October Revolution in 1917 stunned the capitalist ruling classes of the Allied and Associated powers, and their attention was diverted to circumvallating Russia and dealing with the Soviet regime. Consequently, the implementation of relevant provisions in the Treaty of Versailles to penalize war criminals, took a backseat.
2. Disagreements arose among the Allied Powers, especially between Britain and France. After World War I, France appeared to dominate the European continent, which was against Britain's traditional policy of power balance. Curbing French control and protecting German interests thus became the basic motivations of the British foreign policy.
3. The German government stubbornly resisted the idea of extraditing war criminals for international trials.

Consequently, the Kaiser and other major war criminals were not penalized according to the provisions in the Treaty of Versailles. Following the failure to organize an international tribunal as stipulated by the Treaty, the Allied Powers, for their own convenience, entrusted the subject of trials to the German government itself.

The German government did not begin work until May 1921, that is, two and a half years after the War ended. Finally, an inconsequential 'trial', that gained no respect, was conducted in Leipzig by its own supreme court.

In accordance with the Treaty of Versailles, the Allied Powers presented a list of 896 major war criminals to the German government for arrest and prosecution. The German government repudiated it, and reduced the number of proposed war criminals to 45 to perform an 'experimental trial' upon them, following which they promised to try more offenders.

Only 12 of the accused were tried, out of which, only six were convicted. The convicts were mildly punished with imprisonment for a term ranging from six months to four years. Two of the six convicted escaped from prison, presumably with the aid of German officials.

Therefore, the Leipzig Trials only mildly punished four trivial offenders. When Karl Stenger, an infamous and murderous German general, was declared innocent by the court, the spectators cheered and eulogized him as a national hero. Kaiser Wilhelm II, who ought to have borne the greatest responsibility for World War I, fled to the Netherlands before the war ended. The Netherlands refused to extradite him because it would be a violation of its constitution and tradition. He was then allowed to live freely without any legal sanction.

Thus, the Leipzig Trials, the world's first attempt to try major war criminals after World War I,[2] is regarded as a farcical event in history.

We can infer from the above events that the desire to punish the instigators and perpetrators of war had emerged in the international community by the time the Second World War began. Although the Leipzig Trials failed, the new idea of making war criminals accountable for their actions was born. The lessons learnt from their failed attempts enabled the international community to conduct fairly smooth trials of major war criminals, after World War II.

1.3 Preparatory Work During World War II

When World War II was still being fiercely fought, the Allied Powers (at that time, also called 'the United Nations', referring to the countries fighting against the Axis Powers, and not the organization established in New York after World War II) had already reached some agreements, and made the following preparations for the punishment of war criminals after the war:

1. On 13 January 1942, nine countries—Belgium, Czech Republic, Greece, the Netherlands, Poland, Yugoslavia, Luxemburg, Norway and France—issued a joint declaration, affirming that one of the main objectives of the war was to punish war criminals.

---

[2] For details about the Leipzig Trials, see Mullins, *Leipzig Trials* (1921).

2. In October 1943, the United Nations Commission for the Investigation of War Crimes was founded in London. It comprised the above-mentioned nine countries, as well as China, the United States and the United Kingdom.
3. On 1 November 1943, the Soviet Union, the United States and the United Kingdom jointly issued a Statement on Atrocities at the conclusion of the Moscow Conference. In addition to re-affirming that war criminals must be punished, it stated that all the war criminals who committed atrocities 'will be sent back to the countries in which their abominable deeds were done in order that they may be judged and punished according to the laws of these liberated countries and of free governments which will be erected therein'. The Statement also declared that it 'is without prejudice to the case of German criminals whose offenses have no particular geographical localization and who will be punished by joint decision of the governments of the Allies', meaning that the leaders and the war instigators of the Axis Powers should be tried by an international tribunal, jointly organized by the Allied Powers.

In addition to the combined decisions of the above-mentioned governments, the leaders of the Allied Powers issued stern resolutions about the post-war punishment of war criminals, the most prominent ones being:

1. On 30 July 1943, President Roosevelt of the United States issued a diplomatic note warning the neutral nations against giving protection to war criminals.
2. On 6 November 1943, Marshall Stalin of the Soviet Union stated that 'all the fascist criminals responsible for the present war and the sufferings of the people shall bear stern punishment'.[3]

1.4 Process of Establishing the Two Tribunals

Germany surrendered in May 1945. From 17 July 1945, the United Kingdom, the United States and the Soviet Union held a conference in Berlin which concluded with the renowned Potsdam Agreement.

---

[3] For the statements, diplomatic correspondence and declarations, see S. Glueck, *War Criminals: Their Prosecution and Punishment*, Appendix B, pp. 109–113.

Chapter 6 of the Potsdam Agreement, subtitled 'War Criminals', reaffirms the determination of the three governments to 'bring to swift and sure justice' the key war criminals affiliated with Hitler's regime. It states that 'they regard it as a matter of great importance that the trial of these major criminals should begin at the earliest possible date'.[4] Prior to this, at a conference held in Yalta, Crimea, the three powers seriously contemplated the punishment of major German war criminals. The Yalta Conference resolved to 'bring all criminals to just and swift punishment'.[5]

Driven by the Allied Powers' resolve (repeatedly expressed during and after the war), the representatives of the Soviet Union, the United States, the United Kingdom and France convened in London to discuss the establishment of an international military tribunal to try the major Nazi war criminals. On 8 August 1945, they signed the London Agreement for the establishment of the tribunal and its annex, *Charter of the International Military Tribunal* (the 'Nuremberg Charter'), which stipulated the constitution, jurisdiction and powers of the Nuremberg Tribunal, and the principles for the conduct of the trial.[6]

The organizational work was completed about two months after signing the London Agreement and the Nuremberg Charter. On 18 October 1945, the Nuremberg Tribunal accepted the indictment against 22 major war criminals, including Hermann Göring and Rudolf Hess, and the court hearings began on 20 October 1945.

However, the International Military Tribunal for the Far East was founded in a slightly different manner than the Nuremberg Tribunal. It was not formed directly under an international agreement, but by the Supreme Commander for the Allied Powers in Tokyo, as authorized by a series of international documents, including the Potsdam Declaration, the Japanese Instrument of Surrender and the resolutions of the Moscow Conference of Foreign Ministers.

---

[4] For the provision about punishing war criminals, see *Collection of International Treaties (1945–1947)*, World Affairs Press (ed.), pp. 87–88.

[5] For the Yalta Conference Communique, ibid., p. 8.

[6] For the London Agreement and the attached Nuremberg Charter, ibid., pp. 94–103. By the end of 1945, it was signed by Australia, Belgium, Czech Republic, Denmark, Ethiopia, Greece, Haiti, Honduras, India, Luxembourg, the Netherlands, New Zealand, Norway, Panama, Paraguay, Poland, Uruguay, Venezuela and Yugoslavia.

The Potsdam Declaration was jointly announced on 26 July 1945, by China, the United States and Great Britain, and was later adhered to by the Soviet Union. The purpose of the Declaration was to prompt the Japanese armed forces to surrender unconditionally, and provide the requisite terms for their surrender. Paragraph 6 of the Declaration stated that 'there must be eliminated for all time, the authority and influence of those who have deceived and misled the people of Japan into embarking on world conquest, for we insist that a new order of peace, security and justice will be impossible until irresponsible militarism is driven from the world'. Paragraph 10 declared that 'we do not intend that the Japanese shall be enslaved as a race or destroyed as a nation, but stern justice shall be meted out to all war criminals, including those who have visited cruelties upon our prisoners'.[7]

On 2 September 1945, Mamoru Shigemitsu and Yoshijirō Umezu, the foreign minister and the army chief of staff, respectively, signed the 'Instrument of Surrender' for Japan and submitted it to Douglas MacArthur (the representative of the nine Allied Powers), accepting their surrender. The Instrument accepted all the terms as required by the Potsdam Declaration, in the statement: 'We, acting by command of and on behalf of the Emperor of Japan, the Japanese Government and the Japanese Imperial General Headquarters, hereby accept the provisions set forth in the declaration issued by the heads of the governments of the United States, China and Great Britain on 26 July 1945, at Potsdam, and subsequently adhered to by the Union of Soviet Socialist Republics'. Its paragraph 6 stated that 'we hereby undertake for the Emperor, the Japanese Government and their successors to carry out the provisions of the Potsdam Declaration in good faith'.[8]

Since Japan accepted all the provisions of the Declaration, it follows that it should abide by the specification—'stern justice shall be meted out to all war criminals'.

However, while specifying the conditions for Japan's surrender, the Potsdam Declaration did not mention any procedures for their implementation. Although the US government, with General MacArthur as the Supreme Commander for the Allied Powers, had exclusive authority over matters related to the occupation and control of post-war Japan, and

---

[7] Potsdam Declaration, see *Collection of International Treaties (1945–1947)*, pp. 77–78.
[8] The Instrument of Surrender, ibid., pp. 112–114.

the implementation of its terms of surrender, it still needed a legal basis authorized by the Allied Powers to exercise its authority. The agreement made in December 1945 at the Moscow Conference of Foreign Ministers by the Soviet Union, the United States and the United Kingdom, and concurred by China, provided the necessary legal basis for the US government. Moreover, this agreement became a unanimous resolution of the four big powers at war with Japan.

The agreement required the Supreme Commander for the Allied Powers to take the necessary steps to 'issue all orders for the implementation of the Terms of Surrender, the occupation and control of Japan'. While the agreement empowered the Supreme Commander, it also obliged him to implement the provisions of the Potsdam Declaration, including the punishment of war criminals.[9]

Consequently, Douglas MacArthur, the Supreme Commander for the Allied Powers, upon consultation with the Allied Powers, issued a *Special Proclamation for Establishment of an International Military Tribunal for the Far East* on 19 January 1946, reading as follows:

> Whereas, the United States and the Nations allied therewith in opposing the illegal wars of aggression of the Axis Nations, have from time to time made declarations of their intentions that war criminals should be brought to justice;

---

[9] Douglas MacArthur was the Supreme Commander for the Allied Powers in Tokyo after the war. As one of the three five-star General of the Army, he behaved rather arrogantly. He was a field marshal in the Philippines when the Japanese attacked the Pearl Harbour in December 1941, and was after that appointed as Commander-in-Chief of US Army Forces Pacific and the Supreme Commander for the Allied Powers. Douglas MacArthur presided over the war against Japan until it formally surrendered on 2 September 1945, when he served as the general representative of the Allied forces accepting the surrender. Since the US army occupied Japan, he arrogated to himself all the power, acting like an 'emperor's father'. It is true that in the initial stage of occupation when the memory of Japanese aggression was fresh and the US tendency of harbouring Japanese war criminals was not fully unveiled, his actions were congruous with the assigned responsibilities such as democratic reforms and punishment of war criminals. At that prime time, the International Military Tribunal for the Far East was established. But soon after, MacArthur released without authorization, in two times, 40 or so alleged Class-A war criminals who had been arrested and were waiting to be prosecuted in the second and third rounds of trials. When the first group of the 25 Class-A war criminals were sentenced and the seven capital prisoners executed, all those Class-A war suspects were released by him. With no one else to be prosecuted, the Tribunal virtually disbanded.

Whereas, the Governments of the Allied Powers at war with Japan on 26 July 1945 at Potsdam, declared as one of the terms of surrender that stern justice shall be meted out to all war criminals including those who have visited cruelties upon our prisoners;

Whereas, by the Instrument of Surrender of Japan executed at Tokyo Bay, Japan, on 2 September 1945, the signatories for Japan, by command of and in behalf of the Emperor and the Japanese Government, accepted the terms set forth in such Declaration at Potsdam;

Whereas, by such Instrument of Surrender, the authority of the Emperor and the Japanese Government to rule the state of Japan is made subject to the Supreme Commander for the Allied Powers, who is authorized to take such steps as he deems proper to effectuate the terms of surrender;

Whereas, the undersigned has been designated by the Allied Powers as Supreme Commander for the Allied Powers to carry into effect the general surrender of the Japanese armed forces;

Whereas, the Governments of the United States, Great Britain and Russia at the Moscow Conference, 26 December 1945, having considered the effectuation by Japan of the Terms of Surrender, with the concurrence of China have agreed that the Supreme Commander shall issue all Orders for the implementation of the Terms of Surrender.

Now, therefore, I, Douglas MacArthur, as Supreme Commander for the Allied Powers, by virtue of the authority so conferred upon me, in order to implement the Term of Surrender which requires the meting out of stern justice to war criminals, do order and provide as follows:

ARTICLE 1. There shall be established an International Military Tribunal for the Far East for the trial of those persons charged individually, or as members of organizations, or in both capacities, with offenses which include crimes against peace.

ARTICLE 2. The constitution, jurisdiction and functions of this Tribunal are those set forth in the Charter of the International Military Tribunal for the Far East, approved by me this day.

ARTICLE 3. Nothing in this Order shall prejudice the jurisdiction of any other international, national or occupation court, commission or other tribunal established or to be established in Japan or in any territory of a United Nation with which Japan has been at war, for the trial of war criminals.[10]

Soon after this Special Proclamation and the *Charter of the International Military Tribunal for the Far East* (the 'Tokyo Charter') were published, the Supreme Commander for the Allied Powers appointed 11 judges as nominated by their respective home countries: on 15 February 1946—from China, the United States, the United Kingdom, the Soviet Union, Australia, Canada, France, the Netherlands and New Zealand; and in April 1946—from India and the Philippines.

However, as some judges arrived in Tokyo later than others, it was not until 29 April 1946 that the Tribunal accepted the indictment against 28 major war criminals prepared by the International Prosecution Section (IPS) under the Supreme Commander for the Allied Powers. The trial, which was open to public, officially began on 3 May 1946.[11]

1.5 Jurisdiction of the Two Tribunals

1.5.1 Conceptual Evolution of 'War Crimes'

The Tokyo Charter, which was promulgated on 19 January 1946, was divided into five sections and 17 articles; it included topics on the Tribunal's functions and powers (i.e. jurisdiction), its constitution (i.e. internal organization and personnel), and its main principles for the evidence, court hearing, judgement, review, and sentence reduction. The articles on jurisdiction will be first discussed for the following reasons:

---

[10] For the No. 1 Special Proclamation of the Supreme Commander for the Allied Powers in Tokyo (19 January 1946), see US State Department, *Trial of Japanese War Criminals* (Publication No. 2613). It was also reported in Chinese and foreign newspapers at the time.

[11] It was three and a half months between the time when its Charter was published and judges named, and the opening date of the Tribunal, mainly because of the late arrival of some of the judges. The judge from the Soviet Union, accompanied by the Soviet prosecutor and their staff members, arrived only two days before the proceedings started. It was said that his delay was due to the General Headquarters (GHQ) of the Supreme Commander for the Allied Powers deliberately placing obstacles to their entry: the Soviet Union had intended to send a team of 70 people to work for its judge and prosecutor, but the GHQ under the US control considered the team too large and refused to issue visas. Through negotiations back and forth, only about 20 people were allowed to come. This story fully shows the arrogance and dominance of the United States.

1. The jurisdiction provisions in the Tokyo Charter were primarily responsible for the establishment and existence of the Tribunal. The Tribunal's jurisdiction was a fiercely debated topic during trial; the defence lawyers incessantly attacked the Tribunal's jurisdiction and many law scholars in Western countries challenged it. It must be borne in mind that before World War II, the international law principles in this area were not perspicuous.
2. The Tribunal affirmed the jurisdiction provisions in the Tokyo Charter, and exercised them. Consequently, the Nuremberg and Tokyo Trials clarified and developed the traditional concepts of war crimes, and made significant contributions to modern international law. On 11 December 1946, the First Session of the UN General Assembly adopted a resolution that 'affirmed' the principles of international law recognized by the Nuremberg Charter and the Judgement of the Nuremberg Tribunal.[12]

Owing to the above-mentioned reasons, I believe that a preliminary introduction to the jurisdiction provisions in the Tokyo Charter is necessary to understand the work and mission of the Tribunal. Topics pertaining to the constitution and trial procedures will be addressed later in the book.

The jurisdiction of the International Military Tribunal for the Far East is provided in Article 5 of the Tokyo Charter, and reads as follows:

> ARTICLE 5. *Jurisdiction over Persons and Offenses* The Tribunal shall have the power to try and punish Far Eastern war criminals who as individuals or as members of organizations are charged with offenses which include Crimes against Peace. The following acts, or any of them, are crimes coming within the jurisdiction of the Tribunal for which there shall be individual responsibility:
>
> > (a) <u>Crimes against Peace</u>: Namely, the planning, preparation, initiation or waging of a declared or undeclared war of aggression, or a war in violation of international law, treaties, agreements or assurances, or participation in a common plan or conspiracy for the accomplishment of any of the foregoing;

---

[12] *Yearbook of the United Nations*, 1946–1947, p. 254.

(b) <u>Conventional War Crimes</u>: Namely, violations of the laws or customs of war;

(c) <u>Crimes against Humanity</u>: Namely, murder, extermination, enslavement, deportation, and other inhumane acts committed before or during the war, or persecutions on political or racial grounds in execution of or in connection with any crime within the jurisdiction of the Tribunal, whether or not in violation of the domestic law of the country where perpetrated. Leaders, organizers, instigators, and accomplices participating in the formulation or execution of a common plan or conspiracy to commit any of the foregoing crimes are responsible for all acts performed by any person in execution of such plan.

Despite minor differences in phraseology,[13] the jurisdiction provisions in Article 6 of the Nuremberg Charter are similar to that of the Tokyo Tribunal.

In accordance with the specifications laid down by the Charters of the Nuremberg and Tokyo Tribunals (especially, after the Judgements of both Tribunals, and the affirmation by the UN General Assembly), 'war crimes' were categorized as—'Crimes against Peace', 'Conventional War Crimes' and 'Crimes against Humanity'. This was undoubtedly a major development in international law.

Prior to World War II, the concept of 'war crimes' was vague. In addition to the breaches of international laws and customs of war (Item b of Article 5 of the Tokyo Charter and of Article 6 of the Nuremberg Charter), the use of arms by civilians, participation in skirmishes,

---

[13] The differences between Article 5 of the Tokyo Charter and Article 6 of the Nuremberg Charter are as follows: (1) The former defined Crimes against Peace as 'the planning, preparation, initiation or waging of a declared or undeclared war of aggression', with the words 'declared or undeclared' not being used in the latter. (2) The header 'Conventional War Crimes' in the former simply read 'War Crimes' in the latter. (3) The former defined Conventional War Crimes as 'violations of the laws or customs of war', while the latter added 'such violations shall include, but not be limited to...'. (4) The latter defined Crimes against Humanity as including 'or persecutions on political, racial or religious grounds', while in the former, only 'political or racial grounds' were mentioned, without the word 'religious'. Apart from these differences, the provisions on jurisdiction in the two Charters are identical.

espionage and treason ('war rebellion'), marauding, and other similar offences, were considered as war crimes.[14]

After the Charters and the Judgements of Nuremberg and Tokyo Tribunals listed the three types of war crimes, illegal acts such as espionage and treason, although still punishable by the belligerents, were no longer acknowledged as war crimes.[15] Consequently, the scope of international war crimes as defined in the Charters was apparently narrowed. However, due to the explicit recognition of two other types of major war crimes— 'Crimes against Peace' and 'Crimes against Humanity' in the Charters, apart from traditional war crimes, the scope was broadened to a large extent.

The three types of war crimes are discussed below:

1.5.2 Conventional War Crimes

Out of the three types of war crimes, 'Conventional War Crimes' are most easily recognizable. The Tokyo Charter defines them as 'violations of the laws or customs of war', and the Nuremberg Charter elaborates:

> Such violations shall include, but not be limited to, murder, ill-treatment or deportation to slave labour or for any other purpose of civilian population of or in occupied territory, murder or ill-treatment of prisoners of war or persons on the seas, killing of hostages, plunder of public or private property, wanton destruction of cities, towns or villages, or devastation not justified by military necessity.

The additional sentence in the Nuremberg Charter cites only a few examples; this crime category covers a wide range of misdeeds. Formerly, 'Conventional War Crimes' were considered to be the most important, or the only type of war crimes. Atrocities committed by the belligerent countries, such as murder, arson, rape, plunder, ill-treatment of prisoners of war, and injury and killing of civilians were punished, with or without trial; this was a world-wide practice for many ages.

---

[14] See L. Oppenheim, *International Law: A Treatise*, London: Longmans, 1948, Sects. 151, 152, 154 and 155.

[15] Oppenheim's ideas about war crimes in his *International Law: A Treatise* were quite confusing. He still sometimes mistook those acts for war crimes. For criticism of Oppenheim's conception, see И.П. Трайнин, 'War Crimes', *Oppenheim's International Law* (Chinese Translation), Appendix A, Part 2 of Vol. 2, pp. 409–413.

Consequently, it led to the formation of many unwritten principles and customs in the international arena. As wars became frequent, the nature and scope of these war traditions increased. By the middle of the nineteenth century, people began to sense the need to regulate and consolidate those practices as an international convention. Since the last 100 years, a series of international diplomatic conferences have been convened on various matters such as methods of combat, use of weapons, treatment of the wounded, and treatment of prisoners of war (POWs) and civilians. Among a series of international conventions, the most prominent ones were those adopted at the two Hague Peace Conferences in 1899 and 1907 (especially the Fourth Hague Convention and its annexed regulations of 1907), and the four Geneva Conventions adopted at the Geneva Conference in 1949. Excepting some new cases of nuclear weapon usage and air wars, these conventions have primarily dealt with many issues pertaining to war, including the declaration of war, use of weapons, combat methods, treatment of POWs, protection of civilians, position of neutral powers, and rules and formalities to be complied with by countries and individuals during wartime.[16] Having been signed, ratified or

---

[16] Before the Second Hague Peace Conference in 1907, there had been rules and customs of war adopted at different international conferences as conventions, declarations or protocols, which included the Paris Declaration Respecting Maritime Law (1856), the Geneva Convention for the Amelioration of the Condition of the Wounded and Sick in Armed Forces in the Field (1864), the Saint Petersburg Declaration Renouncing the Use of Explosive Projectiles Under 400 Grammes Weight in Time of War (1868), and the three conventions and three declarations signed at the Hague Peace Conference of 1899 (the three conventions being the Convention for the Pacific Settlement of International Disputes, the Convention with Respect to the Laws and Customs of War on Land, and the Convention for the Adaptation to Maritime Warfare of the Principles of the Geneva Convention of 22 August 1864; the three declarations concerning the Prohibition of the Discharge of Projectiles and Explosives from Balloons, the Prohibition of the Use of Projectiles with the Sole Object to Spread Asphyxiating Poisonous Gases, and the Prohibition of the Use of Bullets which can Easily Expand or Change their Form inside the Human Body). At the Second Hague Peace Conference of 1907, the following 14 conventions and declarations were adopted: Convention for the Pacific Settlement of International Disputes, Convention respecting the Limitation of the Employment of Force for Recovery of Contract Debts, Convention relative to the Opening of Hostilities, Convention respecting the Laws and Customs of War on Land, Convention relative to the Rights and Duties of Neutral Powers and Persons in case of War on Land, Convention relative to the Legal Position of Enemy Merchant Ships at the Start of Hostilities, Convention relative to the Conversion of Merchant Ships into War-ships, Convention relative to the Laying of Automatic Submarine Contact Mines, Convention concerning Bombardment by Naval Forces in Time of War, Convention for the Adaptation to Maritime Warfare of

acceded to by most countries in the world, these conventions provide an internationally recognized code of conduct which needs to be adhered to by all. Violation of these wartime regulations amounts to a war crime, that is, a 'Conventional War Crime' as described in the Tokyo Charter, and also referred to as an 'atrocity'.[17]

---

the Principles of the Geneva Convention of 7 July 1906, Convention relative to Certain Restrictions with regard to the Exercise of the Right of Capture in Naval War, Convention relative to the Establishment of an International Prize Court, Convention concerning the Rights and Duties of Neutral Powers in Naval War, and the Declaration Prohibiting the Discharge of Projectiles and Explosives from Balloons. These conventions partially replaced, amended or supplemented the previous conventions. In the period between the Second Hague Peace Conference of 1907 and World War II, important developments in war legislation included the London Declaration concerning the Laws of Naval War (1909) and the Treaty relating to the Use of Submarines and Noxious Gases in Warfare (1922) (these two documents were not ratified by the various countries but, being in nature declarative of international practice, they still amounted to important documents of international law); the Protocol for the Prohibition of the Use in War of Asphyxiating, Poisonous or other Gases, and of Bacteriological Methods of Warfare (1925) (this protocol had 46 contracting countries, including the Soviet Union and the Republic of China; it has not been ratified by the United States or Japan; the People's Republic of China recognized and succeeded to it on 13 July 1952); the Geneva Convention Relative to the Treatment of Prisoners of War (1929) and the Geneva Convention for the Amelioration of the Condition of the Wounded and Sick in Armies in the Field (1929) (these two conventions amended and supplemented the Hague Conventions of 1907: the former had been part of the Fourth Hague Convention of 1907 and now became an independent convention, while the latter had been an existing convention but was now amended and expanded). After World War II, four conventions were signed in Geneva on 12 August 1949: in addition to amending the two conventions of 1929 (now the Third Geneva Convention Relative to the Treatment of Prisoners of War, and the First Geneva Convention for the Amelioration of the Condition of the Wounded and Sick in Armed Forces in the Field), there was also one amending the Tenth Hague Convention of 1907 (now the Second Geneva Convention for the Amelioration of the Condition of the Wounded, Sick and Shipwrecked Members of Armed Forces at Sea), as well as an additional one (the Fourth Geneva Convention relative to the Protection of Civilian Persons in Time of War). The People's Republic of China recognized with reservation, on 13 July 1952, the signature by the Kuomintang government to these four Geneva Conventions, and ratified them on 5 November 1956.

[17] The following acts are typical examples of the more frequently committed atrocities or Conventional War Crimes (violations of the laws or customs of war): (1) Making use of poisoned or otherwise forbidden arms and ammunition. (2) Killing or wounding soldiers disabled by sickness or wounds, or who have laid down arms and surrendered. (3) Assassination and hiring of assassins. (4) Treacherous request for quarter or treacherous feigning of sickness and wounds. (5) Ill-treatment of prisoners of war, of the wounded and sick. Appropriation of such of their money and valuables as are not public property. (6) Killing or attacking harmless private enemy individuals. Unjustified appropriation and destruction

Some people believed that the effectiveness of some conventions, such as the Hague Conventions, was limited because of its 'general participation clause' (i.e. a convention is binding only if all the belligerent countries are parties to it, and not otherwise). It follows that if the provisions of a convention are violated by individuals from a non-party country, they are exempted from punishment. This argument was refuted by the Nuremberg Tribunal:

> The rules of land warfare expressed in the Convention undoubtedly represented an advance over existing international law at the time of their adoption. The Convention expressly stated that it was an attempt to revise the general laws and customs of war, which it thus recognized to be then existing, but by 1939 these rules laid down in the Convention were recognized by all civilized nations, and were regarded as being declaratory of the laws and customs of war.[18]

The Tokyo Tribunal concurred with the Nuremberg Tribunal on the Hague Conventions by stating:

---

of their private property and especially pillaging. Compulsion of the population of occupied territory to furnish information about the army of the other belligerent or about his means of defence. (7) Disgraceful treatment of dead bodies on battlefields. Appropriation of such money and other valuables found upon dead bodies as are not public property, nor arms, ammunition and the like. (8) Appropriation and destruction of property belonging to museums, hospitals, churches, schools and the like. (9) Assault, siege and bombardment of undefended open towns and other habitations. Unjustified bombardment of undefended places on the part of naval forces. (10) Unnecessary bombardment of historical monuments and of such hospitals and buildings devoted to religion, art, science and charity, as are indicated by particular signs notified to the besiegers bombarding a defended town. (11) Violations of the Geneva Convention. (12) Attack on or sinking of enemy vessels which have hauled down their flags as a sign of surrender. Attack on enemy merchantmen without previous request to submit to visit. (13) Attack or seizure of hospital ships, and all other violations of the Hague Convention for the adaptation to naval warfare of the principles of the Geneva Convention. (14) Unjustified destruction of enemy prizes. (15) Use of enemy uniforms and the like during battle; use of the enemy flag during attack by a belligerent vessel. (16) Violation of enemy individuals furnished with passports or safe-conducts, violation of safeguards. (17) Violation of bearers of flags of truce. (18) Abuse of the protection granted to flags of truce. (19) Violation of cartels, capitulations and armistices. (20) Breach of parole. (L. Oppenheim, *International Law: A Treatise*, Part 2 of Vol. 2, annotation to Sect. 252.)

[18] *Judgment of the International Military Tribunal*, London Edition (published by HMSO), p. 64.

Although the obligation to observe the provisions of the Convention as a binding treaty may be swept away by operation of the 'general participation clause', or otherwise, the Convention remains as good evidence of the customary law of nations, to be considered by the Tribunal along with all other available evidence in determining the customary law to be applied in any given situation.[19]

On many occasions, both the Nuremberg and the Tokyo Tribunals cited the provisions of the Hague Conventions, considering them as 'universally recognized rules' with a binding force on Germany and Japan, irrespective of their participation; this is true of other conventions as well. Therefore, these conventions offer a universally acknowledged set of rules and practices pertaining to war, followed by all countries.

Even before World War II, violations of war laws and customs were recognized as war crimes by international law scholars. Although there were few trials of war crimes before World War II, the offenders were often subject to legal sanctions during or after the war. Even the much-ridiculed Leipzig Trials were an attempt to punish war criminals. The Charters of the two international tribunals at Nuremberg and Tokyo attempted to conform to the international tradition by including violations against war laws or customs as a war crime category in their jurisdiction. In the category of 'Conventional War Crimes', the principles of international law remained unaltered except that the scope of their application was clarified and moderately expanded. During the Nuremberg and Tokyo Trials, the defence lawyers did not object to the court's jurisdiction over this subject, and there was no opposition from the international jurists and writers.

1.5.3 Crimes Against Humanity

Apart from 'Conventional War Crimes', the Nuremberg and Tokyo Tribunals were also empowered to adjudicate on the other two war crime categories: 'Crimes Against Humanity' and 'Crimes Against Peace' (also known as 'the Crime of Aggression'). These two types were considered more serious than 'Conventional War Crimes'. After World War II and the two international trials, especially after the affirmation by the UN General

---

[19] *Judgment of the International Military Tribunal for the Far East* (Chinese Translation), Beijing: The 1950s Press, Part A, Chap. 3, p. 40.

Assembly in 1946, the war crime categories 'Crimes Against Humanity' and 'Crimes Against Peace' were unequivocally recognized by the international community; this marked an important development in international law.

First, let us explore 'Crimes against Humanity':

All war crimes are violations against human rights, but 'Crimes against Humanity' have a specific context as elucidated in the ensuing discussion.

The war legislation declared in the Hague Conventions and other international treaties prohibited only certain crimes such as rape, plunder, ill-treatment of POWs, killing of civilians and use of illegal weapons, and excluded serious atrocities such as genocide against a peaceful population and collective persecution on racial, political or religious grounds. During World War II, the atrocities perpetrated by Hitler's gang were unprecedented in history, and their methods of murder and persecution were barbaric. The mass slaughter of the Jews, the Soviets, the Czechs and the Poles was a ghastly episode that was unanticipated by the drafters of the conventions. It is unjust to punish only the perpetrators of conventional war crimes and ignore their instigators, due to a lack of legislation. Therefore, such crimes were classified under 'Crimes against Humanity', which was added as a special war crime category in the Charters of the Nuremberg and Tokyo Tribunals. The crime category complemented as well as extended the scope of crimes that violated traditional laws and customs of war.

For example, this is the narrative of the extermination of the Jews by Hitler's government on racial grounds in the Nuremberg Judgement:

> Evidence was given of the treatment of the inmates before and after their extermination. There was testimony that the hair of female victims was cut off before they were killed, and shipped to Germany, there to be used in the manufacture of mattresses. The clothes, money, and valuables of the inmates were also salvaged and sent to the appropriate agencies for disposition. After extermination, the gold teeth and fillings were taken from the heads of the corpses and sent to the Reichsbank.
>
> After cremation the ashes were used for fertilizer, and in some instances, attempts were made to utilize the fat from the bodies of the victims in the commercial manufacture of soap. Special groups travelled through Europe to find Jews and subject them to the 'final solution'. German missions were sent to such satellite countries as Hungary and Bulgaria, to arrange for the shipment of Jews to extermination camps and it is known that by the end

of 1944, 400,000 Jews from Hungary had been murdered at Auschwitz. Evidence has also been given of the evacuation of 110,000 Jews from part of Rumania for 'liquidation'. Adolf Eichmann, who had been put in charge of this program by Hitler, has estimated that the policy pursued resulted in the killing of 6 million Jews, of which 4 million were killed in the extermination institutions.[20]

There were no war provisions against a large-scale massacre such as this, and they had to reductively call them as 'Crimes against Humanity'. The main difference between 'Crimes against Humanity' and 'Conventional War Crimes' is that the latter is prohibited by international rules and norms in various conventions, while the former is a transgression of universal humanitarian ideals.

Additionally, 'Crimes against Humanity' have two characteristics which are absent in other war crime categories. First, 'Crimes against Humanity' are committed not only against the enemy but also against citizens of the offender's own country. For example, the Germans massacred their own native (German) Jews on a large scale; Second, 'Crimes against Humanity' are committed not only during war, but also before it. For example, the Germans began killing native Jews even before World War II. These murders qualify as triable war crimes, only when they were committed to realize, or were related to, other war crimes. The pre-war murders of Jews which facilitated the German antagonism against Jews, and prompted other war crimes, such as invasion and the Holocaust, were tried as 'Crimes against Humanity'. On the contrary, murders which were not related to wars of aggression or any other war crime did not qualify as war crimes although they were punishable crimes. As the name suggests, a 'war crime' is solely concerned with crimes associated with war.

After it was affirmed that the Germans' killing of native Jews was an expression of their hostility against Jews, it became a 'Crime against Humanity' even though the domestic law of Nazi Germany did not prohibit, but actually encouraged such an act. In fact, most of those tragedies were directly or indirectly instigated by the German laws at that time. Therefore, once an act qualifies to be a 'Crime against Humanity', it can be tried under those grounds even if it is judged differently by the domestic laws that govern it.

---

[20] *Judgment of the International Military Tribunal*, London Edition, p. 64.

Thus, there was a necessity for the establishment and reinforcement of provisions on 'Crimes against Humanity' in the Nuremberg and Tokyo Charters.

The inclusion of 'Crimes against Humanity' in the jurisdiction of the Nuremberg and Tokyo Tribunals was not opposed. There were no serious protests by defence lawyers, or criticism by international law scholars; it was generally agreed that it was proper and imperative to punish the perpetrators of such crimes.

1.5.4 *Crimes Against Peace (the Crime of Aggression)*

Similar to the Nuremberg Charter (Article 6), the Tokyo Charter (Article 5) lists 'Crimes against Peace' as the first and foremost, Item (a) of the court jurisdiction. All the 22 major Nazi war criminals, including Hermann Göring, and the 28 major Japanese war criminals such as Hideki Tōjō, were charged with this Item (a) provision for war crimes, i.e. 'Crimes against Peace', or 'the Crime of Aggression'. Some were also accused of Item (b) ('Conventional War Crimes') and/or Item (c) ('Crimes against Humanity'). Item (a) was the major charge against them, whereas Items (b) and (c) were minor charges in the two international trials. Consequently, the accused were referred to as 'Class-A war criminals', and the two trials as 'the trials of Class-A war criminals of Germany and Japan'. They were known as 'Class-A war criminals' due to their power and status in their respective countries, and also because they were solely responsible for the formulation of aggressive national policies and the instigation of wars.

As observed earlier, there was no objection to the jurisdiction of Nuremberg and Tokyo Tribunals over 'Conventional War Crimes' (Item b) since this crime category had always been considered triable by international or domestic military courts. Similarly, 'Crimes against Humanity' (Item c), despite being a newly established crime category, received a lukewarm response from the defence lawyers and scholars.

On the contrary, the most important jurisdiction over offenses, that is, jurisdiction over 'Crimes against Peace' (Item a) of the Nuremberg and Tokyo Charters was opposed and attacked by defence lawyers. Even Western scholars and writers of international law doubted the provision and debated over it.

In accordance with the provisions of the two Charters, wars of aggression were crimes, and anyone who participated in such a war had to bear individual responsibility for it. This was an unequivocal, and definitive rule.

Individuals who doubted this rule raised the following two objections to it in an attempt to disregard the most important jurisdiction of the Nuremberg and Tokyo Tribunals:

1. Was the war of aggression considered a crime in international law when the accused was involved in it? If such a law was non-existent at the time of crime, and it had only come into force at the time of trial, the accused should be acquitted on the basis of the 'non-retroactivity' principle.
2. Even if the war of aggression was considered a crime by international law when the accused were involved in it, should they be held individually responsible for it? Both aggressive and non-aggressive war was an 'Act of State' and expression of national sovereignty, permissible by international law. It is the state, rather than any individual, that should be held responsible for an 'Act of State'. Moreover, it is the state, and not an individual that is the subject of international law; the latter is not concerned with international law.

During the Nuremberg and Tokyo Trials, these two legal objections created a heated controversy, but assisted the defence's critique of the court's jurisdiction. The claims made by the defence lawyers were: first, the war of aggression was not a crime in international law; second, even if it was a crime, the defendants should bear no individual responsibility for it.

At that time, the international law scholars in the West were also divided in opinion about these two issues. Many of them concurred with the defence.[21] Mr. R. Pal, from India, one of the 11 judges of the Tokyo

---

[21] Shortly before and after the establishment of the Nuremberg and Tokyo Tribunals (from autumn 1945 to winter 1946), there were many articles on the issue of aggressive war and individual responsibility in the Western newspapers and law journals. Judging from the articles that I have read, most writers were in support of the Charters of the two Tribunals (i.e. the war of aggression is a crime, and the participants should be individually responsible), including Lord Wright, Hans Kelsen, William Cowles, Albert Levy, H. Lauterpacht, Q. Wright, and the like. Those who opposed to or doubted the provisions on jurisdiction in the Charters included C. E. Wyganski, Max Finch, Erich Hula and G. Swarzenberg, among others. Sheldon Glueck before the Nuremberg Trial belonged to the conservative opposition minority (see *War Criminals: Their Prosecution*

Tribunal, also agreed with the defence. From the beginning of the court hearing to the issuing of the sentence, Mr. R. Pal refused to agree with the other ten judges; he insisted that the war of aggression was not a crime, and the accused ought to be acquitted.[22]

However, the Nuremberg Tribunal and the Tokyo Tribunal dealt with the above-mentioned objections in a consistent manner. They disregarded both objections, and supported the provisions of their Charters. In Nuremberg, the four judges from the Soviet Union, France, the United States and the United Kingdom, agreed that the individuals involved in wars of aggression should be penalized. In the Tokyo Tribunal, all judges, except the Indian judge, agreed that wars of aggression were crimes in international law, and all participants should be held individually responsible for them.

We will now explore the legal argumentation and interpretation of these problems by the two international tribunals. The Nuremberg Tribunal started its proceedings about half a year earlier, and pronounced its judgement about two years earlier than the Tokyo Tribunal. Additionally, the Tokyo Tribunal concurred with and supported the Nuremberg Tribunal's legal perspectives. The ensuing description of the statements made by the Nuremberg's Tribunal holds true for the Tokyo Tribunal as well.[23]

---

and Punishment, published by Alfred A. Knopf, Inc. in New York in 1944), but by 1945, he changed his view and became an important advocate of the Nuremberg Charter (see *Nuremberg Trial and Aggressive War*, published by Alfred A. Knopf, Inc. in New York in the summer of 1946).

[22] When the Tokyo Tribunal announced its verdict, Mr. R. Pal disagreed with the Judgement passed by the majority of the judges and issued his Dissenting Opinion, which reached a length of over 1400 typed pages, breaking the record of any judges' dissenting opinions. (The Judgement of the Tokyo Tribunal was 1218 pages long, already unprecedented in the judicial history; yet Mr. R. Pal's personal opinion was over 200 pages longer, which was really exceptional.) His Dissenting Opinion was published by A. Sanyal & Co. in Kolkata, India with the title *International Military Tribunal For The Far East—Dissentient Judgment of Justice Pal*.

[23] The Tokyo Tribunal stated in its Judgement: 'In view of the fact that in all material respects the Charters of this Tribunal and the Nuremberg Tribunal are identical, this Tribunal prefers to express its unqualified adherence to the relevant opinions of the Nuremberg Tribunal rather than by reasoning the matters anew in somewhat different language to open the door to controversy by way of conflicting interpretations of the two statements of opinions.' (See *Judgment of the International Military Tribunal for the Far East*, Part A, Chap. 2, Sect. a.)

Although the Nuremberg Tribunal obliged to comply with and apply the provisions of the Charter, it insisted that the Charter conforms to the international law at the time; compliance with and application of the Charter was equivalent to abiding by the principles of international law. It pronounced the Judgement:

> The Charter is not an arbitrary exercise of power on the part of the victorious Nations, but in the view of the Tribunal, as will be shown, it is the expression of international law existing at the time of its creation; and to that extent is itself a contribution to international law.[24]

Thus, it follows that the Nuremberg Tribunal determined that the war of aggression had long been considered as a criminal act in international law. It was not only a crime but, according to its Judgement, 'it is the supreme international crime differing only from other war crimes in that it contains within itself the accumulated evil of the whole'.[25] This is because, without aggression, there would be no international war; without international war, there would be no damage, destruction, rape, ill-treatment of prisoners, killing of civilians, and other war crimes. Hence, the war of aggression was a conglomeration of all evil activities, and the 'supreme international crime'.

However, neither the Nuremberg Tribunal nor the Tokyo Tribunal recognized that it was the imperialist system of exploitation which instigated wars of aggression. Imperialism must thus be condemned because as long as it remained, there was the possibility of war.[26]

The Nuremberg Tribunal identified wars of aggression as war crimes based on the principles of the *General Treaty for Renunciation of War as an Instrument of National Policy* (more commonly known as the Pact of Paris, or the Kellogg-Briand Pact, signed in Paris on 27 August 1928,

---

[24] *Judgment of the International Military Tribunal*, London Edition, p. 38.

[25] *Judgment of the International Military Tribunal*, London Edition, p. 13.

[26] Chapter 2, 'The Modern War Has Its Root in Imperialism', in *Lenin on War and Peace* (published by People's Publishing House in 1960, pp. 16–22). *Selected Works of Mao Tse-tung* (published by People's Publishing House in 1952), Vol. I, pp. 167–168; Vol. II, pp. 464–466.

and ratified or adhered to by 63 countries, including Germany, Italy and Japan); all the three Axis Powers were obliged to comply with it.[27]

According to the preface of the Pact of Paris, for the signatory powers, 'all changes in their relations with one another should be sought only by pacific means ... thus uniting the civilized nations of the world in a common renunciation of war as an instrument of their national policy'.

Article 1 of the Pact: 'The High Contracting Parties solemnly declare in the names of their respective peoples that they condemn recourse to war for the solution of international controversies, and renounce it, as an instrument of national policy in their relations with one another.'

Article 2 of the Pact: 'The High Contracting Parties agree that the settlement or solution of all disputes or conflicts of whatever nature or of whatever origin they may be, which may arise among them, shall never be sought, except by pacific means.'

The Nuremberg Tribunal contended that wars of aggression were illegalized by international law due to the inclusion of these articles in the Pact of Paris, and the law was abided by the majority of civilized nations. The Tribunal stated:

> In the opinion of the Tribunal, the solemn renunciation of war as an instrument of national policy necessarily involves the proposition that such a war is illegal in international law; and that those who plan and wage such a war, with its inevitable and terrible consequences, are committing a crime in so doing. War for the solution of international controversies undertaken as an instrument of national policy certainly includes a war of aggression, and such a war is therefore outlawed by the Pact.[28]

The Nuremberg Tribunal stated that it was immaterial whether the Pact of Paris explicitly used the word 'crime' or not, because the word 'illegal' by itself meant 'criminal'. An example given by the Tribunal was the Fourth Hague Convention of 1907 which prohibited atrocities in war. Although the Convention did not use the word 'crime', the actions prohibited therein were implicitly considered criminal. Accordingly, numerous offenders were arrested, tried and punished as war

---

[27] For the full text of the Pact of Paris, see *Collection of International Treaties (1924–1933)*, pp. 373–374.

[28] *Judgment of the International Military Tribunal*, London Edition, p. 39.

criminals by courts of different countries over the last 40 years. Therefore, the interpretation and application of the law should not be limited to its articulation, but should consider the legislative spirit and the social environment of the time, including public consciousness, human progress and public opinions.

In order to reaffirm that the Pact of Paris regarded wars of aggression as international crimes, the Nuremberg Tribunal listed some important efforts that were undertaken to identify aggressive wars before the enforcement of the Pact:

1. In the year 1923, the draft of a *Treaty of Mutual Assistance* was sponsored by the League of Nations. In Article 1, the Treaty declared that 'aggressive war is an international crime', and that the parties would 'undertake that none of them will be guilty of its commission'.
2. The preamble to the League of Nations 1924, *Protocol for the Pacific Settlement of International Disputes* (the 'Geneva Protocol'), declared that 'a war of aggression constitutes a violation of this solidarity and is an international crime'. The Protocol was recommended to the members of the League of Nations by a unanimous resolution in the Assembly of the 48 members of the League, including Italy and Japan. The Protocol was never ratified, but as was stated by the Nuremberg Tribunal, it 'may be regarded as strong evidence of the intention to brand aggressive war as an international crime'.[29]
3. At the meeting of the Assembly of the League of Nations on 24 September 1927, all the delegates present (including those of Germany, Italy and Japan) unanimously adopted a declaration. Its preamble stated that 'a war of aggression can never serve as a means of settling international disputes, and is in consequence an international crime'.
4. The unanimous resolution taken on 18 February 1928, by 21 American republics at the Sixth (Havana) Pan-American Conference, declared that 'a war of aggression constitutes an international crime against the human species'.

---

[29] *Judgment of the International Military Tribunal*, London Edition, p. 40.

5. We understand from the Treaty of Versailles, Article 227 (to try the former German Emperor) and Article 228 (to try the major war criminals), that the intention to try the instigators of aggressive wars as criminals, existed even in the early post-World War I period.

The Nuremberg Tribunal thus produced the above-mentioned evidences to illustrate the advancement of thinking over the last 20 years. It was evident that the signing of the Pact of Paris implicitly acknowledged wars of aggression as crimes in international law. As was declared by the Tribunal, 'resort to a war of aggression is not merely illegal, but is criminal. The prohibition of aggressive war demanded by the conscience of the world finds its expression in the series of pacts and treaties to which the Tribunal has just referred'.[30] It can be seen that the Pact of Paris did not abruptly modify old principles of international law, or create new ones, but instead it pronounced a timely and mature principle of international law.

The Tokyo Tribunal concurred with the Nuremberg Tribunal on the description and interpretation of the Pact of Paris. Consequently, the Tokyo Tribunal also rejected the claims of defence lawyers that based on the principle of 'non-retroactivity' (aggressive wars had not been declared illegal when the defendants planned, launched or participated in the war), the defendants should not be penalized.

1.5.5 Individual Responsibility

Another attack launched by the defence over the jurisdiction of the Nuremberg and Tokyo Tribunals, concerned the individual responsibility of war criminals. Many international law scholars and writers concurred with the opinion of the defence attorneys.

There was no objection to charging the accused with 'Conventional War Crimes', and 'Crimes against Humanity'; their objections only pertained to 'Crimes against Peace'. Those who claimed that the aggressive war at the time of occurrence was not a crime, also objected to individual responsibility for 'Crimes against Peace'. They upheld a conservative, even outdated, description of traditional international law, which was staunchly rejected by the Nuremberg and Tokyo Tribunals.

---

[30] *Judgment of the International Military Tribunal*, London Edition, p. 41.

Given below are four reasons cited by the defence lawyers and international law scholars for disclaiming personal responsibility in 'Crimes against Peace'.

1. A war of aggression is an 'Act of State' and an expression of state sovereignty, for which the state should solely be held responsible. As the concerned individuals only accede to and execute the state policy and orders, no independent individual can be held responsible for the war.
2. Even though a war of aggression is a crime in international law, the subject of international law is the state and not any individual. Therefore, individuals violating international law should not be punished.
3. International law imposes sanctions against states that violate it, but there is no stipulation on the method of sanctions against individuals. Therefore, it is groundless and impracticable to punish individuals.
4. According to the principles of criminal law, a crime is said to be committed when the accused person has a mens rea ('guilty mind'), but it is impossible for an individual to have the required mens rea when participating in a war of aggression.

These four arguments were untenable and firmly rejected by the Nuremberg and Tokyo Tribunals.

The Judgement of the Nuremberg Tribunal countered the claim that the war of aggression was an 'Act of State' and incurred no individual responsibility, with the argument: 'That international law imposes duties and liabilities upon individuals as well as upon states has long been recognized.'[31] It quoted the Ex parte Quirin case, and furthered its argument that 'individuals can be punished for violations of international law. Crimes against international law are committed by men, not by abstract entities, and only by punishing individuals who commit such crimes can the provisions of international law be enforced'. However, the accountability of individuals did not acquit the state from its role in it. On the contrary, the state has always been held liable for launching aggressive wars, and had to adequately recompense for it. The responsibility of the

---

[31] *Judgment of the International Military Tribunal*, London Edition, p. 41.

state was civil (compensating the injured party for the losses incurred in war) rather than criminal. Demanding a war compensation from the offending state is an outdated method of criminal punishment which is no longer practiced.[32] In order to stop war and aggression we must increase the accountability of warmongers and militarists. It is unfair to increase the civil responsibility of the state, as the necessary compensation would have to be borne by its citizens, who were passive, non-beneficiary participants in the war. Owing to a universal craving for peace, the punishment of war criminals of World War II was seriously undertaken and prioritized over the demand for compensation from offending states.

The second argument, that international law could not punish individuals as they were not subjects of international law, is also untenable. There are several precedents to the practice of punishing individuals under international law. For example, piracy and human trafficking have always been considered crimes in international law, and any country can arrest and punish the concerned criminals. In fact, the alleged war crimes are all individual violations of international law, for which the trial and punishment cannot be governed by the general rules of domestic criminal law. In international courts, international law is directly cited, while in domestic courts, it is applied in a domestic legal form upon conversion of international law into domestic law by generalization or enumeration.[33] In essence, these rules for punishing war criminals are derived

---

[32] It has long been a matter of debate whether the state has criminal responsibility. In the early stage, international law scholars mostly contended that the state could commit crimes and therefore be named 'state-as-a-criminal' (see Van Vollenkoven, *The Three Stages in the Evolution of the Law of Nations*, pp. 8ff). In the peace treaties with defeated nations, there were often provisions for ceding territories and paying indemnities as 'punitive' measures. However, recently most international law scholars and writers have opposed the concept of 'state-as-a-criminal'. In the Nuremberg Trial, the lead British prosecutor Hartley Shawcross had once adopted the old doctrine so as to put the focus of indictment on the defendants' 'accomplice' and 'abetting', i.e. the defendants had aided and abetted their country to commit crimes. In that way, the state became the subject of war crimes, or at least the defendants' co-offender. The Nuremberg Tribunal did not follow Shawcross' view. Its Judgement said that crimes against international law were committed by 'men', not by 'abstract entities' (state). This clearly indicates that the court did not agree with or accept the 'state-as-a-criminal' concept, which position was in line with the standpoint of the international law scholars at the time. Apparently, Shawcross' view represented that of only a few conservative international law scholars (Shawcross' gravamen are outlined in *Proceedings of the International Military Tribunal*, pp. 833–835).

[33] Some countries regularly incorporate all or part of the principles and practices of international law of war into their criminal law and warfare regulations (such as the British

from the Hague Conventions and other internationally recognized laws and customs of war, which are undoubtedly international law.

The third argument, that international law did not stipulate the method of sanctions against individuals and therefore could not punish them, is also invalid. Over 300 years ago, Grotius, known as the founder of international law in the West, agreed that those who captured or tried a violator of international law had the right to execute him.[34] Since a death penalty could be imposed, it meant that milder sentences could also be levied. Moreover, long before the Nuremberg and Tokyo Trials took place, it was a common practice for the military authorities or domestic courts of different countries to impose various penalties on war criminals, with or without trials. This practice was unchallenged then, and it is futile to now quote the lack of legislation against individuals in international law as an excuse to refute the personal liability of the accused.

The fourth argument was that the defendants did not commit crimes for they did not have mens rea ('guilty mind') or any knowledge of international law at that time. This was also rejected by the Nuremberg Tribunal with the following counterstatements: first, each individual shall be obliged to be informed of and to abide by all laws in force (international law included), ignorance of which can never be a valid defence;[35] second, when the defendants carried out an aggressive war in defiance of treaties and agreements, their positions and social status

---

Manual of Military Law and the US Rules of Land Warfare); other countries generally recognize the rules of international law in their domestic law, and even recognize the effectiveness of international law in their constitutions (such as the German Democratic Republic); and still other countries only enact specific laws or orders reflecting the relevant provisions of international law when it comes to the time of trying the war criminals, by way of generalization or enumeration (such as the Soviet Union, France and Canada). In China, the Decision to Deal with War Criminals in Custody in the Japanese War of Aggression Against China passed by the Standing Committee of the National People's Congress on 25 April 1956, also belongs to the last category. Some countries have included the trial of traitors in such laws or orders as well (e.g. Czechoslovakia, Poland, Romania and Bulgaria). Although the way of acceptance varies from country to country, contents of the laws and orders against war crimes have mostly been taken from the Hague Conventions, the Geneva Conventions, and the rules and practices generally recognized by the international world, and thus are essentially international law rather than national law.

[34] Grotius, *De Jure Belli ac Paris*, Book III, Chap. 11, Sect. 10; S. Glueck, *War Criminals: Their Prosecution and Punishment*, pp. 107ff.

[35] Baron Wright, 'War Crimes Under International Law', *Law Quarterly Review*, Vol. 62 (1946), pp. 40, 51. Jackson, a prosecutor at the Nuremberg Trial, once said, 'The

should have made them know or feel what they were doing was wrong or criminal, even though they might not know exactly how serious a crime it was in international law. They could not be said of lacking in 'criminal intention'. According to the Judgement of the Nuremberg Tribunal, it says of a war criminal, 'so far from it being unjust to punish him, it would be unjust if his wrong was allowed to go unpunished'.[36]

After resolutely refuting all the defences against individual responsibility, both the Nuremberg and the Tokyo Tribunals concluded that those who participated in wars of aggression, at any stage of planning, preparation, initiation or waging of such a war, had to bear personal responsibility and be adjudicated as war criminals. Thus, a major principle in international law that is ascertained and proclaimed in the Charters and the Judgements of the two international military tribunals is individual responsibility in a war of aggression.

1.5.6 Official Position and Orders of the Superior

Two subjects associated with the above-mentioned problems: the defendant's official position, and the orders of superiors, are elaborated below.

1.5.6.1 Official Position

Article 7 of the Nuremberg Charter states: 'The official position of Defendants, whether as heads of State, or responsible officials in Government departments, shall not be considered as freeing them from responsibility, or mitigating punishment.' Article 6 of the Tokyo Charter provides: 'Neither the official position, at any time, of an accused ... shall, of itself, be sufficient to free such accused from responsibility for any crime with which he is charged....' The two provisions are similar to each other in essence, confirming and declaring a new principle of international law regarding the trial of war criminals—any person, from the head of state or Prime Minister, to an ordinary soldier or civilian, as long as he is guilty of any war crimes, shall be held personally responsible and be tried and punished as a war criminal.

---

price for the progress of law has to be paid by those who predict wrongly or understand too late.' See *Proceedings of the International Military Tribunal*, p. 116.

[36] *Judgment of the International Military Tribunal*, London Edition, p. 39.

Earlier, the head of a state was regarded as a sacred and inviolable authority; he was not for any reason tried by a foreign court or an international tribunal. This was firmly advocated by the representatives of the United States and Japan in the 'Commission on the Responsibility of the Authors of the War and on the Enforcement of Penalties', which was established by the Allied Powers at the end of World War I.[37] However, their opinions were not adopted at the Paris Peace Conference. Article 227 of the Treaty of Versailles expressly stated: 'The Allied and Associated Powers publicly arraign William II of Hohenzollern, former German Emperor, for a supreme offence against international morality and the sanctity of treaties. A special tribunal will be constituted to try the accused....' Although this provision was not enforced because the Dutch government refused to extradite William II, and the Allied Powers separated, the doctrine of absolute monarchy was shaken. According to the legislation for the other major war criminals beneath the German Emperor as given by Article 228 of the Treaty of Versailles: 'The German Government recognizes the right of the Allied and Associated Powers to bring before military tribunals, persons accused of having committed acts in violation of the laws and customs of war.' Unfortunately, this provision also collapsed due to the failure of the Leipzig Trials where only six low-level officers were sentenced to imprisonment.

From the above events, it can be inferred that before World War II, the purpose of a war crime trial was restricted to the conviction of soldiers and ordinary officers. Senior officials, not to mention the head of a state or the main leaders of a government, were never tried.

However, things changed after World War II; the provisions of the Nuremberg and Tokyo Charters as well as their implementation by the two international tribunals facilitated the enforcement of the principle of equality in determining those responsible for war crimes.

Göring, and 21 other Class-A alleged war criminals adjudicated at the Nuremberg Trial were the most important leaders of Nazi Germany (Hitler was dead at that time or else he would have also been tried). The 28 Class-A defendants before the Tokyo Tribunal were also among the most important leaders of the fascist Japan; four of whom were former Prime Ministers. At Nuremberg, 12 defendants were sentenced to death

---

[37] For the opinions of the US and Japanese representatives, see the official Report of the Commission, pp. 147–152; also see S. Glueck, *War Criminals: Their Prosecution and Punishment*, pp. 121–139.

by hanging, three to life imprisonment, four to fixed-term imprisonment, and three were acquitted.[38] In the Tokyo Trial, seven defendants

---

[38] Twelve defendants were sentenced to death by hanging by the Nuremberg Trial: Göring, Reichsmarschall, Commander-in-Chief of the Luftwaffe (air force), Plenipotentiary of the Four-Year Plan, Vice-Chancellor of Germany, the first successor designated by Hitler; Ribbentrop, Diplomatic Moderator, Ambassador to the United Kingdom 1933–1938, Foreign Minister from 1938 to Germany's surrender; Keitel, Chief of the Armed Forces High Command, Chief of the War Ministry's Armed Forces Office from 1935 onwards; Kaltenbrunner, an Obergruppenführer (general) in the Schutzstaffel (SS), trusted assistant to the head of special agent, leader of the Austrian SS and Chief of the Reich Main Security Office from 1935 onwards; Rosenberg, head of 'spiritual training' of the Nazi Party, Minister for the Occupied Eastern Territories from 1941 to Germany's surrender, theorist and propagandist of fascism and racial superiority; Frank, Minster of Justice from 1934 to Germany's surrender, Governor-General of Poland from 1939 until its liberation; Frick, Minister of the Interior 1934–1943, Protector of Bohemia and Moravia from 1943 onwards; Seyss-Inquart, an important leader of the Nazi Party, Minister without Portfolio and Governor of Austria, Deputy-Governor of Poland from 1939, and Commissioner for the Occupied Dutch Territory from 1940 onwards; Streicher, an important leader of the Nazi Party, editor of Der Stürmer, anti-Semitism thinker and propagandist, organizer and leader persecuting the Jews; Sauckel, General in the SS from 1942 to Germany's surrender, Plenipotentiary for Labour Deployment, organizer of 'slaves and forced labour'; Jodl, General, Chief of the National Defence Section of the Armed Forces High Command 1935–1938, Chief of the Operations Staff of the Armed Forces High Command from 1939 onwards; Bormann, Chief of Staff of Hess, Head of the Nazi Party Chancellery, Hitler's confidential secretary and trusted adviser from 1943 onwards (judgement by default). Three defendants were sentenced to life imprisonment: Hess, Deputy Fuehrer of the Nazi Party and Minister without Portfolio from 1933, a member of Hitler's secret cabinet from 1938, Defence Commissioner from 1939, the second successor designated by Hitler, all until his flight to Britain in 1941; Funk, Minister of Economics from 1938 to Germany's surrender, President of the Reichsbank and Plenipotentiary for War Economy, Defence Commissioner, member of the Central Planning Board; Raeder, Grand Admiral, Commander-in-Chief of the Reichsmarine (navy) 1935–1943, Admiral Inspector from 1943 onwards. Four defendants were sentenced to fixed-term imprisonment: Von Schirach, organizer and head of the Hitler Youth, Governor of Vienna from 1940 onwards; Speer, Hitler's close comrade-in-arms, Minister of Armaments 1942–1943, Minister of Armaments and War Production from 1943 to Germany's surrender, one of the leaders of the Central Planning Board; Von Neurath; Foreign Minister 1932–1938, Protector of Bohemia and Moravia 1939–1943; Doenitz, Grand Admiral, commander of the submarine arm 1936–1942, Commander-in-Chief of the Navy from 1943 to Germany's surrender, Hitler's successor as head of state for a short period in May 1945. Three defendants were acquitted: Schacht, President of the Reichsbank 1933–1939, Minister of Economics 1934–1937, Plenipotentiary for War Economy, Minister without Portfolio 1937–1943, main adviser to Hitler on economic and financial questions; Von Papen, organizer and leader of foreign espionage and sabotage activities, Minister to Vienna 1934–1938, Ambassador to Turkey 1939–1944; Fritzsche, propaganda activist, Goebbels' close colleague, successively Head of the

were sentenced to death by hanging, 16 to life imprisonment, two to fixed-term imprisonment, and none was acquitted of a charge—such massive trials and severe punishments against the state leaders had never happened before. Although the Nuremberg and Tokyo Trials had their shortcomings, their Judgements were based on the concepts of 'individual responsibility' and 'rejection of official status as a reason for being free from one's criminal responsibility'.

1.5.6.2 Orders of the Superior

Another problem closely related to the principle of 'individual responsibility' is orders from one's superiors. This was also one of the defences to absolve the accused from criminal responsibility, especially when they were charged with 'Conventional War Crimes' and 'Crimes against Humanity'.

The argument was: if an individual, such as a soldier or a subordinate officer, did not act out of his own free will when committing a war crime, but only followed the orders of his superior officer or government, should he not be exempted from responsibility and punishment? Responses to this question were confusing in the past.

Famous international jurists in the West, such as Kelson and Smith argued that alleged war criminals who only followed the orders of their superiors should be acquitted of all charges.[39] On account of their preoccupation with the laws of that time, the rigid discipline in the army, and the danger of disobeying orders, the accused individuals simply obliged to do as they were commanded. This was also a stipulation in the British *Manual of Military Law* (Article 443) and the US *Rules of Land Warfare* (Article 366), before 1944. However, in 1944 the laws were revised, and stated that orders from one's superiors cannot serve as a valid defence against criminal liability.

The Nuremberg and Tokyo Tribunals adopted a firm stance towards this problem. Article 8 of the Nuremberg Charter states: 'The fact that the Defendant acted pursuant to order of his Government or of a superior

---

Home Press Division and Head of the Radio Division of the Ministry of Public Enlightenment and Propaganda. The Soviet judge declared his disagreement on the acquittal of Schacht, Papen and Fritzsche, and the life imprisonment (instead of death) sentence of Hess. He wrote a Dissenting Opinion which was attached to the Judgement of the Nuremberg Tribunal. As to the sentencing by the Tokyo Tribunal, a detailed discussion will follow later in this book.

[39] H. Kelson, *Peace through Law*, p. 107; H. A. Smith, *Law and Custom of the Sea*, pp. 176–180; L. Oppenheim, *International Law: A Treatise*, Sect. 253.

shall not free him from responsibility, but may be considered in mitigation of punishment if the Tribunal determines that justice so requires.' Article 6 of the Tokyo Charter has a similar provision: '... nor the fact that an accused acted pursuant to order of his government or of a superior shall, of itself, be sufficient to free such accused from responsibility for any crime with which he is charged, but such circumstances may be considered in mitigation of punishment if the Tribunal determines that justice so requires.'

The underlying motive for such provisions was that one should obey only legal orders but not illegal and criminal orders, and he must bear unavoidable responsibility for violating any obvious and undeniable rules of war by obeying orders. Otherwise, by attributing responsibility to his immediate superiors who issued the orders, who would in turn impute it to their superiors, the responsibility would eventually shift to the head of state or a few top officials. This would make only these few individuals responsible for war crimes—a decision which would hamper the effective implementation of war laws.

Any person who commits a crime against the rules of war or against humanity, whether on his own accord or by following orders of a superior, shall be regarded as a war criminal and accordingly punished. In the case of a war crime committed pursuant to a superior's order, the urge to escape the risk of defying the order may be considered as a valid reason to mitigate the sentence passed; an ordinary soldier or a subordinate officer faces the inevitability of being severely punished for disobeying orders. However, a senior commander, a civilian official or a businessman, would only run the risk of losing his position or business. Sometimes, his resistance to the execution of an illegal order may even lead to the revocation or revision of that order. The court should thus take into account the different and specific circumstances of each case when imposing penalties. The excuse of 'superior's orders' is not valid for state leaders and senior officials, because if they did not agree with an order or policy, they could freely resign without having to face any negative consequences. In fact, in many cases they were the drafters and issuers of such illegal orders.

In short, if an ordinary soldier or a subordinate officer committed a 'Conventional War Crime' or a 'Crime against Humanity', the fact that he acted under a superior's orders shall not free him from responsibility, but it may be considered for mitigation of punishment. However, this is not possible in the case of 'Crimes against Peace'. Theoretically, every person who participates in the planning, preparation, initiation or waging of aggressive wars has committed 'Crimes against Peace', and since the superior's orders cannot free him from responsibility, it follows that an ordinary soldier or officer, when ordered to join an aggressive war, automatically becomes guilty of a 'Crime against Peace'. This was not the proposition maintained by the prosecuting and judicial organs of the Allied Powers, whether domestic or international. The Allied Powers did not prosecute ordinary soldiers and officers on a charge of 'Crimes against Peace' for their participation in the war of aggression, because those individuals could not choose whether to wage a war or not, and it was also difficult for them to identify the aggressive nature of the war with their limited knowledge and exposure. Thus, after World War II, the Allied Powers repatriated millions of German and Japanese POWs to their homeland without detention or prosecution. Only a small number of ordinary soldiers and officers who had committed 'Conventional War Crimes' or 'Crimes against Humanity' were arrested and prosecuted as Class-C war criminals, most of whom were tried by domestic military tribunals rather than international courts.

After World War II, those brought on trial for 'Crimes against Peace' ('the Crime of Aggression') were limited to a handful of state leaders, namely heads of governments, leading politicians, warlords, plutocrats, armament manufacturers, prominent war instigators, commander of important war zones, and other upper-class individuals, who were primarily responsible for the initiation and advancement of aggressive wars.

1.6 Class-A War Criminals and International Trials

Finally, we answer a few essential questions in legal practice: what is a 'Class-A war criminal'? What are the differences between 'Class-A war criminals' and 'Class-B/C war criminals'? Why were 'Class-A war criminals' generally tried by international tribunals whereas the other two types were tried by domestic tribunals (in the country where the crimes were committed)?

The classification of war criminals into classes A, B and C was an academic practice which was not based on any formal international literature. The London Agreement and its annex, the Nuremberg Charter, signed by the United Kingdom, the United States, France and the Soviet Union on 8 August 1945, used the words 'prosecution and punishment of the main war criminals of the European Axis'. Similarly, the Special Proclamation and its annex, the Tokyo Charter, promulgated by the Supreme Commander for the Allied Powers on 19 January 1946, used the words 'just and prompt trial and punishment of the major war criminals in the Far East'. Other official international documents also referred to 'major war criminals' instead of 'Class-A war criminals'.

In general conversations, as well as in academic writings and news reports, people often called such war criminals 'Class-A war criminals' for the sake of convenience and conspicuousness. Class-A war criminals had two characteristics: first, they held high positions and had much power, and were usually state leaders; second, they all committed 'Item (a)' war crimes as defined in the Nuremberg and Tokyo Charters—'Crimes against Peace', i.e. the crimes of planning, preparation, initiation or waging of a war of aggression, which was considered by the two international tribunals as the 'supreme international crime' that 'contains within itself the accumulated evil of the whole'. These two characteristics were interlinked because a person without a high position or much power would not be able to influence the formation of a national policy of aggression or war strategy. Consequently, the 'Class-A war criminals' were usually the prime culprits and instigators of wars of aggression.

Although these 'prime culprits' were often charged with 'Conventional War Crimes' and 'Crimes against Humanity', they were mainly guilty of 'Crimes against Peace'.

In accordance with international practice, many Class-A war criminals were tried by international military tribunals. However, there was no explanation given in official documents or academic writings for trying them in international tribunals. Since peace is a universal value, and world peace can only be maintained through the efforts of an international community, the impact of an aggressive war concerns not only the victim country, but also all other countries involved in the war. The scourge of such crimes is beyond geographical boundaries; it is an atrocity against humanity at large, and for this reason, the offenders should be adjudicated by international tribunals, rather than by domestic tribunals of any particular country.

In accordance with international practice, Class-B and Class-C war criminals who had committed 'Conventional War Crimes' and 'Crimes against Humanity' were tried by domestic courts or military tribunals in the country wherein the crimes were committed. Since the offenders had a lower social status and their offences were not as complex as 'Crimes against Peace', it was unnecessary to organize international tribunals for their trial. Additionally, there were two advantages: first, trying the offenders in the same region where the atrocities were committed meant adhering to territoriality principle of criminal law. This facilitated the processes of evidence collection, witness summons and on-the-spot investigation. Second, it helped to lessen the indignation of the local people who were haunted by memories of the atrocities committed in their homeland. Therefore, the Allied Powers in many declarations and diplomatic notes, emphasized that war criminals who had committed brutal atrocities must be extradited to the place of occurrence to stand trials, and warned the neutral countries against granting them asylum.[40]

The conduct and adjudication of a large number of war criminal trials was a striking phenomenon at the end of World War II. On the international front, there were the Nuremberg Tribunal to try the German Class-A war criminals, and the Tokyo Tribunal to try the Japanese Class-A war criminals. In the domestic arena, the Allied Powers booked numerous cases against Class-B and Class-C war criminals. Some countries (such as the United States), tried as many as 1000 cases; unsurprisingly, many other countries also filed hundreds of lawsuits.[41]

The trials conducted after World War II greatly clarified, and modified the principles of international law on war crimes and war criminal trials. Earlier, the section of international legal principles was vague and

---

[40] For those declarations, notes and statements, see S. Glueck, *War Criminals: Their Prosecution and Punishment*, Appendix B, pp. 109–113.

[41] We have not found accurate and comprehensive statistics or reports on the number of cases against Class-B and Class-C war criminals in the different domestic courts and military tribunals after World War II. According to the US *Time* magazine published on 24 December 1964, during the period when Germany was occupied, the military tribunals of the Allied Powers tried altogether 5025 Nazi war criminals, of whom 486 were sentenced to death; the post-war German tribunals tried 12,882 Nazi war criminals, of whom 5243 were convicted, 12 sentenced to death and 76 to life imprisonment; the Soviet Union tribunals were estimated to have sentenced about 10,000 Nazi war criminals. While the reliability of this report and its estimates are questionable, the huge number of the cases and the severity of punishment of German and Japanese war criminals after World War II were most striking, which were totally different from the situation after World War I.

confusing, and international law scholars and writers had different opinions on it. These principles were elucidated and developed after World War II, especially during the Nuremberg and Tokyo Trials.[42]

Hence, this chapter summarizes the process of and reasons for the clarification, affirmation and development of principles of international law, which were the basic guidelines for the Tokyo Tribunal while exercising its jurisdiction.

---

[42] Mei Ju-ao, 'New Concept of War Crimes: Summary of Some Main Changes and Developments of the Principles of International Law After World War II', *Academic Monthly*, No. 7 of 1957, pp. 57–66.

CHAPTER 2

Charter and Organization of the International Military Tribunal for the Far East

2.1 INTRODUCTION TO THE TOKYO CHARTER

The *Charter of the International Military Tribunal for the Far East*, also known as the Tokyo Charter, was promulgated by the Supreme Commander for the Allied Powers in Tokyo based on a series of international documents, including the Potsdam Declaration, Japan's Instrument of Surrender and the resolutions of the Moscow Conference. It was published in the Special Proclamation on 19 January 1946, whereas the Nuremberg Charter was directly formulated by the United States, the United Kingdom, the Soviet Union and France, as an annex to the London Agreement signed on 8 August 1945.[1]

After the issuance of the Tokyo Charter, the Supreme Commander for the Allied Powers ordered an amendment on 26 April 1946, by adding two judges nominated by India and the Philippines, respectively, to those from the nine countries which signed the Instrument of Surrender, thus increasing the number of judges to eleven.

Except for the above-mentioned amendment (made before the commencement of court sessions), the Tokyo Charter remained unaltered. It served as the standard reference for the organization of the Tokyo Tribunal, and the conduct of its trials during the entire period of its existence.

---

[1] See Chapter 1, Sect. 1.4 of this book.

© Shanghai Jiao Tong University Press 2020
M. Ju-ao, *The Tokyo Trial and War Crimes in Asia*,
https://doi.org/10.1007/978-981-15-9813-5_2

The Tokyo Charter has 17 articles in five sections for the constitution, personnel, administration, and legal matters of the Tribunal. Among the legal articles, some deal with substantive law, such as its jurisdiction and judgement; others concern procedural law, such as the trial procedure, admissibility of evidence, examination of witnesses, range of punishments, and the execution of sentences.

<u>Section I</u> of the Charter stipulates the 'Constitution of Tribunal' in four articles.

<u>Article 1</u> states that the purpose of establishing the Tribunal is 'for the just and prompt trial and punishment of the major war criminals in the Far East'. We must remember that when the Tribunal was established, its intention was to try all major war criminals arrested in the Far East, regardless of their nationalities. In reality, however, only the Japanese war criminals were tried. Therefore, this article refers to 'the major war criminals in the Far East', rather than just 'the Japanese war criminals'.

On 11 September 1945, about ten days after Japan surrendered, the General Headquarters (GHQ) of the Supreme Commander for the Allied Powers published a list of 39 Class-A war crime suspects to be arrested, of whom 27 were Japanese, including Hideki Tōjō, while the rest were non-Japanese, including three Germans, three Filipinos, two Australians, and one Burmese, Dutch, Thai and American. The 12 non-Japanese alleged war criminals included José P. Laurel, President of the Second Philippine Republic, a Japanese puppet state; Benigno Aquino Sr., Speaker of the National Assembly of Laurel's regime; Jorge B. Vargas, Laurel's ambassador to Japan; Heinrich Georg Stahmer, German ambassador to Japan; Colonel Alfred Kretschmer, German military attaché to Japan; Luang Vichitr Vadhakar, Thailand's ambassador to Japan; and Dr. Thein Maung, the puppet State of Burma's ambassador to Japan. They were all arrested to be tried by the Tokyo Tribunal. Due to various reasons (some did not qualify as Class-A war criminals, some were demanded for extradition by their home countries, and technical challenges such as foreign language interpretation) they were released or repatriated before the trial proceedings began.

The lists in the subsequent arrest warrants for Class-A war criminals—the second, on 11 November 1945 for 11; the third, on 2 December 1945 for 59; and the fourth, on 6 December 1945 for 9—comprised only Japanese major war criminals. Twenty-eight major war criminals out of 118 detainees from the four arrest warrants were selected for prosecution by the Tokyo Tribunal. Although all of them were Japanese, the Tokyo

Charter referred to them as 'major war criminals in the Far East', similar to the Nuremberg Charter which referred to the German war criminals as 'major war criminals of the European Axis'.

Article 1 of the Tokyo Charter also stipulates that 'The permanent seat of the Tribunal is in Tokyo'.

Article 2 pertains to the appointment of the members (judges) of the Tribunal. Article 4 stipulates the quorum and the presence, voting and absence of the judges, which will be explained in Sect. 2.3 of this chapter.

Article 3 stipulates the appointment and powers of the Tribunal's President and General Secretary, and the administrative work of the Secretariat, which will be discussed in Sects. 2.3 and 2.6 of this chapter.

Section II (Articles 5–8) covers 'Jurisdiction and General Provisions'.

Article 5, 'Jurisdiction Over Persons and Offenses' and Article 6, 'Responsibility of Accused' illustrate the main reason for the establishment and existence of the Tokyo Tribunal. They also depict a subject in international law which was debated everywhere by defence lawyers and legal scholars. This significant topic has been discussed already in Sect. 1.5 of Chapter 1.

Article 7 provides that the Tribunal may draft and amend its own 'Rules of Procedure'. Accordingly, 'Rules of Procedure' was prepared and announced by the judges' conference on 25 April 1946; Chapter 4 will discuss these rules.

Article 8 concerns the appointment and powers of the 'Chief of Counsel' (chief prosecutor) and the 'Associate Counsel' (associated prosecutors), which will be explained in Sect. 2.4 of this chapter.

Section III (Articles 9–10) provides a 'Fair Trial for Accused'. In order to ensure a fair trial for the accused, Article 9 specifies the 'Procedure for Fair Trial'. For example, the indictment shall meet certain requirements, and each of the accused persons shall be furnished, in adequate time for defence, a copy of the indictment and of the Charter, which shall be translated in a language understood by the accused, i.e. Japanese (Item a); all the proceedings (whether oral or in writing) shall be conducted in English and Japanese (Item b); each accused shall have the right to be represented by counsel of his own selection or as appointed by the Tribunal (Item c); the accused shall have the right, through himself or through his counsel, to conduct his defence, including the right to examine any witnesses, and to apply to the Tribunal for the production of witnesses or of documents in his favour (Items d and e). All these matters will be expounded below in Sects. 2.2 and 2.3 of this chapter, and in Chapter 4.

Article 10 is about applications, motions and other requests addressed to the Tribunal before the commencement of trial. These formalities are only mildly suggested in the Charter.

Section IV (Articles 11–15), under the heading of 'Powers of Tribunal and Conduct of Trial', covers many topics about trial procedures.

Article 11 elaborates upon the 'powers' of the Tribunal. The term 'power' here does not refer to the jurisdiction of the Tribunal (which is the most significant power of the Tribunal, as mentioned in Chapter 1), but the administrative authority possessed by the Tribunal, such as to summon witnesses, interrogate the accused and witnesses, require the production of evidentiary documents, require and administer oaths or declarations of the witnesses, and appoint officers for the execution of tasks designated by the Tribunal, including taking evidence on commission.

Article 12, although titled as 'Conduct of Trial', does not mention the steps, phases or course of the trial (topics that are covered in Article 15), but specifies the measures to be taken, and powers to be exercised by the Tribunal during trial to ensure prompt and fair judgement. For example, the Tribunal shall strive to confine the trial (during representation, evidence production, or debate) to an expeditious hearing of the issues raised by the charges, to prevent any action which would cause unreasonable delay, and rule out irrelevant issues and statements; the Tribunal shall maintain order at the trial and deal summarily with any contumacy, imposing appropriate punishment including exclusion from some or all further proceedings. Additionally, the Tribunal has the right to determine the mental and physical capacity of any accused to proceed to trial.

Article 13 pertains to 'Evidence', and discusses the different types of evidence that may be admitted, and the format and procedure for producing and filing them. Generally, the Tribunal shall not be bound by technical rules of evidence; it shall mostly adopt and apply expeditious and non-technical procedure, and permit any evidence which has probative value. Although these rules were drafted to ensure a swift and smooth trial, the results were not as anticipated; most judges found it hard to break away from the highly technical and complicated common law rules of procedure. The trial extended for two and a half years; an important reason for its delay, among many others, was the fastidious and cumbersome process of evidence submission. This topic will be discussed in detail in Chapter 4.

Article 14, titled 'Place of Trial' mandates that the first trial be held in Tokyo, which is the permanent seat of the Tribunal, and subsequent trials be held at any such place as the Tribunal decides. All trials of the Tribunal were conducted in Tokyo, and therefore this article was never used.

Article 15 stipulates the 'Course of Trial Proceedings'. This significant article outlines the general principles for the steps, phases and course of the trial: the prosecutor reads the indictment; the Tribunal asks each accused whether he pleads 'guilty' or 'not guilty'; the prosecution and each accused or his counsel may make a concise opening statement; the prosecution may offer evidence (including witnesses and documents) against the accused, and the defence may offer counter evidence (including witnesses and documents); the prosecution and each accused or his counsel may examine and cross-examine each witness and any documents; the accused or his counsel may make a closing statement to address the Tribunal; the prosecution may make a closing statement to address the Tribunal; finally, the Tribunal delivers its judgement and pronounces its sentence.

This article provides only a sketch of the procedural steps for the trial; the complexity of the actual proceedings are detailed in Chapter 4.

Section V (Articles 16–17), the final part of the Charter, is about 'Judgment and Sentence'.

Article 16 provides: 'The Tribunal shall have the power to impose upon an accused, on conviction, death or such other punishment as shall be determined by it to be just.' Since the Tribunal can impose the death penalty, it follows logically that it can issue milder sentences as well.

Although the Charter authorized the Tribunal to issue capital punishment, the enforcement of this power triggered fierce debates among the judges. Radhabinod Pal, the Indian judge tried to acquit all accused; a few other judges whose home countries had abolished the death penalty, proposed that the Tribunal impose life imprisonment instead of death, as the maximum punishment. Their proposition was not endorsed by the majority of the judges. Later, the Tribunal sentenced seven convicted war criminals to death by hanging based on the gravity of their crimes. Since some judges (including those who advocated non-application of the death penalty) refused to vote for the capital punishment, and the decision on any sentence required at least six affirmative votes, there were fewer death sentences and a lower sentenced to accused ratio than at the Nuremberg Tribunal.

Sir William Webb, the presiding judge from Australia, proposed the ludicrous idea that all accused should be exiled to an isolated island, on the lines of Britain, Russian and Austria's decision for Napoleon I. Although this idea did not draw much attention from other judges, he refused to vote for capital punishment against any accused, and instead publicized his proposition in his 'dissenting opinion' of the judgement.

The dissenting opinions of President Webb and a few other judges, and the voting of the bench on conviction and sentencing, will be discussed later in the book.[2]

Article 17 pertains to 'Judgment and Review', which provides that 'The judgment will be announced in open court and will give the reasons on which it is based'. As this was a general practice, the Tribunal could not be an exception. The Judgement of the Tribunal, comprising 1200 pages, encompassed all the reasons for the judgement, and took six and a half days to be read out. It not only met the requirement of this article, but also set a historical record in judicial practice across the world.

This article also demands that the record of the trial be transmitted to the Supreme Commander for the Allied Powers for his action thereon. 'A sentence will be carried out in accordance with the order of the Supreme Commander for the Allied Powers, who may at any time reduce or otherwise alter the sentence except to increase its severity.'

This leads to an important legal question: since the Supreme Commander has power to change (reduce) the punishment decided by the Tribunal, can the judgement of the Tribunal still be regarded as final? If so, what is the legal nature of the power held by the Supreme Commander?

The Tokyo Tribunal's judgement should undoubtedly be regarded as the final judgement. The finality of a judgement depends on whether the accused party has an option to appeal against it, that is, whether there exists an authority which can revoke such a judgement and re-try the case. The Tribunal's judgement was not subject to appeal by the parties (defendants or prosecution), and there was no authority (including the Supreme Commander) which could revoke the Tribunal's judgement and re-try the case. The Supreme Commander's capacity was in the nature of executive clemency of the head of a state to reprieve or pardon the punishment imposed by the state's Supreme Court. This power to pardon

---

[2] Editor's Note: As the original manuscript of this book is unfinished, the above-mentioned discussion is not found in the existing four chapters.

or reduce a penalty does not impair the conclusion that 'the judgment of the original court is final'. The Control Council for Germany was assigned a similar power by the Nuremberg Charter for the Nuremberg Trial.[3] The judgement delivered by the Nuremberg Tribunal, similar to that of the Tokyo Tribunal, was non-appealable and final.

Although the Control Council and the Supreme Commander for the Allied Powers were, respectively, empowered by the Nuremberg and Tokyo Charters to reduce penalties, they never implemented it. In Nuremberg, the sentences imposed on the accused were executed completely in accordance with the judgement of the Tribunal. In order to avoid international censure, the Supreme Commander in Tokyo did not amend the judgement at that time (the end of 1948), despite his desire to protect the Japanese war criminals. Consequently, the Japanese war criminals were punished. On 23 December 1948, the day the seven Japanese war criminals were condemned to be hanged, Douglas MacArthur issued a media statement: 'I have no reason to change the penalties imposed by the Tribunal. If such a rigorous procedure and the learned judges cannot be trusted, there will be nothing trustworthy in the world.'[4]

This completes the discussion of select articles in the Tokyo Charter. The rest of this chapter discusses articles on the Tribunal's organization, and Chapter 4 elaborates its procedures.

2.2 Location and Layout of the Tokyo Tribunal

Article 1 of the Tokyo Charter mandates that Tokyo be the permanent seat of the Tribunal, whereas Article 14 permits subsequent trials to be held wherever the Tribunal decides, with the exception of the first trial which should only be conducted in Tokyo. The two articles are apparently contradictory, but in reality they are not. The Tribunal must have

---

[3] *Charter of the International Military Tribunal*, Article 29.

[4] The newspapers published in Tokyo and other cities in Japan, on 23 December 1948, report his pompous statements on the judgement of the Tokyo Tribunal. Shortly after that, he commanded the Chief Prosecutor to release the remaining alleged Class-A war criminals from Sugamo Prison for a 'lack of sufficient evidence for prosecution'. Moreover, a year after the Tokyo Tribunal's judgement was delivered, he released an unauthorized 'Order No. 5', which stated that the war criminals sentenced by the Tokyo Tribunal could be released by a majority agreement of the Allied Powers after they had served one third of their terms (refer the statement of Zhou Enlai, China's Premier, on 15 May 1950).

a fixed official location (chosen to be Tokyo) for external communications and other purposes. However, for the convenience of conducting and efficacy of trials, and with deference to the will of the judges, the Charter authorized the Tribunal to shift a part of, or the entire trial to any place as it deemed appropriate.

Nevertheless, the Tribunal, throughout its existence conducted all trials in Tokyo, except once; it, however, could hardly qualify as an exception. In the spring of 1947, the Tribunal required Lieutenant General Kanji Ishihara, former Chief of Staff of the Kwantung Army, who was then bedridden, to testify at a trial. Instead, the Tribunal sent Harvey Northcroft, the judge from New Zealand, together with a team comprising the court secretary, a stenographer, and representatives of both the prosecution and the defence, to his home at Fukura, Yamagata Prefecture, for a 'bedside court hearing'. It was common practice for a court to send a commissioned judge and obtain evidence outside of court, in case of witness's absentia on valid grounds. Northcroft's expedition was one such instance, and should not be regarded as a deviation from the stipulated norm.

In the warm summer months after the Tribunal's opening in 1946, the judges in their black satin robes, profusely sweated in the courtroom. Some of them suggested shifting the trial temporarily to Karuizawa, a summer resort. Many judges thought that that would be expensive and unfeasible and therefore dismissed the idea. As the courtroom was not air conditioned, the Tribunal decided to strike (by adjournment of the hearing) and demand for air conditioners. Accordingly, the appliances were installed by the GHQ within a week of their resistance, and the trial resumed. Although the public scorned the Tribunal's strike, their reaction would have been worse had the trial been shifted.

Despite the flexibility in location provided by the Charter, the entire trial was conducted only in Tokyo.

The building of the former Japanese Ministry of War in Ichigaya, Tokyo, was deliberately chosen as the permanent premises of the Tokyo Tribunal. Prior to World War II, the building which housed the Imperial Japanese Army Academy, was the nurturing ground for Japanese militarism. During war, the Imperial General Headquarters comprised of the Ministry of War, the Army General Staff Office and the Ministry of Navy, acted as a centre to issue directions for aggressive wars.

More than 75 per cent of the buildings in Tokyo were destroyed by fires and bombs during World War II. Amidst the ashes and war debris, some structures, such as the building that housed the Tokyo Tribunal, were unaffected.

Asahi Shimbun, a popular daily newspaper in Japan with a circulation of about five million, in its article titled 'Traces of a Dream', described the surroundings of the Tribunal headquarters in poetic language:

> In red or white, the Azaleas bloom, filling the air with scents wafting from the grass on either side of the ramp. You may walk across the ramp that leads to the Tokyo Tribunal. There stands before your eyes, a majestic building in concrete and steel, and in front of its gate is a wooden plaque with the words 'INTERNATIONAL MILITARY TRIBUNAL, FAR EAST'.

> The pine trees on the hills near the plaque still flourish. This building used to be the shelter of the Imperial Japanese Army Academy. After the Pacific War broke out, the Ministry of War and the Imperial Japanese Army General Staff Office began using it as the centre for warlords to issue commands and orders (and to talk their lunatic dreams). The Tribunal's trials are conducted in the building's auditorium, the sanctuary of those Japanese warlords whose criminal acts destroyed human civilizations in the 20th century. As spring ceased and summer began, on May 3, the 21st year of Showa era (1946), the trial commenced in Ichigayadai. Alas! The balm of flowers, the burgeoning spring, all are gone like a dream of the past![5]

The headquarters of the Tokyo Tribunal or the 'War Ministry Building' was a magnificent three-storey building with many functional rooms.[6] The Tribunal held its sessions on the first (ground) floor in the 'grand courtroom', and the rest of the floor was used as offices for the Secretariat and its staff. The Tribunal's stenographers, interpreters, typists and printing staff, guards and watchmen, mail clerks, photographers,

---

[5] *The Tokyo Trial* by the Journalist Team of *Asahi Shimbun* in the Tokyo Tribunal, Vol. 1, 1946, p. 1.

[6] The building that the Tokyo Tribunal was housed in, was called the War Ministry Building by the Allied Powers and the Japanese people, because the Ministry of War had been stationed here after the Imperial Japanese Army Academy moved away before the War. Following the outbreak of the Pacific War, it became the location of the Imperial General Headquarters composed of the Ministry of War, the Army General Staff Office and the Ministry of Navy. Therefore, the 'War Ministry Building' was still an appropriate name for it.

recordists and other servicing staff, worked on this floor. The floor also had lounge rooms near the courtroom for the defendants, witnesses, counsel, journalists and spectators.

The second floor was used by the judges to work, rest and conduct meetings. Each judge was allocated two office rooms—one for himself, and an adjoining room, for his secretary and typist. The office of the Tribunal's President was used by Hideki Tōjō. A large room in the centre of the second floor was a conference room for the judges, where the Japanese militarists held frequent meetings during the war for plans of aggression.

The second floor also housed the General Secretary's office and a small canteen which provided lunch and drinks for the judges, prosecutors and other senior court officers. The waitresses employed at the canteen spoke fluent English, and its Japanese chefs were experts in cooking Western dishes of the style served at the Imperial Hotel. However, the judges seldom went there and they usually drove back to their Imperial Hotel for lunch, probably just to enjoy a short break from their long hours in the courthouse.

The third floor of the building was assigned to the prosecution team. The Chief Prosecutor, the associate prosecutors and assistant prosecutors from the Allied Powers had their offices here. Some rooms on this floor were used for archiving documents, and storing the Tribunal's books and records. There were also dormitories for a limited number of senior staff (such as court secretaries, personal secretaries, and clerks for printing, typing and news release) who may be required to stay over.

The grand courtroom, the venue for the Tokyo Trial and the hub of all activity, was at the posterior part of the first floor.

The auditorium of the Imperial Japanese Army Academy had been changed into a courtroom; it was square, with a housing capacity of about 2000 people. The GHQ of the Supreme Commander for the Allied Powers had it refurbished in the style of the Nuremberg Tribunal's courtroom as soon as it was allocated to the Tribunal. The renovation was completed in three months and the courtroom was larger and better equipped than that at Nuremberg.

The interior structure and layout of the courtroom is briefly described below (Fig. 2.1).

The hall had a dais; a long, phoebe wood desk with 11 seats was placed on it. Behind the seats was a large wooden shelf displaying the 11 national flags of the 11 judges on the bench. When the Tribunal opened

Fig. 2.1 Courtroom of the International Military Tribunal for the Far East

its session, they would ascend the stage in a single file and sit down at their respective seats: the President, at the centre, and the judges alternating between his right and left, in the order: the US, China, the UK, the Soviet Union, Canada, France, the Netherlands, New Zealand, India and the Philippines.

In front of the bench was a long desk with some chairs, for the registrar, court secretaries and the judges' personal secretaries.

On the other side of the hall, facing the bench and against the wall was the dock, a two-tiered seating area where the 28 defendants sat in two rows. The erstwhile war makers who were now prisoners were often the focus of everyone's attention during trial.

Near the bench, there was a podium with a lectern for the prosecutors or the defence lawyers; only one person at a time was permitted to speak at the lectern. The lectern had an in-built microphone and a red-light indicator. When the speech was being translated, the red light was on;

after the translation was completed, the light went off so that the speaker could continue speaking. The President was also given a microphone and a red-light indicator because he often needed to speak on behalf of the Tribunal.

On the left of the podium, there was a small witness box, erected slightly above the ground. As only one witness was allowed to testify at a time, the box was designed to accommodate just one person.

When the prosecutor or the defence counsel stood on the podium, the witness could sit in the witness box to testify. The witness was allowed to be seated because he had to stay there for a long time responding to direct examination, cross-examination, re-direct examination, and re-cross examination made by the prosecutors and the defence counsel, after providing his own testimony. In one instance, Puyi, the Emperor of the puppet regime Manchukuo, was summoned to court for eight consecutive days. What a pity if he had to testify standing for five hours every day!

A microphone and a red-light indicator were also installed on the witness stand, and the red light indicated that his testimony was being translated.

On both sides of the podium, there was a large desk with about ten seats. The desk on the left was for the prosecution team, and the other, for the defence team. There were scores of prosecutors (including assistant prosecutors), and about a hundred American and Japanese defence lawyers. Only those who were on duty for the particular session sat at the desks, whereas others found seats elsewhere or were absent for the proceedings.

Between the witness box and the prosecutors' desk, there was a square table for the on-duty interpreters. The interpreters were a group of professionals proficient in both English and Japanese, and they would translate for the speakers during the trial. Occasionally, a witness or lawyer spoke in Chinese, Russian or some other language, which also had to be translated into English and Japanese. On the desk where the interpreters sat was a microphone and a red signal button; they would switch it on while interpreting, and switch it off upon finishing, to allow others to speak.

All the seats were equipped with earphones; the listener could switch to the language that he understood or wanted to listen to—English or Japanese, and sometimes even Russian or Chinese.

Language translation had always been a problem for the Tribunal, and had caused frequent disputes between parties. Hence, the Tribunal established a Language Arbitration Board with three members to resolve language problems. They were seated in front of the VIP spectators' area and attended all the court sessions to render services whenever needed.

Behind the interpreters' desk, there was a small desk for the court stenographers. They transcribed speech into writing with a stenographic device instead of manually.

On the right side of the hall, and against the wall, a large, rectangular fenced area was demarcated for the journalists. The seats within were grouped into two halves: one half of the seats for journalists from the Allied Powers, and the other half, for Japanese journalists. They often brought with them cameras, typewriters and transmitters. They hustled about, chatted and used their contraptions, making this area the noisiest and most crowded part of the courtroom.

On the left of the hall, opposite to the journalists' area, there was a rectangular platform which was reserved exclusively for the special (VIP) spectators from the Allied Powers. It had two rows of about a hundred seats. Given the strict eligibility criteria for VIP spectators, the seats were sparsely occupied, thus making it the quietest corner of the courtroom.

A row of seats in front of the elevated platform for VIP spectators was designed for other prosecutors and counsel, and the three members of the Language Arbitration Board.

This completes the discussion on the main floor in the grand courtroom (Fig. 2.2).

There was a balcony on one side of the hall, to the right of the judges' bench. It was designated for ordinary spectators, with two separate sections, one for the Japanese and the other for non-Japanese people. It had a seating capacity of about 600, and was always filled with people. Eager relatives of the accused, and curious residents and tourists from Tokyo, occupied the seats and watched the criminals being tried, at a distance.[7]

---

[7] Among the spectators on the balcony were Kōki Hirota's wife and daughter, and Shigenori Tōgō's wife, a German woman who came to all the sessions for the entire two years of trial. The hapless women sat facing their husbands or fathers, and exchanged sad smiles when their eyes met. When Hirota heard his death sentence, he shivered and turned pale. He looked for his wife and daughter on his right, but they were seated on his left. He was bewildered and could not figure out where they sat; he could hardly walk out of the courtroom and had to be dragged out by two sturdy military policemen.

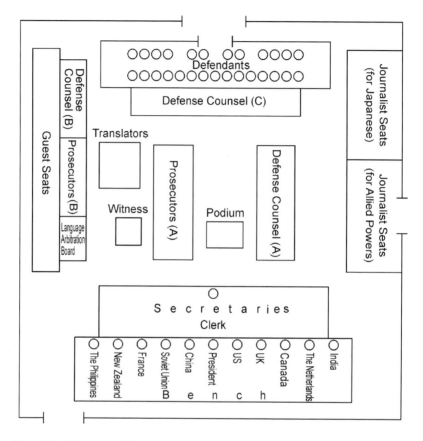

Fig. 2.2 Diagram of the courtroom (*Note* On the right of the judges' bench, there is a balcony with about 600 raked seats for ordinary spectators, Japanese and non-Japanese separated, which is not depicted here)

At the corner of the balcony, there was a glass room for recording the trial proceedings. Apart from a written recording of the court sessions of two years in more than 50,000 pages, there was also a wire recording of the entire Tokyo Trial. Hence, the Trial was an expensive affair.

There was no seat allotted for the Marshal of the Court. He often walked about to maintain order, announced the opening and closing of the session, and when a witness had to testify, ushered him in and administered his oath.

The security of the courtroom and of the entire Tribunal was maintained by the military police corps of the GHQ. When the Tribunal was in session, about 20 MPs (military policemen) stood in their designated positions in the hall; most of them faced the bench, and the remaining few positioned in front of the journalists' section and the spectators' seats on the balcony stood menacingly, facing the audience. Although this arrangement annoyed the journalists and spectators, it was retained for security reasons.

This completes the description of the courtroom and offices located in the former War Ministry Building.

2.3 MEMBERS OF THE TRIBUNAL: JUDGES AND PRESIDENT

2.3.1 Introduction to the 11 Judges

The Tokyo Charter promulgated on 19 January 1946 stipulated that the Tokyo Tribunal should 'consist of not less than five nor more than nine members, appointed by the Supreme Commander for the Allied Powers from the names submitted by the Signatories to the Instrument of Surrender'. Therefore, within one month of the Charter's issuance, that is, on 15 February 1946, the Supreme Commander appointed nine judges, one each from China, the Soviet Union, the US, the UK, Australia, Canada, France, the Netherlands, and New Zealand.

In the amendment to the Charter on 26 April 1946, two members were added from India and the Philippines, respectively, thus making a total of eleven judges.[8] On the same day, the Supreme Commander made the aforesaid appointments upon nomination by their home countries. When the Tribunal officially opened on 3 May 1946, there were eleven judges (Fig. 2.3).

---

[8] India and the Philippines did not sign the Instrument of Surrender. They were allowed to join the Tribunal because they had been admitted to the Far Eastern Commission (FEC), the supreme policy-making body over the control of Japan. To make the membership of the Tokyo Tribunal and the FEC consistent, India and the Philippines were each entitled to a judge's seat. On the other hand, Pakistan, Burma and Ceylon were excluded from both organizations. Indonesia and Vietnam were respectively Dutch and French colonies, struggling for their independence, and they also had no representation in the two organizations.

Fig. 2.3 The judges

Sir William Webb, from Australia, President of the Tribunal
John P. Higgins, from the United States (who resigned three months later and was succeeded by Gen. Myron Cramer)
Mei Ju-ao, from China
Lord Patrick, from the United Kingdom
Gen. Ivan Michyevich Zaryanov, from the Soviet Union
E. Stuart McDougall, from Canada
Henri Bernard, from France
B. V. A. Röling, from the Netherlands
E. Harvey Northcroft, from New Zealand
R. M. Pal, from India
Delfin Jaranilla, from the Philippines

All judges, excepting the US judge, Higgins, served for the entire duration of the Tokyo Tribunal. Higgins was the chief justice of the Massachusetts Superior Court. He assumed office at the Tokyo Tribunal after delegating his duties to a deputy chief justice. Owing to the sudden death of his deputy, and the illness of his counterpart, he was compelled to resign office at the Tribunal. Higgins wrote to the US government and the Supreme Commander for the Allied Powers requesting resignation, and upon their approval, returned to Massachusetts. Gen. Myron Cramer, former Judge Advocate General of the US Army, replaced Higgins. It was rumoured that the United States sent a military person this time to match the military judge from the Soviet Union.

The replacement of the US judge took place in mid-July, 1946, not long after Higgins had assumed office in Feb 1946. On the day when Gen. Cramer first presented himself in court, the defence counsel submitted an urgent motion to debar Cramer from attending the Tribunal on the grounds that: (1) the maximum number of judges that the Tribunal could have was eleven, but Cramer was the 12th appointed judge, which was a violation of the Charter; (2) the intermediate replacement of judges made the fairness of the trial questionable; (3) as a General of the victory state and former Judge Advocate General, he could not act impartially in a court such as the Tokyo Tribunal.

The Tribunal firmly dismissed the motion after a judges' conference.

Even before this event, and at the very beginning of trial, the defence counsel had challenged the President of the Tribunal and the Filipino judge. They also threatened to do the same against other judges. The defence counsel requested Webb to withdraw from the trial because Webb was priorly appointed by the Australian government and served as the chairman of an investigation committee on Japanese atrocities; he was liable to be prejudiced against the Japanese military force and hence could not impartially conduct the trial. As for Jaranilla, the defence counsel found that he had been captured by the Japanese troops and was forced to join the Bataan Death March.[9] As he was a survivor of that episode, he was presumed to be antagonistic towards the Japanese army and thus could not be an impartial judge.

After the rejection of the first two motions against the judges, the defence had found no reason to make further accusations against other judges. In less than three months after the judges' induction, however, they took the opportunity of the replacement of the US judge to launch another attack. This was merely their strategy to delay the trial's progress as far as possible. The judges could have escaped censure if the Tokyo Charter, like the Nuremberg Charter, had prohibited attacks against them.[10] Unfortunately, the Tokyo Charter did not foresee the onslaughts, and unnecessarily exposed their limitations to the defence.

The 11 judges, nominally appointed by the Supreme Commander for the Allied Powers according to the nominations by the Allied Powers, were actually selected by the governments of their respective home countries. The Supreme Commander's role was limited because he had no choice, but to appoint the sole candidate nominated by each government. Although they were international judges, they represented their home countries, and displayed their national flag behind benches and on cars.

All the 11 judges, excepting the two military officers from the United States and the Soviet Union, were civilians who had long served as judges in domestic courts, as legal practitioners, instructors, or activists. Sir

---

[9] Bataan Death March was one of the greatest atrocities committed by the Japanese troops during World War II, on the lines of the Nanking Massacre. In the spring of 1942, when the Japanese troops took over the Bataan peninsula in the Philippines, the prisoners of war and civilian Filipinos, regardless of their age or physical conditions, were forced to march under the scorching sun to the concentration camps in San Fernando. They marched a distance of 120 km in nine days. During the march, the Japanese soldiers not only refused to provide them with food and water, but also brutally beat them and shot anyone who secretly obtained water from the ditches. Over 8000 Filipinos and Americans died in the march, and their bodies were scattered along the road. This event was therefore called the 'Bataan Death March'.

[10] *Charter of the International Military Tribunal*, Article 3. It stipulates that no judge can be challenged.

William Webb (59 years old), the then chief justice of the Supreme Court of Queensland, had been committed to judicial services since 1913; the UK judge (57 years old) was a judge of the Supreme Court of Scotland; the judge from New Zealand (62 years old) was a judge of the Supreme Court of New Zealand; the Filipino judge (63 years old) was the deputy chief justice of the Supreme Court of the Philippines and had once served as the Attorney General and Minister of Justice; the Canadian judge (58 years old) was a judge of the Quebec Court of Appeal. All five had been judges in domestic courts and had a profound experience in trials. The Indian judge (58 years old) had been a professor of mathematics before he switched to law; he had also acquired about thirty years of experience in legal practices and participated in many international activities. The Chinese judge (42 years old) and the Dutch judge (40 years old) were the youngest among the judges; they both were university professors and legal researchers, apart from being, respectively, a legislator and legal practitioner. The French judge (47 years old) had been a colonial magistrate after law school graduation, and was a passionate advocate of De Gaulle's Free France. He served as a prosecutor or the chief prosecutor in several military tribunals.

The two judges who were in active military service wore their military uniforms instead of black robes in court. Although they were military men, they both were law graduates and had many years of experience in judicial and prosecutorial work.

The Soviet Union judge (62 years old), from the Military Collegium of the USSR (Union of Soviet Socialist Republics, also known as Soviet Union) Supreme Court, had served as the chief prosecutor of the Wartime Military Collegium and the president of the Red Army Military Academy of Law, and was involved in the trial of the followers of Leon Trotsky and Nikolai Bukharin. Gen. Zaryanov received the Order of Lenin, Order of the Red Banner, Order of the Red Star, Medal of Twenty Years' Service in Red Army, Medal for the Defence of Moscow, and Medal for the Victory Over Germany.

The US judge (65 years old) was the eldest member judge of the Tribunal. He graduated from Harvard Law School, and had a long stint as a legal practitioner. During World War I, he joined the US Army and fought in France, after which he remained in the army and spent over twenty years as a judge advocate and a teacher of military law. In the years between the outbreak of the Pacific War and the end of World War II, he was Judge Advocate General, the top legal post in the US Army, where he conducted effective and fruitful reforms on the wartime military legal system. He retired in November 1945, but was recalled to active duty in August 1946 to act as a judge in the Tokyo Tribunal, in replacement of Higgins. He received the Labour Glory Cross, Distinguished Service Cross and an honorary JSD (Doctor of Juristic Science) degree.

This completes the description of the member judges in the Tokyo Tribunal.[11]

2.3.2 *Working Relationship and 'Judges' Conference'*

Throughout the existence of the Tribunal, the eleven judges worked diligently and cooperatively. For instance, even after the Indian judge expressed peculiar views on almost every major legal problem, and quarrelled with his peers in conferences, he was still treated well outside the meetings. Although the Soviet judge, who was the only representative from a socialist country, expressed ideas that were contrary to his peers, and made lengthy, controversial speeches arousing resentment and criticism, he was not held in contempt. This liberality of manner among them was perhaps possible because they were a group of highly educated and experienced judges, with an average age of over 50.

The judges' conferences were conducted in English. According to the Tokyo Charter, all proceedings of the Tribunal must be in English and Japanese, where Japanese was the language commonly understood by defendants. In interest of the defendant's right to a fair trial, he is informed of the trial proceedings in Japanese. The judges' conferences, however, were privately held in the absence of the defendants, excluding the requirement for Japanese translation. During conferences, the judges discussed in English, and the Soviet judge who did not understand English, brought his interpreter.

Language did not pose much trouble for the Tribunal's judges. Most of them were educated by the Anglo-American legal system. Judges from Great Britain, the United States, Canada, Australia and New Zealand were conversant in English. Even those from countries such as India and the

---

[11] On 23 October 1946, the Civil Intelligence Bureau of the GHQ posted a press release on the resumes of justices. This article was reprinted in *Japan Times* and other Japanese newspapers. For the Tribunal members' experience and life in Tokyo, Xie Shuangqiu, a special reporter of *News Daily* (《新闻报》) in Shanghai, wrote a long article, published in series on 23–25 March 1948.

Philippines, due to long-term European and American colonization, had had English as their language of instruction in universities. The Indian and Filipino judges not only spoke English, but they had also received a common law education. Judges from non-English speaking and non-common law countries such as China, France and the Netherlands, could manage to speak English and grasp the common law procedures, although they came from the civil law system—the other major legal system in the world, apart from the common law system of the Anglo-American countries. This was because the US government, which had been occupying and controlling Japan, had formerly suggested to the Allied Powers the desirable criteria for the selection of the Tribunal's members.

On 18 October 1945, the US Department of State sent a long, confidential note to the embassies of the Allied Powers. The note explained in detail the policies of and measures taken by the US government to deal with Japanese war criminals. It stated that the Supreme Commander for the Allied Powers would organize an international tribunal for the trial of Class-A war criminals, and asked the Allied governments to nominate the judges for appointment by the Supreme Commander. The note requested that the Allied Powers recommend an English-speaking legal expert; this clearly affected the selection process in non-English speaking countries. China, for instance, sent an US educated, J.D. graduate who had taught common law in China.

Consequently, most of the judges in the Tokyo Tribunal spoke English, except the Soviet judge who was supported by a fluent interpreter and some efficient translators. He avidly debated with the other judges, and sometimes sent them memorandums; his opinions and proposals, however, were rarely accepted.

The judges who did not have an opportunity to speak at the judges' conference, or were unsatisfied with the majority opinion, would write memorandums after the meeting and send them to other judges. The memorandums focused on expounding the author's own ideas and sometimes attacked the opinions or proposals made by others during the meeting. Every time an important topic was discussed, memorandums were frequently exchanged between the judges. This was jokingly called as the 'Battle of Memorandums'. Some judges indulged in this to display their literary skills and stubborn opinions, while others were less enthusiastic about writing memorandums.

It was the President's duty to process the memorandums. If a memorandum had a specific suggestion or requested reconsideration of a previous resolution, the President had to convene a judges' conference to discuss it. If, however, a memorandum only elaborated on opinions, justified a rejected proposal, or expressed hostility, the President might just ignore it without convening a meeting.

The members of the Tokyo and Nuremberg Tribunal were differently organized. In Nuremberg, every judge had an alternate who could function in place of the principal judge with full authority when the latter was unable to attend a court session or a judges' conference. Therefore, in the Nuremberg Trial, four judges (or their alternates) representing the four Allied Powers were present on all days. The Nuremberg Charter also required all important resolutions to be made by affirmative votes of at least three members of the Tribunal.[12] The Tokyo Tribunal, however, had no such rules for alternate judges. The Tokyo Charter stated that more than half of the members being present shall constitute a quorum, and their majority vote was necessary for the adoption of any resolution.[13] Only six of the 11 judges were therefore required to be present to open a court session or convene a judges' conference; only four of the six judges present had to cast their affirmative votes to make any decision. In addition, the Tokyo Charter stated that 'In case the votes are evenly divided, the vote of the President shall be decisive'.[14] This paved the way for manipulation by any four judges or the President and two judges, and could jeopardize the organization of the Tribunal—a drawback which was called to attention by some astute writers.[15]

Although there was room for manipulation, it never happened. Throughout the functioning of the Tokyo Trial, judges were rarely absent for trial proceedings. Apart from a short vacation to their home countries that the President and the Indian judge took, the bench was mostly occupied. Some judges had never asked for leave; the Chinese judge had been absent for only a few times out of 818 court sessions. The judges arrived on time for the sessions and filed into and out of the court, eight times a day, like school pupils entering and leaving classrooms. All the judges were responsible and diligent; when they voted on a specific matter, it always

---

[12] *Charter of the International Military Tribunal*, Article 4(a) and 4(c).

[13] *Charter of the International Military Tribunal for the Far East*, Article 4(a) and 4(b).

[14] *Charter of the International Military Tribunal for the Far East*, Article 4(b).

[15] Raginsky and Rozenblit of the Soviet Union had this idea. See М. Ю. Рагинский and С. Я. Розенблит, *International Trial of the Japanese Major War Criminals* (Chinese Translation), World Affairs Press, 1954, p. 55.

resulted in a majority/minority, and the casting vote by the President was never resorted to.

During the President's absence, the US judge acted on his behalf, because he was second in hierarchy and sat to the right of the President. The Chinese judge was the next in rank, and sat to the left of the President.

2.3.3 Seating Arrangement of the Bench

The seating arrangement of the bench was not stipulated in the Tokyo Charter, but it was heatedly discussed before the official opening of the Tribunal. Unless arranged alphabetically, questions over the order of seating at international events and court sessions are unavoidable because it involves not only an individual's dignity, but also the status of their nation.

For the Tribunal, apparently, an easy solution would be for the judges of different nationalities to sit according to the signing order of their respective countries when the Allied Powers accepted Japan's Instrument of Surrender (i.e. the US, China, the UK, the Soviet Union, Australia, Canada, France, the Netherlands and New Zealand, where the Australian judge served as President of the Tribunal). As a reasonable arrangement, this was supported by many judges including those from China, the US and Canada.

The President of the Tribunal, however, disliked the proposal and instead wished to have the British and American judges, especially Lord Patrick, sit beside him. Therefore, he worked hard to oppose the aforesaid arrangement by proposing different alternatives. He first suggested that the seating sequence follow the order of the Five Powers of the UN Security Council (the US, the UK, the Soviet Union, China and France). It was, however, drawn to his attention that the five permanent members of UN Security Council were arranged alphabetically in the UN Charter (China, France, the Soviet Union, the UK and the US), which would mean that the judges from China and France (both non-common law countries) sat at his side, instead of the preferred British and American judges. The President then proposed that the Tribunal arrange all member judges in the alphabetical order of their nations; as it was not an UN-affiliated agency, it need not follow the UN Security Council. In this way, the central seats would be occupied by the judges from Canada and China, followed by France, India, the Netherlands and New

Zealand …; this arrangement further distanced him from his favoured judges. Another judge suggested that, instead of considering the country names, the seating arrangement be on the basis of the judges' seniority. 'Seniority', however, could mean either the judge's age or his experience; for the latter, there were the questions—how to calculate the years of services of a judge? Were the years in a local court to be regarded the same as those in a national supreme court? Moreover, were the years in which he practised law in a firm or taught in a university to be included as experience? A special committee would be required to investigate the legal and political systems of the 11 different countries and resolve these questions. The Chinese judge believed that 'the most reasonable solution would be to arrange the seats according to the sequence of signatories on the Instrument of Surrender'. If that was unacceptable to the President and its peers, he suggested that 'we might find a scale to weigh us and put the heavier ones to the middle. In this way, we would have a fairest and most objective standard'.

On hearing this, the judges burst into laughter. The President remarked that it was a good idea 'but only suitable for boxing games'. As they were at an international tribunal, and not a 'boxing stadium', it was not a feasible solution. The Chinese judge retorted, 'Should the order for signing the Instrument of Surrender not be followed, then this, in my opinion, would be the only applicable criterion. Even if I would be placed at the end of the bench, I would be able to sit there at ease and explain to my government, who should not blame me. If China wanted a central seat, it would have to send a fatter man to replace me.' It was evident that the Chinese judge had understood the President's prejudices and motivations.

The seating arrangement was frequently discussed at several judges' conferences in a partly serious and partly jocular style. The President neither made a decision nor put it to a vote, thus leaving it in disputatious chaos. Only on the day before the Tribunal commenced, were his real intentions revealed.

The second of May 1946 marked the culmination of the debate over the seating arrangement. The General Secretary sent an urgent notice that morning, asking the judges to prepare for a rehearsal and photo session of the Tribunal's opening ceremony at 4 p.m., with their formal robes on. The judges gathered at the lounge at the specified hour; the President then announced that they should enter the courtroom and sit down in the following order: the US, the UK, China, the Soviet Union,

France, Canada, the Netherlands, New Zealand, India and the Philippines, explaining that this arrangement was made with the consent of the Supreme Commander for the Allied Powers. According to this arrangement, the judges from the US, China, France, the Netherlands and India sat on the President's right, and the judges from the UK, the Soviet Union, Canada, New Zealand and the Philippines, on his left. Apparently, the arrangement was in accord with the idea of the Five Powers of the UN Security Council taking the central seats, but in reality, it was just a ploy to secure the two central seats for the British and American judges, with China in the third position, and Canada, the sixth following France (Canada signed ahead of France on the Instrument of Surrender).

His announcement came as a shock to most of the judges; the Chinese and Canadian judges were the most piqued. The Chinese judge remarked that the arrangement was absurd 'because it was made neither in the signing order of the Instrument of Surrender, nor in order of the Five Powers in the UN Security Council. It was not even according to the alphabetical order of the nations—a system usually adopted by international conferences'. He concluded by saying, 'It is unintelligible. I cannot accept this arrangement; and I am unable to join in today's rehearsal.' He then returned to his office and removed his black robe to show his defiance. The Canadian judge also criticized the arrangement.

Noticing that things had become unmanageable, and surprised by the Chinese judge's reaction, Webb went to Mei's office and said glibly, 'The Supreme Commander's intention of putting the British and American judges in the centre is based on their understanding of common law procedures. This arrangement is adopted only to facilitate our work, and not to discriminate against China. China will still have a better position on the bench than the Soviet Union and France, as it is the central force of the Five Powers.' The Chinese judge remarked that it was 'an international tribunal, and not a British or American one'. Therefore, it was unnecessary to assign them the central positions. He further questioned that if there was really a need to do so, why the judges from common law countries like Canada and New Zealand would be placed at extremities. The President argued, 'Under the current arrangement, your neighbouring seats will be occupied by the American and French judges, and not the Soviet general, which will be agreeable to you.' Mei retorted that he had 'not come to Tokyo for pleasure', but to fight the injustices done to China by the Japanese war criminals. As 'China had suffered from over fifty years of Japanese invasions conducted by war criminals, it had the serious mission of trying the Japanese war criminals'. He continued to say that unlike the Westerners, the Chinese did not resent the Soviets. He personally felt that his Russian colleague was 'an amiable person' who could 'talk and joke well'.

Webb firmly told him that this was the Supreme Commander's idea and 'it would be a pity if your refusal were to entail any unpleasant situation for Sino-US relations. Your government might not endorse your decision'. The Chinese judge replied, 'It is a different matter whether my government endorses it or not, but I cannot accept such an arrangement which has no proper grounds, in law or in facts. A soldier is only obliged to obey legitimate orders, and this applies to a judge as well. Moreover, China was inflicted by disastrous Japanese aggression, fought the longest war of resistance, and suffered the greatest losses. It is inconceivable that China's deserving place in an international tribunal against Japanese war criminals will be lower than Britain's—a nation that only surrendered during the wars. I don't believe that the Chinese government will agree with your arrangement. Moreover, I doubt that it was issued by the Supreme Commander himself.' His last sentence challenged the President's honour and integrity. Annoyed by Mei's firm stance, Webb left the room saying, 'Please allow me to discuss with the others and see what they think.' On seeing Mei prepare to leave, he requested him to remain till he returned.

The President returned in ten minutes and smilingly explained that after discussing with the others, he had come to the conclusion that that day's rehearsal was 'a temporary and unofficial event'. Hence, they could proceed with the original arrangement, and the next day's formal opening could be discussed in a meeting that evening. The Chinese judge still mistrusted him; he felt it was a ploy to orally confirm the validity of the original arrangement, then cancel the evening's meeting, and declare that the Supreme Commander refused to change the 'effective' arrangement on the next day. He therefore persisted in his argument: 'Even if the rehearsal is temporary and unofficial, there are many photographers and journalists waiting in the courtroom. They will take a lot of photos and post them in newspapers. These photos may well be seen by Chinese people, who will be surprised to see such an unfounded arrangement that does not match China's reputation and status, and will then scorn me for my ineptitude. Although the Tokyo Charter does not stipulate the seating order, our Tribunal's establishment and its power to try the major Japanese war criminals are founded on Japan's Instrument of Surrender.

To arrange the bench seats according to the sequence of signatories on the Instrument of Surrender is the one and only legitimate and reasonable solution. I have discussed it several times in the judges' conferences, and most colleagues have expressed no objection, nor have they offered a better approach. However, you have been unwilling to put it to a vote. I see no need to hold another meeting. The only solution is to apply the sequence of signatures for the rehearsal. If the Supreme Commander does not agree, we can convene a conference to discuss it tomorrow. If things are not done like this, I will definitely not join the rehearsal. Meanwhile, I have to consider carefully what I am going to do in future, either to ask for instruction from my government and see if it supports me, or to submit my resignation and request to be replaced by another person. That is my personal business, though.'

Webb again anxiously requested Mei to stay back till he returned after consulting others.

All this delayed the scheduled rehearsal by twenty minutes, and the participants became impatient. The Chinese judge knew that the rehearsal would not take place without his presence. Even if the rehearsal was hastily held, the official opening of the Tribunal would be postponed, which would cause a great disturbance as the date had been fixed, and announced to the world. Additionally, the Tribunal did not fix the opening date until the Soviet judge had arrived in Tokyo, because the GHQ and President Webb repeatedly stated that the Trial would commence only when all the judges were present. Going by that principle, the Chinese judge's refusal to participate would also stall the official opening of the Tribunal and create room for suspicion in Japan and across the world. The Supreme Commander or the President of the Tribunal could not afford to withstand these consequences. Therefore, Mei's firm standpoint was taken at a critical juncture.[16]

The President returned to Mei's office for the third time and said, 'We agree with you; the rehearsal will be conducted in the sequence of signatures on the Instrument of Surrender. I will report it to the Supreme Commander tonight and see whether he agrees.' He then sullenly left the room. The Chinese judge wore his robe and went to the conference

---

[16] For the dispute over the bench's order and the Chinese judge winning the battle against marginalization by the President and the common law judges, see the report by Liu Pusheng, a special reporter in Tokyo sent by *Yishi Daily* (《益世报》) in Tianjin, 'Introduction to the Judges in the Tokyo International Tribunal' (3 August 1947).

room. The rehearsal started thirty minutes behind schedule, and many photographs of the event were taken.

At 9:30 a.m. on the following day, that is, May 3, the Tribunal officially opened. This was a major event in Tokyo. Journalists, photographers, guests from the Allied Powers and Japanese spectators crowded both inside and outside the courtroom. The judges had already gathered in their conference room at 9:15 a.m., and the President announced, 'The Supreme Commander has agreed; the sequence of entering the courtroom and the seating order will be the same as in yesterday's rehearsal.' On hearing this, the judges felt relieved, for the debate over the seating arrangement was finally resolved. The Canadian judge was especially excited, and he thanked the Chinese judge. He said, 'I should thank you. If not for your resolute stance, I would have sat behind the French judge, a disgrace for me indeed. I think that ridiculous arrangement was William's [Webb's] idea, and he mentioned Mac [MacArthur] just to intimidate us.' It remained a mystery whether the idea to retain the original arrangement was the President's alone, or the President and MacArthur's together.

The battle over the seating arrangement was narrated, not to highlight the victory of the marginalized nations, but to draw lessons from it. First, we should realize that such struggles, open or closed, occur frequently and sometimes unavoidably, in any international occasion. They should not be treated lightly because they concern a country's status and honourability in the international community. Second, despite being one of the Five Powers, China had to deal with discrimination. Despite being a big country, its rights and interests were often overlooked under the corrupt and impotent administration of Chiang Kai-shek. Determination and persistent efforts of China's representatives in the international arena were thus necessary to safeguard China's rights and interests. Finally, a legitimate reason to fight for national interests is paramount to display one's resilience and courage. A strategy should be built from the present situation and after evaluating the consequences of changing it. Courage without wisdom will not take us far, and may even hinder our efforts.

This concludes the discussion about the seating arrangement of the bench. Next, we shall discuss the appointment, roles and powers of the President of the Tribunal.

2.3.4 Appointment, Roles and Powers of the President

As stipulated in Item (a) of Article 3 in the Tokyo Charter, the President of the Tribunal was appointed by the Supreme Commander for the Allied Powers from the 11 members of the Tribunal. In the Nuremberg Tribunal, however, the president was elected by the members.[17]

Whether elected or appointed, the President was the first member of the Tribunal and his basic responsibility was to conduct the Trial. He had the same rights and obligations as other judges while exercising the power of adjudication. Additionally, the President was authorized to perform specific functions and roles in procedural and administrative matters.

The Tokyo Tribunal's President, Sir William Webb, was an Australian judge. There was much speculation on the reasons for his appointment. First, the Chief Prosecutor, the concerned authority for criminal investigation and prosecution, was an American. Therefore, a non-American President had to be chosen to posit the impartiality of the Tribunal. Among those non-American judges, it was also necessary to find a jurist who was experienced in the common law system. The common law traditions had an advantage over civil law in terms of the procedures, the working language and the number of Tribunal members, although the Charter states that the international Tribunal need not be bound by technical rules of procedure. Among those judges from common law countries, MacArthur considered William Webb as an ideal candidate. Lord Patrick was also an astute, knowledgeable and honourable person, but being educated in the Scottish legal tradition, he was not considered a typical common law jurist. Other judges, such as Northcroft from New Zealand and McDougall from Canada, were experienced, but lacked the prowess and stature that Webb had. Although India and the Philippines were a part of the common law traditions, they had for long been British and US colonies; thus, they had a low international status and only marginally contributed to the war against Japan. Hence, there was no possibility that MacArthur would consider their judges for the post.

Australia had geographical advantages due to its vast land and rich natural resources, despite its small population. It was part of the British Empire and had served as a major base for the Allied Powers' war against Japan. During the Pacific War, MacArthur's general headquarters was stationed in Australia, which helped foster his appreciation for the place.

---

[17] *Charter of the International Military Tribunal*, Article 4(b).

He also befriended some Australians during that time; he was believed to have met Webb then. The rapport they shared, perhaps prompted his choice; but his primary motivation to appoint Webb as President was Australia's international status and Webb's experience and expertise as a judge.

Webb was not only a standard professional judge of the West who was upright and sincere, but also an efficient and energetic individual. Although he looked like a British gentleman, he portrayed the roughness of an Australian. His attitude and language were explicit and sometimes rash—a temperament which triggered conflicts during the trial. For instance, on the second day of the court hearing, when Chief Prosecutor Keenan was reading his lengthy opening statement, Webb said, 'Your inflammatory phrases are of no benefit to our trial.' Annoyed, Keenan responded harshly and even threatened to resign. When the Tribunal asked the defendants to plead guilty or not guilty, Sadao Araki replied, 'In my life of over sixty years, I have never committed any crime against peace, nor conventional war crime or crime against humanity.' The President rebuked him by saying, 'We only want you to plead guilty or not guilty, not give a speech.' Kijurō Shidehara, a former Prime Minister of Japan, was once called to testify before the Tribunal. He was one of the few Japanese politicians who could speak fluent English and thus was allowed to testify in English. On hearing a few words, Webb stopped him saying, 'Witness, your English is impossible to understand! Please revert to Japanese.'

From the above examples, we can see that Sir William Webb could be rude to prosecutors, defendants and witnesses. He was also impolite to some defence counsel. For example, when Kenzo Takayanagi, defence counsel for Teiichi Suzuki and a well-known legal scholar, was permitted to read his lengthy and bombastic plea regarding the Tribunal's jurisdiction, and he began reading it slowly and gravely, the President told him, 'You don't have to assume airs as if it had some significance. We have already known every word you will say. So, read it fast and do not waste our precious time.'[18] During the Trial, David F. Smith and Owen Cunningham, two American counsel, were forced to resign due to

---

[18] Takayanagi's defence statement was published by Yuhikaku in English and Japanese under the title of *The Tokyo Trials and International Law*. As a senior renowned professor of the Tokyo Imperial University, his statement represented the defence's overall stance, opinions and claims.

verbal conflicts with the President. Smith was suspended by the judges' conference because he disrespected the Tribunal and remained defiant even after the President reprimanded him. Cunningham was dismissed as 'foolish' by Webb when they had an argument; this infuriated him and he asked the President to apologize, which caused an uproar in the courtroom. The President adjourned the court and said, 'This matter will be discussed and decided by the judges' conference, from which I shall excuse myself.' Although the President was absent, the judges chose to ratify his behaviour, and agreed that he need not apologize. The Tribunal then re-opened and announced its decision. An angry Cunningham, submitted his resignation then and there, and the Tribunal immediately accepted it.

The above examples depict Sir William Webb's nature and attitude towards all parties in court. This attitude was often supported by the other judges because it was effectual in countering the counsel's intention of endlessly protracting the trial. The apparently smooth progression of the Tokyo Trial could be largely attributed to Webb's attitude and disposition.

Being a member of the Tribunal, the President's duty was to try the war criminals. He had the same rights and obligations as the other judges for issuing rulings and preparing the judgement for the Trial. As mentioned before, the President also had other special functions in trial procedures and administrative matters.

The President presided over the court hearing and spoke on behalf of the judges. When the session began and the judges entered the courtroom, one after another, the President walked ahead and occupied the central seat of the bench. He also led the judges out during recess. During the session, he would speak on behalf of the Tribunal, question the prosecution, defence and witnesses, and announce the Tribunal's rulings over their motions or petitions. Rarely, a direct inquiry was made by any judge to a speaker—a prosecutor, counsel or witness. In the common law system, almost all questions would be raised by the prosecution or the defence. For example, the defence might denounce or challenge the prosecution's statement or claim, which would ensue in a verbal debate. The defence could also exhaustively cross-examine the witness called by the prosecution to undermine his testimony. The prosecution would do the same to the defence. Thus, through repeated inquiries and cross-examinations, the factual truth and crux of the problem could be discovered. The judges on the bench only listened passively; this was different from the civil law system in which the judge directly questioned the parties. Here, a judge could ask a question only after both parties finished their examinations. His question would be passed on as a note to the President, who would read it aloud and demand an immediate reply from the concerned party. However, the judges rarely posed questions.

Although there was hardly any direct inquiry by the bench, the Tribunal had to continually address the numerous extempore motions or petitions brought by the prosecution and the defence. Such motions or petitions were frequent, especially when an important witness was under examination. For example, a prosecutor (often called 'prosecution counsel') would first make his direct examination of a witness for the prosecution. When a question was asked and if the defence counsel felt that the witness' response would harm the interests of the defendant, he could quickly make a motion to prevent the witness' response. His words could be, 'I object to the question asked by the prosecution counsel as it is irrelevant or immaterial to this case. I request the Tribunal to disallow it.' After direct examination, any defence counsel could cross-examine the witness to obtain information beneficial to the defendants, or to lessen the probative value of the testimony by exposing its inherent contradictions. Similarly, the prosecutor could propose a motion against any question raised by the defence counsel in the cross-examination if he considered it detrimental to his case. He could say, 'I object to the question brought to the witness as it is irrelevant or immaterial to this case. I request the Tribunal to disallow it.'

This also applied to any witness for the defence. In the course of the direct examination by the defence counsel and the cross-examination by the prosecutor, the opposite party could ask the bench to stall a question by claiming that 'it is irrelevant or immaterial to this case'.

Not only the witnesses, but also the documentary evidence presented by one party was often objected to by the other party. Every time a party submitted a document to the Tribunal as evidence, the other party could make a motion to reject it, saying that 'it is irrelevant or immaterial to the case, and therefore has no probative value'. In addition, speculation about the authenticity of a document may be a reason to prevent the submission of it.

Extempore motions made by both parties were continual and numerous because hundreds of witnesses and thousands of documents were presented before the Tribunal during the Trial. The defence used it as a useful method to protract the trial.

All motions required the Tribunal to make a ruling immediately, even those raised without cause, as otherwise the trial could not continue.

The President announced the ruling, but it was based on the majority opinion of the Tribunal members. For a short period after the Trial commenced, each time when a ruling was needed, the Tribunal would break for a recess to hold a judges' conference for discussion and voting. Regardless of the gravity of the subject, each ruling delayed the trial by 20 minutes. Moreover, the frequent recesses were inconvenient for everybody in the courtroom. When the judges realized that a motion could not be resolved effectively, they decided to pass a ruling for the motions in the court session itself, except for those important motions which demanded a judges' conference.

In order to pass a ruling in the court session itself, the judges were required to vote in court. Each judge wrote his opinion and handed it over to the President; the President made a ruling based on the majority opinion and immediately announced it. In this way, a simple motion was resolved in less than three minutes.

Initially, the judges wrote perfect letters which began with 'dear President', followed by 'I agree to accept...' or 'I oppose this motion...', concluded by 'on the grounds that...' or 'because...', and signed by the author. Later, the opening and closing sentences were thought to be unnecessary and the reasoning seemed redundant; therefore, they limited themselves to the words 'agree' or 'oppose'. Eventually, the two words were also considered unnecessary, and so they replaced them with the signs: '+' (agree) or '−' (oppose). Once a motion was launched, the judges made their choices by marking the appropriate signs on notes and handed them to the President; the President then counted the notes for and against the motion and announced their decision straight away. In this manner, the motion could be resolved in less than a minute.

Although the decision-making process was simplified, it was still time-consuming and troublesome for the judges because of the number of extempore motions proposed. This was especially true for the President, as he had to collect and calculate the votes, and announce the decisions on behalf of the Tribunal.

All the ordinary rulings (which were more than 90 per cent of all rulings) were made by in-court voting. Only when a significant issue arose, the court would convene a judges' conference at recess. Any judge who considered it necessary to hold a meeting could send a note to the President, who would adjourn the trial session immediately. Any judge who had a question about a party's statement in court could also send a note to the President, and the President would question that party on his behalf. This was the President's responsibility because he presided over the trial, and was the sole speaker for all the judges.

Some trivial motions or requests which were unconnected with the proceedings were resolved by the President himself. For example, a witness requested the Tribunal to stop using flashlights because they irritated his eyes; the President consented and cancelled the use of flashlights. Once a defence counsel had an urgent request to use the toilet. The President agreed but taunted him by saying, 'This is a strange request from the Tribunal.' Minor matters were decided by the President himself without voting or a judges' conference. No judge had protested against the President's 'ultra vires acts' or called it as 'undemocratic'.

Apart from presiding over the court sessions and speaking on behalf of the Tribunal and the judges, the President had to convene and chair the judges' conference. This task was not as tiring as the first one, because the judges' conferences were not frequently held; the trial sessions, however, took five hours a day (from 9:30 to 12:00 a.m. and 1:30 to 4:00 p.m., with two 20-minute intervals). Smaller matters were discussed in the lounge, or the President would consult the judges during leisure, avoiding the necessity of a judges' conference.

The President convened a judges' conference only under the following circumstances:

1. The prosecution, the defence (or any defence counsel), or the General Secretary made requests or proposals in writing concerning some important matters, such as requesting the Tribunal to adjourn for several days to prepare proceeding materials, to cease application of some part of the procedures over a certain matter, or to summon someone to testify before the court (usually, before each phase of the proceedings, the prosecution and the defence would make long lists of witnesses to be summoned, for the judges' conference to review and approve, but separate requests were also accepted).
2. An extempore motion made by a party could not be resolved by in-court voting, thus necessitating a judges' conference. The two common scenarios were: First, if the President, on hearing the motion considered it too important to be resolved by an in-court voting, he would adjourn the trial, convene a judges' meeting, and announce the decision when the court was resumed. Second, if

one or more judges were dissatisfied with the result of the in-court voting and thereby requested a meeting, then the President would adjourn the court session immediately, and declare that the previous ruling was invalid and an official one would be announced after the judges' conference. Under the principles of collective responsibility and equal rights and obligations, any judge had an absolute right to request a judges' conference at any time, in writing or orally, and the President must convene it as requested, without any resistance or delay.
3. In the 'Battle of Memorandums', the President would convene a judges' conference to discuss or debate on the content of a memorandum if it involved reconsideration of a certain ruling or fact-finding, or if he felt that a memorandum was worth reviewing at a meeting. Most of such discussions were theoretical; they served as a reference for the Tribunal's future work, but had never altered the Tribunal's existing rulings.

Only in the above occasions would the President convene a judges' conference. These meetings were not onerous like the court sessions in which the judges were clad in their robes and sat attentively for about five hours a day. During the course of the trial which lasted for two years, the judges' conference was conducted less than one hundred times, and each lasted for 30 minutes to one hour or even as short as 10–20 minutes (excepting the whole-day meetings at the final stage of the Trial, when the judges were discussing the Tribunal's judgement and sentencing of the defendants).

The judges' conference was often confidential, and the agenda was executed without any written record. The judges had to attend it alone, unaccompanied by any secretary or assistant. The Soviet judge Zaryanov, however, was allowed to bring in his interpreter, Mrs. Bernstein because he did not speak English. Aged over 60 years and fluent in English, French and German, Mrs. Bernstein spoke rapidly, like an automatic translating machine, and had never caused any delays in the meeting. She had to take an oath of confidentiality which was guaranteed by the Soviet judge. The General Secretary could not participate in any judges' conference unless he was invited or, at his request, approved by the conference.

Owing to the confidentiality measures adopted at the judges' conference, the Japanese called it a 'secret court' (as opposed to 'open court' or 'court for public trial'). However, it was not a 'court' in any sense because there were no written records of the meeting and it was not attended by the concerned parties or their representatives.

The atmosphere at the judges' conference was informal, and the judges could freely express their thoughts. After they reached a consensus or expressed a dominant opinion, the President would pronounce the majority opinion. If there was no objection or resistance to it, he would declare it to be the Tribunal's decision or ruling. In general, there was no voting at the judges' conferences, and the Charter's provision for a decisive vote by the President was never applied.

We have discussed the President's duties of presiding over the Tribunal sessions and convening judges' conferences. Another task handled by the President was daily businesses and signing important documents such as declarations, orders and summons. This was not a difficult task because all important matters concerning the proceedings were already decided in the judges' conferences, and the administration, management, personnel and funding details were controlled by the American General Secretary; the President only had to sanction them.

As an institution established by the Supreme Commander for the Allied Powers, the Tokyo Tribunal was under the control of the GHQ. Apart from the judges who were recommended by their governments and appointed by the Supreme Commander, all the Tribunal staff, including the General Secretary were appointed by the GHQ directly, or indirectly through the General Secretary. The administrative work, personnel arrangements, and matters of funding and expenditure were handled by the General Secretary, under the guidance of the GHQ. These matters were executed independently by the General Secretary without the involvement of the judges. The President only listened to the General Secretary's report, signed his approval of it, and affixed the Tribunal's seal.

As the President spent the same amount of time as the other judges in court sessions and judges' conferences, his working hours were as much as them. He had to be, however, more alert and vigilant than the other judges. After the closure of court on Friday afternoons, the President, like the rest of them, would prepare for a weekend vacation.

(The Tribunal had a two-day weekend. On weekends, the judges usually toured cities or suburban areas outside Tokyo. Some of them hunted, swam or played golf. Japan's beautiful landscapes, scenic hot springs and excellent services attracted many tourists. Moreover, the administration of the Tribunal personally arranged pleasant weekend vacations for the judges. The judges thus looked forward to the weekend tours and recalled them as their best time in Tokyo.[19])

[19] The GHQ of the Supreme Commander for the Allied Powers was very considerate and generous in making arrangements for the judges' tours on weekends and holidays. Once informed by a judge about where he planned to go, what type of transportation he would take, where he would stay, how many companions he would bring, and how many rooms and cars he would need, the General Secretary would notify the GHQ, and the latter would inform the relevant parties to make arrangements. All their travels were free of charge. It was said that those travel expenses were kept on the account of the judge's country, which would be deducted from Japan's war reparations. During a longer Tribunal recess, the judges could make bigger travel plans. In May 1946, when the Tribunal adjourned for two weeks, judges from China and the United States requested an airplane, accompanied by about ten people (along with five crew members) to travel in China, touring Shanghai and Peking for 10 days. Before the Tribunal officially opened, judges from China, the United States, New Zealand, Canada and the Netherlands also used a plane to travel across Japan. In the spring of 1947, when the Tribunal had another short adjournment, the Chinese judge along with 14 companions toured Kyoto, Osaka and Kobe for about one week. Apart from two secretaries, most of his companions were his Chinese friends and the Tribunal staff who were eager for free travels. For their convenience, the GHQ arranged a carnival float named 'Paradise' (originally used for the emperor's travels), a number of rooms in Kyoto's most luxurious hotel, and cars and jeeps according to their ranks, all free of charge. The GHQ's great care and generosity towards the judges' tours might be for two reasons: First, the Americans wanted to express their respect and preferential treatment for the representatives of the Allied Powers, which could lessen the exposure of the US military's total control over the occupation of Japan. Second, the judges' travel expenses were covered by the occupation fees provided by the Japanese government and would incur no additional cost to the United States. As for the threat to have the travel expenses deducted from future Japanese reparations, the judges knew it was an empty statement because Japan's reparations was not guaranteed. Therefore, they were only glad to take the opportunity to enjoy the privilege. However, the modest indulgences of the judges paled before the extravagance of the US generals of the occupation force. For instance, the Chief of Staff of the Allied Powers occupied a garden mansion that used to be owned by a Japanese prince, and spent a luxurious time there. He had 60–70 Japanese servants, which was later reduced to about 40 after it was reported by the US journalists and condemned by public. The Commander of the Eighth US Army also lived luxuriously in occupied Japan. Two of his numerous Japanese servants were famous ice cream masters in Japan, who could make ice cream in the shapes of animals, plants, airplanes and warships. The judges were once treated by the Commander to those exquisite ice creams, and they were deeply impressed. Douglas MacArthur, the Supreme Commander for the Allied Powers, led a royal lifestyle; when he dined alone or with guests, there were at least eight Japanese servants in traditional Japanese garments, waiting on his table. These examples partly reveal the US military officials' profligacy through exploitation of Japan's resources. Even the American journalists felt unhappy and exposed their wastefulness in Japan. For example, they reported in the newspaper that in

On occasion, the President also performed a social function; this was another small task that he had to do. When the eleven judges were invited for dinner by the senior officials or delegates of the Allied Powers, the President sat at the head table, spoke to the hosts graciously, and gave them a thank-you speech on behalf of the judges. On rare instances, when some special guests (such as a prime minister, a foreign minister or a senior military official) attended the court session, the President informed the judges, and after consulting with the General Secretary or a judge from the guest's nation, arranged a simple welcoming ceremony for them in the lounge, during recess. This happened only less than once a month on average. The judges were often invited to celebrations, receptions, banquets and cocktail parties; the Tribunal or the judges as a group, had never hosted a party because in the Western legal tradition, judges were supposed to be solemn, and ill-fitted for hosting parties. Any association with the Japanese was unacceptable; the Imperial Hotel where the judges stayed, restricted Japanese people other than their hotel attendants, from entering.

This completes the description of the roles of the President and other judges, their work style and daily life in Tokyo.

2.4 International Prosecution Section

The International Prosecution Section (IPS) was a part of the GHQ of the Supreme Commander for the Allied Powers. It also served as a prosecution organ for the Tokyo Tribunal, as the plaintiffs for the eleven countries during the Tokyo Trial.

The GHQ had set up many specialized sections or groups to implement Japan's Instrument of Surrender. There were two sections relating to legal affairs and war criminal trials: the Legal Affairs Section and the IPS. In order to avoid confusion between the two similar sections, we will discuss each section's individual nature and its corresponding powers.

Apart from the general legal affairs arising from the daily operations of GHQ, the Legal Affairs Section was also in charge of the extradition of Japanese war criminals, the identification, arrest and investigation of Class-B and Class-C war criminals, and the organization of tribunals for their trials. Most of these tribunals were established ad hoc, and each often

---

the Imperial Hotel where the senior staff of the GHQ and the judges stayed, each guest had on average three and a half hotel attendants serving him.

consisted of three to five military judges with one or more defendants accused of atrocity, i.e. the conventional war crimes. Often, the trials were swiftly conducted by summary process. Since many of the trials against Class-B and Class-C Japanese war criminals were held in Yokohama, they were collectively called as 'Yokohama Trials' by the Japanese, to differentiate them from the Tokyo Trial, which was against the Class-A war criminals held by the International Military Tribunal for the Far East.

The organization of the Yokohama Trials and the associated arrests, investigation and prosecution of criminals were undertaken by the Legal Affairs Section, and indirectly controlled by the Americans. In a spirit of liberality, they sometimes invited representatives from other Allied Powers. For example, two Chinese were assigned for investigation and collection of evidence in the Legal Affairs Section. During the Yokohama Trials, the Chinese Military Delegation was also requested to send a judge to participate in some of the cases. This was only an eyewash because, from indictment to adjudication, the trial processes of Class-B and Class-C criminals at Yokohama were managed only by Americans. The Allied Powers who wished to avoid being subject to such manipulation, extradited the war criminals to their own countries for trial. This was done on the grounds that as those war criminals had inflicted direct damage to their countries, it was appropriate that they are tried in the victim countries. For example, in 1946, pressurized by the Chinese people, the Kuomintang government requested extradition of some Class-B war criminals such as Hisao Tani, Takashi Sakai and Rensuke Isogai, to China. Unless they had a valid excuse, the GHQ could not refuse the Allied Powers' request for extradition.[20]

---

[20] According to general principles of international law, the declarations by the leaders of the Allied Powers during wartime, and the resolutions of the Far Eastern Commission, if a country requested the GHQ to extradite the Class-B and Class-C Japanese war criminals who conducted atrocities in that country, the GHQ could not reject it. The Chinese government requested extradition of those criminals, because they had during the Japanese invasion committed multitudinous atrocities, among which Hisao Tani was one of masterminds of the Nanking Massacre. The Chinese government had also intended to extradite Iwane Matsui, the principal criminal of the Nanking Massacre, Kenji Doihara and Seishirō Itagaki, for whom the Chinese people had an undying hatred. The government gave up this idea as those three were listed as Class-A war criminals to be tried by the Tokyo Tribunal. Subsequently, they were all sentenced with capital punishments. Had they been extradited to China, the incumbent Kuomintang government would have been likely to give them more lenient sentences, even acquittals, as was the case with Yasuji

Except for a small number of war criminals who were extradited to stand trial in the Allied Powers, most Class-B and Class-C suspects in Japan were arrested, interrogated, investigated and prosecuted under the direction of the Legal Affairs Section. The Legal Affairs Section also had the power to organize and arrange the trials of Class-B and Class-C criminals.

The IPS had very different duties and powers, as it was specifically established to deal with major Japanese war criminals (Class-A war criminals). The Potsdam Declaration (or Proclamation Defining Terms for Japanese Surrender) had demanded that 'stern justice shall be meted to all war criminals', and accordingly, an international tribunal must be organized to try them. An international tribunal, however, could only conduct the trial process, not the creation of itself, where its 'international' status made its organization complicated. Meanwhile, the preparatory work for such a trial including the drafting of the indictment required a specialized unit and an extensive staff; the IPS was thus established for this purpose.

The tasks of the IPS were complex although it was vested with great powers. In Allied-occupied Japan, before the Tokyo Charter was published, the IPS was commissioned to select the site for the future tribunal, renovate the building, and furnish its interiors. More importantly, it compiled the list of Class-A war criminals, arrested and investigated them, and collected detailed statements from them. After the Tokyo Charter was promulgated, the IPS sent staff to relevant places in Japan and in the Allied Powers to look for evidences and analyse them. It then finalized the list of defendants and drafted the indictment. After the Tribunal officially opened, the IPS handled the prosecution work during the Trial, such as providing documentary (and other kinds of) evidence and witnesses to support the criminal charges in the indictment, direct examining its own witnesses and cross-examining the defence witnesses, debating in court, and making closing statements concerning the defendants' individual cases and the whole case under trial.

Owing to the large number of cases, defendants and witnesses, and the complexity of subjects, the prosecution work required adequate human resource and financial support from the GHQ. The head of the IPS had to have an influence over the prosecution of Japanese war criminals and the operation of the Tokyo Trial, and a close relationship with the Supreme

Okamura, Commander-in-chief of the China Expeditionary Army and the creator of the Three Alls Policy (to kill all, burn all, loot all).

Commander of the Allied Powers, Douglas MacArthur. The American lawyer, Joseph B. Keenan was thus the ideal choice for the post.

Keenan was the chief prosecutor of the IPS and the legal counsel to the Supreme Commander. He was also a trusted and close friend of MacArthur's. Before the Tribunal was established, he was assigned a series of preparatory work, including the selection of the site, renovation of the building, arrest and investigation of Class-A suspects, collection of evidence, drafting of the Charter and the indictment. Although he may have referred to the Nuremberg Tribunal for his preparatory work, the differences between the German and Japan contexts made it a laborious task.

When the Tokyo Charter was published on 19 January 1946, Keenan was appointed as the Chief of Counsel (Chief Prosecutor), with an overall responsibility for the prosecution work.

Unlike the Nuremberg Charter, the Tokyo Charter provided sufficient powers to the Chief Prosecutor.

According to the Nuremberg Charter (Article 14), the four countries (the Soviet Union, the US, the UK and France), each having their own chief prosecutor, who were equal in status, undertook duties individually and acted in collaboration. They adopted a collegiate system by majority voting for making decisions.[21] This was similar to the practice of judges in an ordinary court, who had equal status and voting rights.

Although the Tokyo Charter provided a similar collegiate system as the Nuremberg Charter for the judges, the prosecutors had a single-head system or 'autocracy'.

Article 8 of the Tokyo Charter states, 'The Chief of Counsel designated by the Supreme Commander for the Allied Powers is responsible for the investigation and prosecution of charges against war criminals within the jurisdiction of this Tribunal....' It also provides, 'Any United Nation with which Japan has been at war may appoint an Associate Counsel to assist the Chief of Counsel.'

---

[21] Article 14 of the Nuremberg Charter provides: 'Each Signatory shall appoint a Chief Prosecutor.... The Chief Prosecutors shall act as a committee.... The Committee shall act in all the above matters by a majority vote and shall appoint a Chairman as may be convenient and in accordance with the principle of rotation: provided that if there is an equal division of vote concerning the designation of a Defendant to be tried by the Tribunal, or the crimes with which he shall be charged, that proposal will be adopted which was made by the party which proposed that the particular Defendant be tried, or the particular charges be preferred against him.'

As indicated by this article, all war criminals within the jurisdiction of the Tokyo Tribunal, i.e. the major or Class-A Japanese war criminals, were to be investigated and prosecuted by the Chief Prosecutor, who was 'designated' by the Supreme Commander. Although the IPS was a large organization with many staff members, only the Chief Prosecutor had the supreme authority and the final decision-making power. Each Allied Power (the 'United Nation' in the Charter) could appoint one 'Associate Counsel' (associate prosecutor) to assist the Chief Prosecutor. Apparently, the associate prosecutors were subordinate to, and not given equal status as the Chief Prosecutor, which was different from the relationship between the President and the other judges of the Tribunal. Therefore, it was not a collegiate system like the judges had at the Tokyo Tribunal or any other court, or the prosecutors had at the Nuremberg Tribunal, but a single-head system, or 'autocracy'. The associate prosecutors were only advisers, consultants or assistants.

Additionally, there are two more significant points. First, with regard to the countries which were entitled to recommend judges, the Tokyo Charter specified the 'Signatories to the Instrument of Surrender, India and the Commonwealth of the Philippines' (11 countries in total); the associate prosecutors, however, could be sent by 'any United Nation with which Japan has been at war'. Despite such provisions, only those 11 countries appointed associate prosecutors. Second, the Charter stipulated that the judges, the President and the Chief Prosecutor should be appointed by the Supreme Commander, but the associate prosecutors were not. Therefore, an associate prosecutor could easily resign and be replaced during the trial, without any public opposition. For instance, the associate prosecutors from the Soviet Union and India resigned halfway through the Trial, and were immediately replaced by others. It was also common for associate prosecutors to absent themselves when their work was temporarily managed by other staff members.

Although the Tokyo Charter did not grant the associate prosecutors high status or great powers, the Allied Powers carefully selected them, because the entire world, and especially the Asians who were victimized during the war, were keeping track of the prosecution of the Japanese war criminals. Most of the associate prosecutors had a good legal background and their average age was about 50.

Joseph B. Keenan, the Chief Prosecutor, also assumed the role of the US associate prosecutor. Keenan was a wealthy American lawyer and had once served as Deputy Attorney General of the United States. The other

Allied Powers appointed the following persons as their associated prosecutors—China: Hsiang Che-Chun, the chief prosecutor of Shanghai Higher Court; the United Kingdom: A. S. Comyns-Carr, a Liberal member of the parliament and a King's Counsel; the Soviet Union: S. A. Golunsky, a corresponding member of the USSR Academy of Sciences; Australia: A. J. Mansfield, a judge from the Queensland Supreme Court; Canada: H. G. Nolan, a brigadier and the Vice Adjutant-General at the National Defence Headquarters; the Netherlands: W. G. F. Borgerhoff-Mulder, a judge of the Hague Special Court; New Zealand: R. H. Quilliam, a prosecutor of the Supreme Court; India: Govinda Menon; the Philippines: Pedro Lopez, a Member of Parliament[22] (Fig. 2.4).

Most of the above associate prosecutors, excepting a few, served for the entire period of the Tokyo Trial. S. A. Golunsky resigned in less than six months due to poor health, and was succeeded by his assistant prosecutor, Nicolai A. Vasiliev, a third class national judicial counsel. Govinda Menon, who did not contribute much to the Tribunal, returned to India, and his work was handled by his British colleague Arthur S. Comyns-Carr. At the final stage of the Trial, A. J. Mansfield requested R. H. Quilliam from New Zealand to handle his work and returned to Australia. Since the IPS had a single-head system, the absence of a few associate prosecutors did not hamper its work.

The offices of the IPS were on the third floor of the War Ministry Building. Apart from a fairly large room for Chief Prosecutor Keenan, each associate prosecutor and his assistants had one independent room and formed groups, such as the China Group and the Soviet Union Group. The grouping had questionable significance because most of the associate prosecutors came to Tokyo alone, with neither staff nor documents. The prosecution work was directed by Keenan and performed by his American assistant prosecutors, most of whom were US military men or civilian officers with legal training and lawyers' qualifications. Sometimes, they had higher powers than these associate prosecutors. For instance, Frank Tavenner, David Sutton and Thomas Morrow were Keenan's trusted followers and right-hand men, who were well esteemed

---

[22] Editor's Note: R. L. Oneto, the French associate prosecutor, is missing in Mei's draft.

Fig. 2.4 The prosecutors

in the IPS.²³ When Keenan was on leave, he usually deputed Tavenner; sometimes Keenan deputed Comyns-Carr because in addition to his knowledge and experience, he was sophisticated, intelligent and articulate. He excelled both in legal arguments and witness examinations (including direct examinations of the prosecution witnesses and cross-examinations of the defence witnesses). Although he was not a friend of Keenan's, or an associate of the Supreme Commander, the Chief Prosecutor often had to rely upon him. His popularity was much more than that of the Chief Prosecutor and the American assistant prosecutors.

As mentioned before, the requisite for country-wise grouping in the IPS was not very sensible. First, the prosecution work required a comprehensive approach, for which the Chief Prosecutor and his many American assistant prosecutors assumed an overall responsibility—a practice that was different from the Nuremberg Trial, where each nation independently did their prosecution work. Second, most of the 10 associate prosecutors came to Tokyo alone, without the personnel necessary to form a group. Each associate prosecutor was only allocated work that they could independently do by the Chief Prosecutor. In respect of his country's prosecution work, he did nothing more than provided some guidance and collaborated with the people of his country for presenting necessary evidences and witnesses.

The Soviet Union Group, however, meticulously handled their country's prosecution work. First, its associate prosecutor arrived at the Tribunal with about a dozen competent staff. The Soviet Group could thus handle their own prosecution work without having to depend on anyone. Second, unlike the capitalist countries, the Soviet Union's isolation policy and secrecy system made it hard for prosecutors from other nationalities to collaborate with them. Therefore, with regard to the Japanese invasion of the Soviet Union, the Soviet Union Group independently collected and provided documentary evidence, presented and direct-examined its own witnesses, verified the defence's evidence, and cross-examined the defence's witnesses. Moreover, it also handled

---

²³ The American assistant prosecutors were the most favoured assistants of the Chief Prosecutor and the backbone of the IPS. Moreover, their turnover was high. They served at the GHQ and were often summoned and dismissed by the Chief Prosecutor as he deemed necessary. Once they completed their term of service, they left Tokyo and were soon replaced by others. Efficient prosecutors, such as Tavenner and Sutton, served at the IPS for the entire period of the Tokyo Trial.

the prosecution against Japan's invasion of the People's Republic of Mongolia. The Soviet Group, headed by Golunsky, and then Vasiliev and comprising members such as Raginsky, and Rozenblit, contributed significantly towards the Soviet Union and Mongolia's prosecution work.

Although the China Group also had good human resources, because of the long history of Japan's occupation of China and the complexity of the prosecution process, most of the prosecution work was done by the Chief Prosecutor and his American staff; the China Group, however, assisted them. The corrupt Kuomintang government of China did not heed the Tribunal at first, and sanctioned only two secretaries (Qiu Shaoheng, a.k.a. Henry Chiu, and Liu Zijian) for its associate prosecutor, Hsiang Che-Chun. At a later stage of the Trial, and after repeated requests, China sent some additional counsel (Ni Zhengyu, a.k.a. Judson T. Y. Nyi, Wu Xueyi, E Sen and Gui Yu). The new additions helped the China Group to perform better, and it began to play an important role in collecting additional evidence against Japan's invasion of China and in cross-examining the defence witnesses. In the classified archives of the Japanese government, Wu and Liu found convincing evidences on the crimes committed by Kenji Doihara and Seishirō Itagaki, which was presented in court as additional evidence. Mr. Ni made a spectacular cross-examination of Itagaki when he was called to testify, which eventually led to his capital punishment.

Except for the aforesaid Soviet Group (which worked quite independently on the prosecution relating to the Soviet Union and Mongolia) and the China Group (which contributed greatly to prosecution work related to China), the groups of other countries were led by uninfluential associate prosecutors (which did not mean that these associate prosecutors were not important individually). The Chief Prosecutor assigned specific tasks to them. For example, when the prosecution wanted to present a critical but defective document as evidence (which might be opposed by the defence), or needed to cross-examine an artful defendant or defence witness (whose testimony had to be rebutted), Keenan engaged the services of the British associate prosecutor, Comyns-Carr. The frequency and complexity of the tasks assigned to the associate prosecutors were in proportion to their respective capabilities. In general, these associate prosecutors surpassed the American assistant prosecutors in their capabilities. However, due to Keenan's self-centred motives, the American assistant prosecutors were frequently allowed to showcase themselves before the Tribunal, thus consuming two-thirds of the time for prosecution. Keenan was predominantly an American politician. His sectionalism was evident in his attempts to orchestrate the prosecution work of the Tokyo Tribunal. A non-American associate prosecutor was his last choice for any assignment. Consequently, the neglected associate and assistant prosecutors from the other Allied Powers were angry and resentful from time to time during the long Tokyo Trial proceedings.

The IPS held a weekly meeting which was attended by the associate prosecutors from the Allied Powers and some specially invited American assistant prosecutors. The meetings were chaired by Chief Prosecutor Joseph B. Keenan, or by Frank Tavenner or Arthur S. Comyns-Carr when Keenan was absent. At these weekly meetings, the prosecutors discussed the activities to be completed inside and outside of court for that week, allocation and management of workload, and coordination of tasks. For example, when the prosecution had to present evidence before the Tribunal, the meeting determined the documentary evidences to be submitted, the prosecutor who should present and validate it, the witnesses who could testify it, and the prosecutor who could conduct the direct-examination and protect the witness from the defence's cross-examination. The meeting also determined the prosecutor who should object to the documentary evidence when the defence presented it, and the prosecutor who should cross-examine the witnesses.

During the meeting, the associate prosecutors and specially invited American assistant prosecutors (non-American assistant prosecutors, advisers and secretaries were never invited) could voice their opinions; the Chief Prosecutor carefully listened to them, although he could independently manage all critical issues and finalize them. When his decisions were challenged by any associate prosecutor, he would remind them of the Tokyo Charter's stipulation that the Chief of Counsel was responsible for the investigation and prosecution. The associate prosecutor who challenged him had to submit. It is believed that a duel of this kind frequently took place between himself and the associate prosecutor from the Soviet Union.

Keenan had good political acumen and often adopted a fake demeanour. He was a close friend of MacArthur's, and an associate of President Truman. Although he appeared to respect the opinions of the Allied Powers on the conviction of Japanese major war criminals and build a good rapport with the other prosecutors, he preferred to follow the

US government's policy of shielding the criminals and restoring Japan's militarism. Every decision of his was prompted by Truman or MacArthur.

Keenan presided over the heavily-staffed IPS by implementing the single-head system or 'autocracy' with an American supremacist mentality. His supercilious attitude was not limited to the IPS, but extended to the Tribunal. When addressing the press, Keenan projected himself as the sole authority in the Tribunal.[24]

Keenan's attitude was repulsive to most of the judges, especially to the President, Sir William Webb, who took every opportunity to disgrace him. It has been quoted before that at the beginning of a trial, when Keenan was pompously reading his opening statement, Webb had snubbed him saying that his words were of no benefit to the Trial. Keenan had been embarrassed and had threatened to resign. In another instance, he was again taunted by Webb for his speech on the lives of Japanese businessmen, tycoons and arms dealers, uninvolved with the Japanese war policies, but under the control of warlords. As the Tokyo Tribunal followed the common law system in which the prosecutors and the defence counsel had equal status (Keenan was often called 'chief counsel of the prosecution'), no special treatment was given to the Chief Prosecutor or other prosecutors, unlike in the civil law system wherein the prosecution received more importance. Therefore, Keenan had to mutely endure Webb's behaviour. As for the other judges, they all supported

---

[24] The following two cases best illustrate Keenan's character: Four days before the Tribunal's official opening, the bench met with him. He handed over the Indictment to the President, gave a brief summary of it, and explained that he had distributed copies in the Japanese language to the defendants, 48 hours ago. The President accepted it, requested the General Secretary to register it, and informed Keenan to read it out when the Tribunal session began. In the common law system, this was a normal procedure called 'proceedings in chamber' (as opposed to 'proceedings in court'). This was the first gathering of all the judges and their first meeting with the Chief Prosecutor. In less than 30 minutes, the gathering dispersed jubilantly. However, Keenan met the press that evening and said that the Indictment was 'handed down to the Tribunal'. The judges were annoyed with his phrase 'handed down' (instead of 'submitted' or 'delivered'), which was apparently a self-proclamation of superiority. This incidence might have prompted Webb to rebuke him on the first open session of the Tribunal. Keenan's arrogance was evident in another instance. According to the Tokyo Charter, any document handed over to the Tribunal should be in both English and Japanese. One day, when Keenan was making a statement to the Tribunal, he said, 'The American version of this document has been made and delivered to all parties concerned.' Instead of referring to it as the 'English version', he called it the 'American version', an expression which portrayed his chauvinism. Hence, it was no surprise that he was often reprimanded by the bench.

and concurred with Webb's treatment of him, because they also disliked his arrogance and assertion of American superiority. Moreover, the President's behaviour towards the Chief Prosecutor and the prosecution might reinforce the supremacy of the Tribunal and contribute towards a fair trial—a consequence which was beneficial to the image of the Tribunal.

After several castigations before the Tribunal, Keenan was considerably humbled. However, as the Chief Prosecutor of the Tribunal, head of the IPS and legal adviser to the Supreme Commander, he had a leverage over the treatment of major Japanese war criminals and attempts to shield Japanese militarism. He made a list of the defendants, drafted the indictment, and led the investigation, evidence provision, cross-examination and court debates. On the other hand, in the capacity of the Chief Prosecutor, and as directed by the US government and MacArthur, he released about 40 alleged Class-A war criminals who had been arrested but not tried, on the basis of 'insufficient evidence for prosecution'. We will discuss more about Keenan's attempt to shelter and release the Class-A war criminals, later in this book.[25]

2.5 The Defence: Japanese and American Counsel

The large number of defence counsel was a distinguishing feature of the Tokyo Trial, unlike at the Nuremberg Trial. The aberrant organization of defence counsel and their strategy of protracting the proceedings were the main reasons for the prolongation of the Tokyo Trial.

The Nuremberg Charter contains simple provisions for the defence in Item (d) of Article 16: 'A Defendant shall have the right to conduct his own defence before the Tribunal or to have the assistance of Counsel.' The defendant under criminal charges has the right to defend himself or appoint a lawyer to defend him, which is a general practice adopted by legal systems around the world, to ensure a fair trial. Article 23 stipulates the qualifications of the defence counsel: 'The function of Counsel for a Defendant may be discharged at the Defendant's request by any Counsel professionally qualified to conduct cases before the Courts of his own country, or by any other person who may be specially authorized thereto by the Tribunal.' Although it permitted any person authorized by the Tribunal, all the attorneys defending the alleged war criminals were in

---

[25] Editor's Note: As the original manuscript of this book is unfinished, the above-mentioned details are not found in the existing four chapters.

fact, qualified German lawyers, and each defendant had only one counsel that he had chosen for himself.

This was not the case in the Tokyo Trial. In Item (d) of Article 9, the Tokyo Charter stipulates: 'An accused shall have the right, through himself or through his counsel (but not through both), to conduct his defence....' And Item (c) states:

> Each accused shall have the right to be represented by counsel of his own selection, subject to the disapproval of such counsel at any time by the Tribunal. The accused shall file with the General Secretary of the Tribunal the name of his counsel. If an accused is not represented by counsel and in open court requests the appointment of counsel, the Tribunal shall designate counsel for him. In the absence of such request, the Tribunal may appoint counsel for an accused if in its judgment such appointment is necessary to provide for a fair trial.

The similarity of the Nuremberg and the Tokyo Charters was that both recognized the defendant's right to conduct his own defence or to be assisted by a lawyer. In fact, in both the Nuremberg and Tokyo Trials, all the defendants were represented by their counsel. The only occasion when they spoke in court by themselves was to testify in their capacity as witnesses.[26]

There were, however, significant differences between the provisions for the defence in the two Charters.

First, the Nuremberg Charter expressly stipulated the qualifications of the defence counsel, while the Tokyo Charter did not. Despite the difference in wording, the counsel for defence in the Tokyo Trial were professionally qualified to conduct cases before the courts of their own

---

[26] The Tokyo Charter assured the defendant of his right to conduct defence through himself or through his counsel, 'but not through both'. The Nuremberg Charter did not stipulate it, but it implied something similar. This is a feature of the Western judicial system, particularly in Britain and the United States, which the Chinese may find difficult to understand. Since the defendants before the Tokyo and Nuremberg Tribunals chose to be defended by their counsel, they no longer had the right to defend themselves, either in the court arguments or in making any petitions, motions, direct examinations and cross-examinations. All of these were handled by their counsel. The defendants, however, could sometimes be called as witnesses to speak or testify in court. While doing so, they were treated by the Tribunal as witnesses rather than defendants, and the rules of procedure of ordinary witnesses, such as the counsel's direct examinations and cross-examinations, were applied to them. Hence, their statements would naturally be regarded as testimonies rather than confessions.

countries and were formally approved by the Tribunal, similar to the defence counsel in Nuremberg.

Second, the Tokyo Charter provided that if the defendant could not select his counsel, he might request the Tribunal to designate one for him; even if he did not make any request, the Tribunal could still appoint counsel for him if the Tribunal considered it necessary for the conduction of a fair trial. The Nuremberg Charter did not have similar provisions. As the attorneys were appointed by the defendants themselves in both the Nuremberg and the Tokyo Tribunals, this provision in the Tokyo Charter was never applied.

Finally, the Tokyo Charter also stipulated that the Tribunal might disapprove any counsel that the defendant had appointed—a provision was not included in the Nuremberg Charter. As mentioned, the Tokyo Charter disqualified two American counsel (Smith and Cunningham) on the basis of this article. In fact, according to general legal practices, any court can take disciplinary action against any lawyer who has displayed contempt of court or has behaved otherwise improperly in court, including termination of his authority to represent his client in court. Although no such stipulation was exercised by the Nuremberg Tribunal, it had the right to do so. Therefore, the provision in the Tokyo Charter was not a unique judicial stipulation.

Although the two Charters were differently articulated, they were essentially the same. The application of these provisions, however, was different for each Tribunal.

Since neither the Nuremberg Charter nor the Tokyo Charter specified the number and nationalities of the defence counsel, the two Tribunals adopted different policies with regard to the counsel's representation. In Nuremberg, each defendant was represented by only one German lawyer, whereas in Tokyo, each defendant was represented by two to six Japanese lawyers, and at least one American lawyer. A large number of attorneys for defendants, and consequently, confusion and delays in the courtroom, were common during the Tokyo Trial.

Owing to the complexity of cases, each defendant had more than one Japanese counsel. It was odd that each defendant was simultaneously represented by one or more American counsel.

The defendants and their Japanese counsel requested American lawyers because the entire Tokyo Trial proceedings were greatly influenced by the common law traditions; the Tokyo Charter and the Rules of Procedure were drafted by common law specialists and the majority of the judges and prosecutors were common law jurists, although the Charter did not stipulate application of the common law, and even stated that the Tribunal should not be bound by technical rules of procedure.[27] Japan was a civil law country, so Japanese lawyers were not familiar with the common law procedures; they requested the Tribunal to assign for each defendant an additional counsel from an Allied Power under the common law system, to assist the defence with common law procedures, for a fair and swift trial.

The request was soon approved by the GHQ and the Tribunal. In the beginning, the GHQ intended to invite lawyers from the British Commonwealth nations in addition to American lawyers to counter the impression that the Americans dominated the Tokyo Trial. The British Commonwealth nations, including the UK, Australia, Canada and New Zealand, were reluctant to aid the war criminals and refused to send their lawyers to the defence team. Therefore, the defence counsel from 'common law Allied Powers' comprised only Americans.

As mentioned earlier, each defendant before the Tokyo Tribunal had two to six Japanese and one or two American counsel. Therefore, the Trial was crowded, noisy and chaotic, unlike at the Nuremberg Trial or any other international courts.

The following is a list of the Japanese and American counsel for each defendant:

Sadao Araki
Japanese counsel: Yutaka Sugawara, Komei Kato and Jiro Deoka
American counsel: L. G. MacManus
Kenji Doihara
Japanese counsel: Kinjiro Ohta, Takahisa Kato, Shigeharu Kimura and Toshio Kitade
American counsel: F. N. Warren
Kingorō Hashimoto
Japanese counsel: Itsuro Hayashi, Hachiro Okuyama, Kunji Kanase, Toshiko Sugai and Hirairi Iwami
American counsel: E. R. Harris

---

[27] Article 13(a): 'The Tribunal shall not be bound by technical rules of evidence. It shall adopt and apply to the greatest possible extent expeditious and non-technical procedure, and shall admit any evidence which it deems to have probative value. All purported admissions or statements of the accused are admissible.'

Shunroku Hata
Japanese counsel: Masayoshi Kanzaki, Koji Kunitomi and Taitaro Imaari
American counsel: A. G. Lazarus
Kiichirō Hiranuma
Japanese counsel: Rokuro Usami, Yasuo Yasushi, Nori Mori, Tsuneo Yanai and Toshio Kitade
American counsel: F. N. Warren
Kōki Hirota
Japanese counsel: Tadashi Hanai, Shinichi Sawa and Masao Hirota
American counsel: George C. Yamaoka
Naoki Hoshino
Japanese counsel: Goichiro Fujii, Masao Masuda and Akira Masuda
American counsel: G. C. Howard and G. C. Williams
Seishirō Itagaki
Japanese counsel: Hanzo Yamada, Tomoharu Sasagawa, Kunkichi Banno and Kenji Okoshi
American counsel: F. G. Mattice
Okinori Kaya
Japanese counsel: Tsuruo Takano, Yasudo Tanaka, Kunji Fujiwara, Masamichi Yamagiwa and Wataru Narahashi
American counsel: M. Levin
Kōichi Kido
Japanese counsel: Shigetake Hozumi and Takahiko Kido
American counsel: W. Logan
Heitarō Kimura
Japanese counsel: Tokisaburo Shiohara, Coretsune Takkem, Akira Abe and Toshio Kitade
American counsel: G. C. Howard
Kuniaki Koiso
Japanese counsel: Shohei Sanmonji, Kazuya Takagi, Kyoichi Kobayashi, Tokihiko Matsuzaka and Makoto Saito
American counsel: A. W. Brooks
Iwane Matsui
Japanese counsel: Kiyoshi Ito, Takuzem Kamishiro and Ryoichi Omuro
American counsel: F. G. Mattice
Jirō Minami

Japanese counsel: Toshio Okamoto, Tatsuo Matsuza and Giichi Kondo
American counsel: A. W. Brooks
Akira Mutō
Japanese counsel: Shoichi Okamoto and Chihiro Saeki
American counsel: R. F. Cole
Takazumi Oka
Japanese counsel: Shinji Somiya, Seiichiro Ono and Tetsuichi Kurashige
American counsel: S. A. Roberts and G. G. Brennan
Hiroshi Ōshima
Japanese counsel: Tatsuoki Shimanouchi, Takao Uchida and Nobuhiko Ushiba
American counsel: O. Cunningham
Kenryō Satō
Japanese counsel: Hyoichiro Kusano, Isaburo Sekiga and Masutaro Inoue
American counsel: G. G. Brennan and G. N. Freaman
Mamoru Shigemitsu
Japanese counsel: Tsuneo Yanai, Shizuo Kanaya, Kazuichi Miura and Rokuro Usami
American counsel: G. A. Furness
Shigetarō Shimada
Japanese counsel: Yoshitsugi Takahashi, Hachiro Okuyama, Masajiro Takikawa, Otoko Kyojima, Shigeto Yasuda and Isamu Suzuki
American counsel: G. G. Brennan and E. R. Harris
Toshio Shiratori
Japanese counsel: Nobuo Naritomi, Makoto Sakuma and Yoji Hirota
American counsel: C. B. Carlyle
Teiichi Suzuki
Japanese counsel: Kenzo Takayanagi, Tsuko Kaino, Ippei Kato and Jyum Fukushima
American counsel: M. Levin
Shigenori Tōgō
Japanese counsel: Haruhiko Nishi, Denjiro Kato and Motoharu Shichida
American counsel: George C. Yamaoka and B. B. Blakeney
Hideki Tōjō

Japanese counsel: Ichiro Kiyose, Hiroshi Uchiyama, Tokisaburo Shiohara and Kenjiro Kahoku
American counsel: G. F. Blewett
Yoshijirō Umezu
Japanese counsel: Mitsuo Miyata, Yoshikage Ono, Sumihisa Ikeda and Miichi Umezu
American counsel: B. B. Blakeney
Shūmei Ōkawa
Japanese counsel: Shinichi Ohara, Ryosuke Kanauchi and Fumiko Fukuoka
American counsel: A. W. Brooks
President of the Japanese Defenders Association (General Counsel): Somei Uzawa
Vice President of the Association (counsel for Hideki Tōjō): Ichiro Kiyose

As observed from the list, there were about 100 Japanese counsel and 20–30 American counsel, nearly amounting to a total of 130 counsel. The list did not include the counsel for Yōsuke Matsuoka and Osami Nagano, both of whom died during the Trial. Shūmei Ōkawa was excluded from trial because of mental illness, but as it was possible for him to recover and stand trial in the future, the Tribunal retained his Japanese and American counsel. The strong defence squad was a unique feature of the Tokyo Trial that set it apart from other international tribunals.

The Japanese Defenders Association of the Japanese counsel was established before the Tokyo Trial. On 4 May 1946, a day after the Tribunal's first open session, the Association held its first meeting; Somei Uzawa, a silver-haired lawyer, was elected as its president and general counsel for all defendants. Uzawa had served as the president of the Tokyo Bar Association, was respected for his age and manner, and was thought to have had a clean record under the Japanese fascist regime. He was courteous and unassuming, like a Confucianist gentlemen, and discussed political philosophy, such as the differences between the 'king's way' and hegemony, and the interpretation of *hakko ichiu* (all the world under one roof). He argued that the Japanese government had always given importance to peace and democracy, harmonious relationships based on trust, holistic approaches, and had resisted use of force and aggression. He also hailed China as the origin of charitable thoughts and praised the Chinese judge for his learning.

The Association also appointed as its vice president, Ichiro Kiyose, counsel for Hideki Tōjō, at its first meeting. Kiyose was a wily, old-fashioned Japanese politician, who was distinct from the other Japanese defence lawyers; we will discuss him later.

Most of the Japanese counsel were renowned legal experts in Japan before the War. Some of the lawyers were not well known, but were selected because they were relatives of, or known to the defendants. The Japanese lawyers were usually familiar with the work and worked tirelessly to collect supporting evidence (witnesses and documents) for the defendants. They were, however, lethargic in court, and allowed their ambitious American colleagues to fight in the forefront, while they themselves hid behind the scene and supplied weapons for defence outside the court. Therefore, compared to their American colleagues, they appeared better behaved in court.

Some Japanese lawyers, such as Kiyose, were aggressive; Kiyose had been a famous politician and an accomplice of the fascist regime before the War.[28] It was strange that a person of that background was allowed to work as a defence counsel before the Tribunal. In the Nuremberg Trial, all lawyers were strictly scrutinized; anyone who had been associated with Hitler in any way was not permitted to defend the accused at the Trial. As the Tokyo Tribunal was not strict on this criterion, the defence team was high-handed and overbearing.[29]

---

[28] Kiyose became even more politically active after the Allied occupation of Japan came to an end; he was ranked among the most important figures of the Liberal Democratic Party. During the administrations of Nobusuke Kishi and Hayato Ikeda, he served as the Speaker of the House of Representatives, and in Nagoya, built a monument for the seven war criminals executed by the Tokyo Tribunal, and glorified them as martyrs and national heroes. Kiyose, Shohei Sanmonji (Koiso's counsel) and Itsuro Hayashi (Hashimoto's counsel) raised a fund of 5 million yen for the monument's construction, and Kiyose presided over its opening ceremony.

[29] The Tokyo Tribunal barely scrutinized the counsel because the GHQ was assigned the task of selecting Japanese and American lawyers. Consequently, some politicians serving the warlords, such as Kiyose, were appointed as defence counsel. Moreover, some of the war criminals' former colleagues or subordinates were also permitted to defend them. For example, Umezu's counsel, Sumihisa Ikeda was a lieutenant general who acted as the head of Division V of the Chief of Staff of the Kwantung Army and subsequently as the Deputy Chief of Staff under Umezu. In 1942, under Umezu's command, he led a group of officers to Southeast Asia to study the military occupation systems established by the Japanese and to formulate a plan to occupy a certain territory of the Soviet Union. Like Umezu and other military leaders of the Kwantung Army, Ikeda was extremely hostile to the Soviet Union. It is said that the Soviet prosecutor wanted to submit an

Kiyose made vehement statements, protested against evidences, and conducted cross-examinations of the prosecution witnesses; therefore, he was often stopped and reprimanded by the bench. In his lengthy defence statement for Tōjō, he tried to justify Japan's imperialist theories and embellish fascist Japan's war policies. On the cover page of his defence statement, he proclaimed, 'This is a historical document.' This drew criticism from the Tribunal. President Webb asked him why he had absurdly referred to it as a historical document. Nevertheless, to ensure impartiality, the Tribunal allowed him to read his statement.

Among the 100 Japanese attorneys, another lawyer worth mentioning was Kenzo Takayanagi. A renowned professor at Tokyo Imperial University, he had authored many works and was well-versed in Japanese law. He was Teiichi Suzuki's counsel during the Tokyo Trial, but did not appear in court much, except when he read his lengthy essay 'The Tokyo Trial and International Law' in the final stage of trial.[30] For his knowledge and disposition, he was probably the most respectable one among the Japanese lawyers.

Except for these above-mentioned lawyers, most of the other Japanese counsel were mediocre and inconspicuous during the Trial. They allowed their American counterparts to handle critical evidences and witnesses, although they sometimes explained, objected and examined less important cases.

The American counsel did not have a formal organization like their Japanese counterparts, but they had a representative, Beverly Coleman (Tōjō's counsel) who was then replaced by George Yamaoka, an America-born Japanese who took Coleman's position after the latter returned to the US. However, the true leader of the American counsel was George Blewett, Tōjō's counsel and a board member of Columbia University. Blewett was a rich American lawyer, and the most respected American counsel—one wonders whether his wealth influenced his reputation.

Coleman, being very ambitious, requested the GHQ and Tokyo Tribunal to establish an 'International Defence Section' equivalent to

---

application to forbid Ikeda from appearing in court, but Keenan was not willing to make that application, with the excuse that a midway replacement of a defence counsel would be deemed as unfair by the Japanese.

[30] His paper was included in *The Tokyo Trials and International Law* published in English-Japanese by Yuhikaku Publishing House. His famous book, *The Philosophy of Law*, was translated into Chinese and published by China's Dadong Publisher before the War.

the IPS (International Prosecution Section) before the official opening of the Tribunal. The judges held a special meeting to hear his request, but eventually rejected it because the legal obligation of the Allied Powers to prosecute the Japanese war criminals and to give them a fair trial did not include providing them defence. The Tribunal permitted the American lawyers to join the defence in litigation procedures for the purpose of assisting the Japanese counsel chosen by the accused. Therefore, it was unnecessary to establish such a section in the GHQ.

The GHQ also rejected Coleman's request based on the consensus of opinion in the judges' conference. Coleman then resigned and returned to the US. Other than Coleman, nine American counsel: Guyder, Young, Alen, Dill, Haynes, Kleiman, McDonnel, Ruchik and Williams also tendered their resignations and went home.[31] Their names are not included in the list of American counsel mentioned earlier. (If they were included, there would be a total of about 40 American lawyers.) Along with 100 Japanese counsel, the defence team had as many as 140 lawyers. It was unlikely that one hundred and forty attorneys would ever be assigned to defend less than 30 accused, in Nuremberg or any other trial. The Tokyo Tribunal was thus generous in their measures to ensure that the accused were adequately defended.

As mentioned before, each defendant was permitted to have an American counsel to assist his Japanese counsel with trial procedures and techniques. Some of the American lawyers were recruited directly from the United States, while others had been working at the GHQ before the Trial. However, all their salaries were paid by the Legal Affairs Section of the GHQ, and not by the defendants or the Japanese government. Therefore, they were supposed to act as assistants or technical advisers, and play second fiddle to the Japanese counsel appointed by the defendants themselves.

As the Trial proceeded and the international situation changed, the American counsel overpowered their Japanese counterparts who obligingly worked in the background during open sessions. During the Trial,

---

[31] Most of them were military men with legal qualifications. When their service terms expired, they were eager to go home, and their positions had to be handed over to other people. However, some of them chose to stay and continue their service as defence counsel. As for non-military lawyers, such as Blewett, they were recruited directly from the US without fixed terms, and could continue their jobs until the Tokyo Trial ended.

most of the arguments were instigated by the American counsel. Below is an example of their perfidious behaviour.

On 14 May 1946, the defence counsel demanded that Count 39 be removed from the indictment. The crime alleged in it was the killing of Admiral Kidd and other naval officers and sailors when Japan bombed Pearl Harbor. Counsel Blakeney argued, 'If the killing of Admiral Kidd by the bombing of Pearl Harbor is murder, we know the name of the very man whose hands loosed the atomic bomb on Hiroshima, we know the chief of staff who planned that act, we know the chief of the responsible state.'[32] It was obvious that the last person who was being alluded to was President Truman who was the Commander-in-Chief of US Army according to the US Constitution. It was President Truman who decided to bomb Hiroshima and Nagasaki. It was impudent of Blakeney to compare his own country's actions to the Japanese war crimes in a tribunal that was trying war criminals.

The use of atomic bombs is indeed unpardonable, but the Tokyo Tribunal was established for another reason—to prosecute the Japanese war criminals. It was shocking and inappropriate to compare a war crime to a US military operation during the war.

The American attorneys were also unbelievably foolish sometimes, as illustrated in the following example:

> The IPS wanted to demonstrate that the Japanese imperialists had been instilling aggressive ideas into their youngsters through schools; so, it called Tamon Maeda, a Japanese educator, to testify before the Tribunal. On 2 August 1946, Counsel Kleiman cross-examined him after Maeda presented his affidavit.
>
> He questioned, 'You said that the military officers instructed the principals of the schools as to the courses and the administration of the school system. Among the courses that were taught in an elementary school, was not the Japanese language taught?' This triggered a surge of laughter in the courtroom.
>
> The President lost his cool on hearing the question. He exclaimed that it was a ridiculous question to ask.

---

[32] *Transcripts of Proceedings and Documents of the International Military Tribunal for the Far East* (14 May 1946), p. 212.

Kleiman continued, 'May it please the Tribunal, now I am truly trying to get answered a question that the Court asked, itself, about two months ago—what are these courses that were taught? It has never been brought out by the prosecution, and we, of the defence, wish to make the picture clear for the Tribunal. If the Tribunal does not wish to have the questions asked, I will refrain from them.'

The President responded by saying, 'The Tribunal does not wish to have that question asked.'

Kleiman accepted and posed another question. 'Was arithmetic taught to those students?'

This annoyed the President even more and he chided him for his audacity. He rudely reminded Kleiman that he was 'before the International Military Tribunal for the Far East trying former leaders of Japan of the greatest series of crimes ever committed against men'.

Kleiman continued, 'May it please your Honour, is it not important at this stage to show ... these courses which are taught in schools of every country in the world.'

The President in a tone of resignation said, 'Please continue with your questions.'

Kleiman questioned next, 'Was music, penmanship, drawing, Japanese history, needle work, taught in the schools?'

The spectators burst into more laughter. The President was furious with the proceedings and said, 'The witness need not answer to it.'

Knowing that his well-rehearsed, amusing questions would not be answered, Kleiman declared that he had 'no further questions'.[33]

Although the American counsel were often snubbed or criticized by the bench for their occasional absurdity, they managed to delay the Tokyo Trial and skilfully exploit the complex common law procedures.

---

[33] *Transcripts of Proceedings and Documents of the International Military Tribunal for the Far East* (2 August 1946), pp. 3145–3146.

As mentioned earlier, the defence employed the strategy of lengthening the trial proceedings, and consequently, the Trial took place for many years. The international climate was also conducive to their manipulative strategy.

First of all, the US policy to shield Japanese war criminals and rebuild Japanese militarism had become evident. As the Trial progressed, it became clear that the American government and the GHQ intended to protect the Japanese imperialists and use them to strengthen the US's objectives. They released the alleged Japanese war criminals from prison in batches, and stopped purging the militarists from the Japanese government. This prompted the defence to delay the Trial with the hope that it may be concluded prematurely by the GHQ, and the defendants are released and rehabilitated.

Second, the increasingly tense relations between the United States and the Soviet Union since World War II, was portrayed during the Trial. Newspapers reported stories about their antagonism for each other, and foresaw a third world war, particularly during the Berlin Blockade. This gave the defendants and their counsel the hope that if the Trial was delayed enough, a new war might break out and the international relationships would change. A militant Japan associated with the United States would be appreciated by the Western world; this would mean that the defendants could freely employ their war skills, wield power, embrace a new life and help the United States fight future wars.

A third world war did not take place, and the Berlin Blockade was finally resolved. The United States did not dare to disrupt the international circumstances or interrupt the Tokyo Trial. Nevertheless, the intentions of the defence encouraged them to protract the Trial.

Although the judges were anxious about the delay, they were helpless because the Charter's provisions had many loopholes, such as many lawyers to represent the accused, cumbersome procedures, and lengthy speeches from the defence, for the sake of a fair trial.

The Tribunal tried to counter the 'protraction strategy' by altering some tedious rules of procedure, simplifying the judges' voting method, preventing unnecessary remarks, and dismissing two American lawyers pursuant to Article 9 (c) of the Tokyo Charter.[34] These measures had a limited influence, and did not negate the defence's 'protraction strategy'.

Moreover, such a strategy not only wasted the Tribunal's time and resources and delayed its progress, but also gave the defendants the opportunity to distort facts, and spread false theories about imperialism in Japan; this was an unfortunate circumstance in the Tokyo Trial.

2.6 Administrative and Personnel Arrangements

The administrative and personnel arrangements of the Tokyo Tribunal were conducted by the General Secretary, an American, under the command of the GHQ. Although nominally reported to the President, the General Secretary's work was directed by the GHQ. Small matters were decided by the Chief of Staff of the GHQ, whereas big ones were referred to the Supreme Commander via the Chief of Staff for approval. The President of the Tribunal only signed his name or authorized the General Secretary to seal the necessary documents; most of the documents were on matters related to the trial, such as summoning a

---

[34] The Tribunal, to maintain an image of a fair trial, did not fully utilize the provisions of the Tokyo Charter. For example, Article 12 stipulates, 'The Tribunal shall: (a) confine the trial strictly to an expeditious hearing of the issues raised by the charges; (b) take strict measures to prevent any action which would cause any unreasonable delay and rule out irrelevant issues and statements of any kind whatsoever'; Article 13(a) provides: 'The Tribunal ... shall adopt and apply to the greatest possible extent expeditious and non-technical procedure ...'; and Article 9(c) demands: 'Each accused shall have the right to be represented by counsel ... subject to the disapproval of such counsel at any time by the Tribunal.' These articles were never seriously applied. The dismissals of Smith and Cunningham by the Tribunal (as mentioned in the preceding chapter) occurred only in the final stage of the trial, which had little influence on their protraction strategy. Smith was forced to resign in March 1947 due to his offensive language in court, while Cunningham was suspended from duties in October 1948, not because of his misbehaviour in court, but for his offensive remarks outside the Tribunal. On 7 September 1948, Cunningham attended a conference of the American Bar Association in Seattle and made a report of the Tokyo Trial. In his report, he criticized and defamed the Tokyo Tribunal, claiming that it was not objective or fair, and that it was prejudiced against the defendants and deprived the counsel's right of full defence. His report was later published in some US newspapers and made known to the judges. After Cunningham returned to Tokyo, he was ordered to explain it before the Tribunal; but he was unconvincing. Owing to his unsatisfactory explanation, the judges decided to suspend his service for 'defamation of court'. However, by that time, the Trial had already concluded its hearing and entered the judgment-drafting stage; so, his suspension was only symbolic, and without any actual effect on the trial proceedings.

witness, retrieving a document, verifying or dismissing the prosecution's or the defence's plea, altering the procedures, and contacting the Allied Powers for evidence. The administrative matters, personnel arrangements, expense control and archive keeping, were not the President's tasks; they were the concerns of the General Secretary who was obliged to obey the GHQ's orders. Therefore, in terms of administration and personnel, the Tokyo Tribunal was a subsidiary of the GHQ.

The GHQ was an American-managed organization, with almost all positions occupied by Americans. Likewise, the Tribunal's administration was also controlled by the Americans, who were in charge of most things except some less important jobs like translation and service, which were done by people from other Allied Powers or by the Japanese. Consequently, the Tokyo Tribunal was neither independent nor 'international' in the domain of administrative and personnel matters.

Unlike other organizations that establish several departments under a president, with each department divided into several sections, the Tokyo Tribunal did not have a regular, systematic administrative structure; its department names were also not standardized. Its administrative structure and personnel arrangements were realistic and yet modelled on conventional Western courts. Given below is a brief account of some important personnel and departments, their functions and duties, and their characteristics.

General Secretary and Secretariat: The appointment and powers of the General Secretary were stipulated in 'Officers and Secretariat' of the Tokyo Charter.[35] The General Secretary was directly appointed by the Supreme Commander; although he was a legal member of the Tribunal, and led by the Tribunal or its President in certain matters, he was more influenced by the Supreme Commander in his work. As indicated previously, he would convey important concerns to the GHQ and promptly implement its decisions.

The General Secretary was the top officer of the Tribunal's administration, and the director of all the Secretariat's staff and work.

The Charter had given much powers to the General Secretary; unlike the secretariat of an ordinary court, the Tribunal's Secretariat was responsible not only for the regular tasks, such as record keeping, sending and receiving documents, and archiving them, but also for the administration

---

[35] *Charter of the International Military Tribunal for the Far East*, Article 3(b).

and management of the Tribunal's personnel. The General Secretary of the Tokyo Tribunal was comparable to the Director of General Affairs in a government agency, who is ultimately responsible for the agency's administration and personnel affairs. The General Secretary, however, differed in that he was not led by the Tribunal's President or the judges, but by the GHQ (i.e. the Supreme Commander and the Chief of Staff).

The General Secretary of Tokyo Tribunal was Col. Walbridge, a reserved American man who hardly came to the Tribunal other than for attending some important judges' conferences regarding administrative matters.(Incidentally, judges' conferences that were convened for legal discussions and decisions prohibited anyone other than the judges, including the General Secretary.) Walbridge's main duty was to consult the GHQ; he was often shuttling between the Tribunal and GHQ. Any major administrative measures or personnel substitutions would be reported by him to the Chief of Staff or to the Supreme Commander via the Chief of Staff. The GHQ trusted him and he mutely complied with its orders. He rarely contacted the President, judges or the public.

The next in line after the General Secretary was the Assistant General Secretary, or the Deputy General Secretary, Col. Haney. Unlike Walbridge, Col. Haney was friendly and approachable, and usually seen in the Tribunal. Therefore, the prosecutors, defence lawyers and others often consulted him for minor matters concerning the Tribunal's administration (major application or requests had to be made to the Secretariat in writing). The judges also presented their suggestions or requests, such as printing documents or arranging tours. Col. Haney was esteemed by the judges for taking a keen interest in their concerns.

Another officer in the Secretariat, closer to the judges was Capt. Colbert, the Judges' Aide, a special position created to administer to the judges' daily concerns, and official or private matters. When the judges went on tours, he provided for their security, correspondence and escort. In May 1946, when the American and the Chinese judges travelled to Shanghai, Nanking and Peking by the GHQ's plane, Colbert accompanied them and arranged for their transportation, accommodation and visiting schedule. Although the trip was arranged after the war and China was one of the Five Powers, China was still controlled by the United States. All deluxe hotels and conveyances along the route were occupied or monitored by the US Army. If not for Capt. Colbert's arrangements and cooperation with the US Army, the trip would not have been possible.

Translation Section: The two most important units under the Secretariat were the Translation Section and the Administration Department. The written and oral translation work in the trial was complex and laborious, and required much human and material resources.

According to the Charter, English and Japanese were the official languages of the Tribunal. Every statement by the President, prosecutors, defence counsel and witnesses had to be immediately interpreted into its counterpart official language. The listeners could choose their desired language by turning on the headphone at their seats. If the speaker spoke Chinese, Russian, German, French or Mongolian, the translators would translate them into English and Japanese. The court hearing often lasted for about five hours daily, and the urgency required, made the translation job complex and demanding.

Apart from interpreting during the trial, the translators had to translate every document that the Tribunal received into Japanese or English, and sometimes into both the languages, if it was written in a third language. Although some documents were submitted by the prosecution and defence with their translated versions, the work was still laborious because of the huge volume of documents accepted or issued by the Tribunal.

The Translation Section was crucial to the Tribunal's daily operations, because it could influence the quality and efficacy of the trial, which was prone to protests and conflicts. In addition to staff strength, the Translation Section required efficient personnel with excellent language skills.

The Translation Section was headed by Anderson and his deputy Jones, both Americans. For their convenience, they hired some Japanese American personnel, such as Ytami, who were known as 'the second generation' Americans ('nisei' in Japanese), because they were born to Japanese immigrants. Moreover, most of the translators working for the Trial were renowned Japanese scholars who were proficient in English, such as Kisaburo Yokota, senior professor of international law at Tokyo Imperial University.[36] These Japanese translators were knowledgeable and could quickly interpret the words during the trial. Since most of the translators (20–30 of them) were introduced to the Tribunal by the Japan's Ministry

---

[36] Prof. Yokota was a well-known international law scholar and a member of the UN International Law Commission. He served as the director of Japanese translation group for the entire period of the Tokyo Trial.

of Foreign Affairs, they were not entirely trusted by the representatives of the Allied Powers, and especially their judges.

The Translation Section was the only administrative unit that used non-American employees (except for the Japanese servants and handymen hired by the Administration Department).

The Translation Section also temporarily engaged people from other nationalities to assist in difficult situations. For example, when the Russian and Mongolian witnesses testified before the Tribunal, translators for them were hired from the Russian military delegation in Japan. When Puyi (emperor of the puppet 'Manchukuo'), Chin Teh-Chun (Mayor of Peking when the Marco Polo Bridge Incident broke out), and Wang Len-Chai (Special Commissioner and Magistrate of Wanping County) stood in the witness stand, most of their testimonies were translated by members of the Chinese military delegation in Japan and the Chinese judge's personal secretary.

Language Arbitration Board: It was established to address the disputes arising from translations and interpretations. Given the grammatical differences between English and Japanese, translation errors or misunderstandings were common. A sentence spoken by a Japanese witness provided by the prosecution was translated into English, and if the defence counsel believed it was incorrect and could damage the defendant's interests, he had the right to object and ask for arbitration from the Tribunal. The Tribunal would immediately convene the Language Arbitration Board, who would report the result of their discussion. If the report decided to change the translation, the President would order for the change of translation recording. The prosecution could exercise the same right at any time. This applied not only to the oral interpretation but also to errors or misunderstandings in the translation of any document, for which the concerned party could request arbitration.

The three-member Language Arbitration Board was the unit designated to address language disputes, and which was completely trusted by the Tribunal. The members could not leave the courtroom but had to remain for the entire court session.

The Board's decision was final.

The Board was chaired by Maj. Moore, an American who had taught in Japan for about 20 years. He was succeeded by Larft after he returned to the United States. Sano and Kakei were the other two Japanese members with an excellent command of English.

Administration Department: This was an important department under the General Secretary with the most complex and extensive functionality. In addition to its specialized tasks, it also handled matters which were omitted by other departments. In this sense, it was similar to the general affairs office of a government agency.

Typing, printing and record keeping were laborious tasks due to the great volume of documents produced and received by the Tribunal. Moreover, such tasks often had to be finished within a strict time-frame. When a document was written and then translated by the Translation Section, the Administration Department handled its printing and distribution.

The daily shorthand recording of the proceedings was an onerous task; when the session commenced, highly skilled stenographers from the Administration Department took records, transcribed and printed them after the session ended in the late afternoon. They were bound into volumes (a record of 80–100 pages for a five-hour daily session), and delivered to the judges and concerned parties (the prosecution, defence and others concerned) before eight in the evening to give them sufficient time for perusal. If a party detected a mistake, they had to apply for correction by bringing it to the notice of the Tribunal at the beginning of the session on the following day. If the Tribunal approved the application, the President would announce it and call for the immediate correction of the recording.

This was the only procedure provided for the record correction before it was finalized. As the Tokyo Trial did not follow the principle of 'discretional evaluation of evidence' but 'evidentialism', records were crucial to the entire trial process and became the only basis for the Tribunal to make its final judgement.[37] Therefore, the evidences were of interest to all parties; the judges would find time to review the records before they

---

[37] The principle of 'discretional evaluation of evidence' implies that a judge should base his judgement not only on the evidence accepted by the court, but also on his own (subjective) conviction of the evidence that he deems proper, and his understanding of the facts. It is a system generally adopted by the civil law countries, under which the judge has more judicial discretion. On the contrary, the common law countries generally follow the 'evidentialism' doctrine, which means that the judge in reaching a decision, should be objectively and strictly bound by the evidence provided by both parties and accepted by the court. The latter system gives the judge little discretion but forces him to base every decision on evidence. The Tokyo Tribunal adopted the common law system; therefore, evidence and records of the trial were the deciding factors for the judgment.

retired for the day. After years of court hearings, the records ran to 50,000 pages and 10 million words.

In addition to shorthand records, the Tribunal also had audio recordings. The audio recorder was operated by the Administration Department, which also stored the documents, records and archives of the Tribunal for review.

The Administration Department had to manage hundreds of working staff, Japanese servants, cooks, drivers and cleaners. It was responsible for their employment and dismissal, assignment of work, remuneration, work duties, work schedule, and labour disciplines.

When guests from the Allied Powers arrived to visit the Tribunal or watch the trial, the Administration Department would attend to them. Additionally, when the President or some judges wished to host a cocktail or tea party for dignitaries from the Allied Powers, the Department would make the necessary preparations and arrangements for it.

This Department was also responsible for distributing ordinary and VIP seat tickets to the visitors from the Allied Powers—apparently a small task, but mistakes could create dissatisfaction and trigger protests. As the sections of seats reserved for the Allied Powers were not crowded, especially during the final phase of the trial, ticket distribution was not difficult. The Japan's Ministry of Foreign Affairs distributed tickets for the Japanese spectators, without interference from the Administration Department.[38]

Apart from the above-mentioned tasks, the Administration Department managed the sending and receiving of documents, food and refreshments distribution and procurement, cashier services, and accounting. In conclusion, matters that were disregarded by the other departments, fell under the purview of the Administration Department.

The ordeals and procedures, rules and regulations of the court sessions, and the management and supervision of the prison and prisoners, were

---

[38] During the Tribunal's open sessions, the seats for Japanese spectators were always full. It was difficult for the Japanese to get tickets. It was said that the Ministry of Foreign Affairs allocated two tickets to each defendant's family each day, and distributed the rest of tickets to the people who queued outside the Ministry's gate every morning. Some people lined up in queues at midnight or even at dusk the day before to receive the tickets. Some of them would sell their tickets for money. According to the reports of *Asahi Shimbun*, the ticket for hearings against Hideki Tōjō was as expensive as 800 yen in the black market. Of course, 'smuggling' and back-door trades also occurred among the officers who controlled the ticket distribution.

assigned to specialized units and personnel, outside the domain of the Administration Department.

E. R. Harris, a US naval officer was the head of the Administration Department. Next in line was the deputy director, B. A. Hargaden. The busiest senior staff of the Tribunal, Harris and Hargaden, worked under the direction of the General Secretary and reported major issues to him.

During the court sessions, there was another batch of staff that reported to the Secretariat and followed instructions from the General Secretary; they also abided by the President's directions during the trial. The General Secretary, who was rarely present, was not allowed to intervene in the Tribunal's sessions.

Among the staff who had to be present in court (in addition to the interpreters, language arbitrators, recorders and photographers), the most important members were: the Marshal of the Court, the Clerk, and the Provost Marshal.

Marshal of the Court: His duties were to conduct ceremonial procedures when the Tribunal opened its session, and to administer oaths and maintain the court's order. Fifteen minutes before the court session began and the spectators were seated (they had to arrive half an hour before the session), the Marshal announced some important rules to be followed by the spectators, such as maintaining silence, remaining inside the courtroom for the entire session, and standing up when the judges entered. He would also briefly explain how to use the headphones at the seats.

When the judges filed in, he proclaimed, 'All rise!' After the judges were seated, he called out, 'Be seated!' He then announced, 'The International Military Tribunal for the Far East is now in session.' When the Tribunal closed its session, he again called out, 'All rise!' Only after the judges walked out of the court, could the rest leave.

Except on Saturday and Sunday, the Tokyo Trial was held in four slots: 9:30–10:40 and 10:55–12:00 in the morning, and 1:30–2:40 and 2:55–4:00 in the afternoon. Therefore, the Marshal would formally and ceremoniously direct the audience, four times a day.

The Marshal also performed the tasks of ushering the witnesses into the courtroom, seating them, and administering their oaths before they testified. The oath was simple and secular, attesting that the witness would faithfully give testimony out of his conscience and accept punishment if there was any deception. It was bereft of religious phrases such as 'before God', 'punishable by God', or 'so help me God', because not all the Allied

Powers which participated in the Tokyo Trial were Christian countries, nor were most of the witnesses Christians.[39]

The oath was taken in a simple way. The witness and the Marshall stood facing each other, and raised their left hand; the witness repeated what the Marshal said. Upon finishing, the witness sat down and gave his testimony by reading a note prepared for this purpose. Once he had read it, he could be examined and cross-examined by the lawyers from both parties. This could last for several days. During the entire process of testifying, the Marshal would be near him, like a custodian. When the process ended, the President said, 'The witness' obligations are now dissolved.' The Marshal would then guide him out of the courtroom.

In the open sessions, if anyone's behaviour or words produced confusion or laughter from the audience, the Marshal would holler, 'Silence, silence!' For instance, when a counsel requested the Tribunal to excuse him for two minutes as he had to attend nature's call, the President remarked, 'Your application is truly strange to us, but we nevertheless approve it.' The spectators broke into laughter, and the Marshall had to shout, 'Silence, silence!'

The President also had the power at any time, to request the Marshal to summon the military police to remove anyone who transgressed the Tribunal's rules or court orders. This power was never exercised by the President during the two years of trial proceedings. Even when the two American lawyers were dismissed from court, they walked out of the court unaided.

The Marshal of the Court in the Tokyo Tribunal was Van Meter, a burly, bearded and grave US military officer, who spoke in a loud and powerful voice, and appeared to enjoy his monotonous duties. He was esteemed by all parties.

Clerk: The Clerk sat in the middle of the row of secretaries, and in front of the judges' desk. Generally, the term 'clerk' is used for a

---

[39] The oaths made by the staff of the Tribunal and the witnesses were quite different. Before assuming their positions, the staff would swear an oath or make a commitment. In the oaths of the General Secretary and the Secretariat's personnel, there were no references to God. This was also the case in the oaths of the Japanese clerks and translators. However, the oaths taken by the non-Japanese clerks and translators, concluded with 'so help me God'. However, if a non-Japanese clerk or translator was an atheist, he could replace the phrase with an affirmation of different wording. In this sense, they had a choice of wording when swearing before the Tribunal (see Rule 8 of _Rules of Procedure of the International Military Tribunal for the Far East_).

secretary, an assistant or a court recorder; but in the Tokyo Tribunal, the title had a special meaning. He was assigned the sole task of registering all evidentiary documents and materials admitted by the Tribunal (namely the 'exhibits'); he was, in fact, an exhibit registrar. As explained earlier, the documents were the most essential materials for arriving at a judgement, and their admissibility was often the reason for disputes between contesting parties. Therefore, the Tribunal established this position to safeguard and manage the evidentiary documents. Any document provided by either party to the Tribunal as evidence, regardless of whether or not it was challenged, could be admitted and registered as a valid evidence only after the Clerk announced and numbered it in court.

When the prosecution or the defence provided a document and asked the Tribunal to accept it as evidence, and if there was no objection from the other party, the Clerk would announce, 'Prosecution Document No. X (or Defence Document No. Y) is admitted and will be marked as Exhibit No. Z.' If any objection was raised, the Tribunal would allow the contesting parties to debate over it and then the judges would vote to decide its admissibility. If the other party did not intend to debate after raising an objection, the bench could also decide its admission by voting. On the few occasions when there were complexities and heated arguments, rulings were mostly made by voting at a judges' conference, after the court session was adjourned. At other times, particularly when the matter was simple and there was no debating, the judges would cast their votes on the evidence admissibility by marking on slips of paper (a simple way to express 'yes' or 'no' in letters or marks) and passing them to the President.[40]

The result of majority voting, whether through a judges' conference or on the spot, was deemed as a formal ruling, and the President would announce, 'we have decided to admit the document' or 'we have decided to refuse the document'. The decision once announced, was final and could not be overridden.

If the document was rejected, the party that provided it (the prosecution or the defence) had to withdraw it, and step down from the podium. If the document was accepted, the Clerk would announce, 'Prosecution Document No. X (or Defence Document No. Y) is admitted and will be

---

[40] As to the methods of voting in making a ruling by the judges, see Sect. 2.3 of this chapter.

marked as Exhibit No. Z.' Every one of the thousands of exhibits accepted by the Tribunal was announced in this manner by the Clerk.

The announcement and numbering by the Clerk appeared to be a mere formality, but it was significant in that it registered the evidence as a legal and effective exhibit, beyond any dispute. The party that provided the evidence could choose to read it entirely or partially in court, and the portion read out became part of the trial records. As the Tokyo Tribunal did not follow the principle of 'discretionary evaluation of evidence', the trial records were the main basis on which the bench made its final judgement.

The Clerk had the responsibility of announcing the Tribunal's admission of a documentary evidence and assigning it an exhibit number. In this sense, he was the 'gatekeeper' of the Trial's evidence. For the nearly 5000 exhibits the Tribunal accepted, each of them passed through the 'gate' of the Clerk.

The Tribunal's Clerk was an American named Dell. He had been an American judge in a local court and had worked as a civilian officer for the GHQ before being transferred to this Tribunal. He was, however, inconspicuous outside the courtroom because the nature of his job inside court was mechanical and involved little interaction with others.

Provost Marshal: Apart from the Marshal of the Court and the Clerk, the Provost Marshal was yet another important administrative officer who could not be absent from the courtroom even for a moment.[41] The Provost Marshal played a duel role—inside and outside of the Tribunal.

The Provost Marshal was responsible for the security of the whole building; he had to take the necessary measures, such as deploying the military police, arranging for gate guards and conducting entrance checks for the security of the Tribunal. The military policemen assigned to the Tribunal were under his command.

The Provost Marshal had the important task of safeguarding the Tribunal's open sessions. Before the session commenced, he checked every corner of the courtroom, searched the spectators, arranged for the

---

[41] Since the Tokyo Tribunal was essentially a military court, it did not entrust the bailiffs with the tasks of securing the courtroom and guarding the prisoners as other courts did, but engaged a team of military police appointed by the GHQ to perform these functions. There were 80–100 MPs stationed in the Tribunal and Sugamo Prison, all of whom were tall, competent and handsome American soldiers selected by the GHQ and acting under the command of the Provost Marshal.

military police, and escorted the defendants from the prison to the courtroom. During the session, he ensured that the defendants and spectators maintained order and avoided accidents in the courtroom. He was not empowered to expel anyone who broke rules or defied the court, but had to abide by the orders of the President and the Marshal of the Court.

During the session, the Provost Marshal often stood in the middle of the pathway leading to the dock and faced the bench, which represented that the defendants were under his watchful eye and could not escape. He did not leave that post unless an accident took place.

These were the Provost Marshal's responsibilities inside the Tribunal. However, he had another difficult, and more important task outside the Tribunal—custody of the defendants in prison.

Although the defendants stood for trial every day, they were not detained at the Tribunal, but sent to the Sugamo Prison, which was quite a distance away from the Tribunal.

Sugamo Prison was the most prominent detention centre in Tokyo, with a capacity for 1000 prisoners. It usually housed over 400 inmates. During the occupation of Japan, the GHQ expropriated it for the detainment of Japanese war criminals (including Class-B and Class-C war criminals, and those Class-A suspects who were not yet prosecuted) as well as some other criminals.

The nearly 30 prisoners who were tried at the Tokyo Tribunal received special treatment at Sugamo Prison. Being under the custody of the Provost Marshal, they were not bound by the general regulations of the Prison or subject to the authority of its staff.

The Provost Marshal was nominally led by the orders of the President in performing this function, but was primarily under the control of the GHQ. He reported to and received instructions from the GHQ.

As the Class-A defendants detained at Sugamo Prison were prominent personalities such as warlords, bureaucrats and plutocrats before the War, the custodial treatment given for them was far better than that for ordinary prisoners.

For example, each Class-A defendant was given a clean and spacious independent room.[42] They ate the same Western-style meals as the occupation army, and during holidays, they were served specially prepared Japanese food. They were given the best of medical facilities in Japan. They could converse with each other during breaks, meet their family members and friends at noon every day, and answer interviews. The leniency shown here was seldom displayed at other detention centres for war criminals.

The US policy to shield Japanese war criminals and restore militarism in Japan ensured that these defendants were treated well at Sugamo Prison; eventually, even the Provost Marshal became their friend.

The Provost Marshal of the Tokyo Tribunal was an American officer, Col. A. S. Kenworthy. He was a grave man in his 40s and of medium build. As he had served in Philippines as the Provost Marshal of the military tribunal where Tomoyuki Yamashita (nicknamed Tiger of Malaya) was tried, the GHQ appointed him as the Provost Marshal of the Tokyo Tribunal.

Kenworthy strictly complied with the GHQ's instructions while overseeing the accused war criminals, and fully demonstrated the US policy towards Japan. At the beginning of the trial, he adopted a stern stance and implemented drastic measures against the defendants, but after the changes in the US policy towards Japan, he became more lenient towards them.

Kenworthy was a duplicitous person; at open court sessions and while escorting the defendants from prison to court in a bus, he appeared strict and harsh. This was only an attempt to please the representatives from the Allied Powers and Japan. In his report to the President and other judges,

---

[42] When they were first put in Sugamo Prison for custody, each defendant was assigned a fixed single ward. But they had to change their wards once a week after the Nuremberg Trial ended in October 1946. It was said that the change was prompted by Hermann Göring's suicide. He had used the poison hidden in his ward to commit the act. (Göring was sentenced to death by hanging by the Nuremberg Tribunal but managed to kill himself the day before his execution.) From then on, the military police at Sugamo changed their rooms to prevent them from hiding or burying any drugs or tools in there that could help them commit suicide. Apart from changing their rooms frequently, the MP also often searched their clothes and daily articles. It was rumoured that Göring had used cyanide that was hidden within a gold dental crown in his mouth; therefore, the MP often searched their persons as well. Articles and foodstuffs sent by their families were also carefully checked for hidden poison. It may sound strange today, but it was a priority then, to prevent the prisoners from committing suicide.

he clearly explained the custodial measures and treatment meted out to the prisoners. Inside Sugamo Prison, however, the scenario was different; he was not only amiable to the defendants, but also responsive to all their requests. He took such good care of the war criminals that towards the closure of the hearing, on 1 February 1948, the defendants wrote him a three-metres-long scroll of 'letter of appreciation'. It was a brush-pen written, exquisitely bound letter with their signatures, that praised him for his 'style of an ancient knight' and 'heart of a loving father'.

Kenworthy's undue leniency towards the defendants and duplicity of manner stemmed from the ambitious US policy to rearm Japan and restore its militarism. Being an astute American military officer, Kenworthy understood the policy well and faithfully adhered to it.

This completes the description of the administrative organization and personnel arrangements of the Tokyo Tribunal and the personalities of some important administrative officers. Finally, we will discuss the Tribunal's financial and archival problems within the scope of the Tribunal's administration.

<u>Finance</u>: The Tokyo Tribunal had no exclusive budget; the total expense incurred was drawn from the GHQ's account.

This does not mean that the Tribunal had no independent expenditure. The amount of money payable by the Tribunal, however, was limited to administrative expenses. The major expenses of the Tribunal was borne by the GHQ, the Allied Powers, or the Japanese government.

For example, salaries of the Tribunal employees (from the President and judges, to the security guards and servants) comprised the greatest part of the Tribunal's expenditure, but the Tribunal had no responsibility towards it. Salaries of the President, other judges and prosecutors from different countries, and their secretaries, assistants and translators were paid by their respective accrediting countries. Salaries of the US assistant prosecutors (most of them being servicemen or civilian staff of the GHQ) were paid by the GHQ under occupation army expenses. Salaries of the Japanese defence lawyers were financed by the Japanese government. Salaries of the administrative staff of the Tribunal, from the General Secretary, the Marshal of the Court, the Clerk, to the stenographers, typists, photographers (more than 90 per cent of them being Americans, transferred and appointed by the GHQ) were directly drawn from the GHQ. Salaries of the American defence lawyers (either transferred from the GHQ or recruited directly from the US) were also paid directly by the GHQ. The Provost Marshal and the military police of the Tribunal, who had priorly served in the occupation army and were temporarily deputed to the Tribunal, received their remuneration from the GHQ. The Japanese technicians (translators, printers, and electricians) and workers (chefs, maids, and cleaners) were conscripted into the Tribunal by the GHQ, and were paid by the Japanese government. The costs of refurbishment, maintenance and equipment of the Tribunal were entirely paid by the GHQ.

Therefore, the remuneration of all the Tribunal staff and a substantial amount of the Tribunal's infrastructural expenditure was borne by other organizations. The Tribunal had to bear only some administrative expenses. These expenses did not include the cost of board and lodging of the judges and their entourage, or their transportation and hotel charges during vacations or weekends. The GHQ paid for these expenses from the occupation fee, stating that it would be deducted later from Japan's war reparation which was due to their home countries.[43]

Out of the few expenses incurred by the Tribunal, the charges on the witnesses and printing paper were the highest.

In the entire process of open sessions, the Tribunal summoned about 500 witnesses to testify. Some of them were Japanese, others were from the Allied Powers; some lived in Tokyo or other Japanese cities, and some others lived overseas. The Tribunal had to pay only a little amount for witnesses living in Tokyo or other Japanese cities. However, it was expensive to finance overseas witnesses because in addition to their travel tickets, the Tribunal had to fund their board and lodging, and provide a dollar per day for each person as pocket money. Moreover, overseas witnesses could not testify upon arrival, but had to wait until a particular stage of trial when they were summoned by court. Consequently, some witnesses had to stay in Tokyo for a long time, and some even had to visit home for a short period before returning to Tokyo. All these contributed to the Tribunal's expenses.

In addition to the expenses incurred on witnesses, the cost of printing paper was also high. Each evidentiary document admitted by the Tribunal had to be made into many copies (photocopying, stereotyping or printing) for distribution to the judges, the prosecution and the defence, and other concerned parties. Daily proceeding records, memos, petitions and other documents were numerous, and needed to be duplicated into

---

[43] Regarding 'deduction from Japan's war reparation', see Footnote 19 under Sect. 2.3.4 of this chapter.

many copies. Consequently, printing (stereotyping and photocopying) and typing became the busiest section of the Administration Department, and a staggering amount of paper was used. According to the newspapers, the Tribunal used about three to five tons of paper per day for printing and typing. The colossal paper usage and printing ink, film, liquid solution, and carbon paper consumption resulted in much expense. As the Japanese paper industry had been destroyed during the war, the quality of paper produced locally was poor; the Tribunal, therefore, imported paper from the United States and Sweden, which added to the total expenditure.

Except for the two major expenses (witness fees and printing paper), other expenses, such as refreshments for the judges, receptions for important guests, and material procurement were negligible.

Although the Tribunal handled only a few expenses, it was reported that even that amounted to about US$7.5 million for the entire trial—a 'shocking expenditure'.

Expenses that were directly paid by the Tribunal and those covered by the GHQ were consolidated into an 'occupation fee' which was charged to the Japanese government by the United States. The total amount and the itemization of the 'occupation fee' was kept a secret because the Americans regarded management of the GHQ as its 'internal affairs', and did not want to reveal its financial conditions.

The 'Peace Treaty with Japan', signed by the United States and 47 other countries in September 1951 in San Francisco, stipulated that the signatories waive off all the reparation claims.[44] Later, the 'mess account' of the United States in the occupation of Japan was completely ignored and since there was no war reparation from Japan to the judge's home country, there were no deductions from it.

Archives. We shall now discuss the archives of the Tokyo Tribunal and their management.

The Tokyo Tribunal had extensive archives; according to the Japanese, there were 'so many as to fill a house to the rafters' and they were 'as vast as a misty sea'.

Following were the sources of the Tribunal's archives:

---

[44] See the Peace Treaty of San Francisco, Paragraph 2 of Article 14. For the full text of this illegal treaty, see *Collection of International Treaties (1950–1952)*, World Affairs Press, pp. 333–350.

1. There were nearly five thousand volumes of original (or 'authentic') evidentiary documents presented by both parties (prosecution and defence) at the proceeding and admitted by the Tribunal. These were registered and maintained as archives for future reference. Photocopies or printed copies were distributed to all concerned parties. Some of these evidentiary documents were read out by the presenting party at the open court session, and then added to the proceeding's records. Many lengthy documents were only partially read out, and only those relevant sections were included in the proceeding's records. For example, the famous *Kido's Diaries* (one of the most important documents admitted by the Tribunal) had more than a dozen volumes, out of which only a small part was read out in court. In any case, all evidentiary documents which were formally admitted by the Tribunal, had probative value and were archived as evidences.
2. The secret files of the Japanese government seized by the GHQ in the early days of the occupation of Japan, such as minutes of the Imperial Conference, the cabinet meetings and the wartime core cabinet meetings ('Five-Minister Meetings'), decisions and tactical plans of the Imperial General Headquarters, secret instructions and statements of the Ministry of War, and secret reports and telecommunications of the Ministry of Foreign Affairs were hitherto hidden from public scrutiny; these confidential documents were never revealed during the pre-war or wartime Japan. When the Japanese surrendered, their government had made every endeavour to conceal those documents by storing them in metal safes that were hidden in a secret place. Eventually, they were discovered by the occupation army.[45]

---

[45] In order to erase evidences, the Japanese government burned most of the archives before their surrender. Some of them had already been destroyed during the Allied air raids when tens of thousands of bombs bombarded Tokyo day and night, for a couple of months before Japan surrendered. More than 75 per cent of the buildings (including government buildings) in Tokyo and Yokohama were destroyed. However, the most confidential and important archives with great historical value to the Japanese government were stored in metal safes, and buried underground. They were buried under the basement of an insurance company in Tokyo, which had also been destroyed. The government officials thought that it would be difficult to excavate the safes, now that the buildings had collapsed and the basement was covered with debris. Within four months after the occupation of Japan, their 'secret basement' was discovered by the patrolling military police of the Allies. Although it was an accidental discovery, the news described it as a planned

Since those confidential documents were important for the trial of major Japanese war criminals, the GHQ handed over most of them to the Archives Office of the Tokyo Tribunal (except military secrets, such as the Japanese wartime army organizations, production of military supplies, and tactical plans). A large part of the evidence produced by the prosecution and the defence was derived from those archives. The Archives Office on the third floor of the Tribunal building became a repository for both the parties, and their staff diligently rummaged through the numerous documents on shelves for suitable evidences. Even if the papers had scattered information, as long as they were relevant to their purposes, the prosecutors and the defence lawyers retrieved and submitted them to the Tribunal. It was a different question though, whether they would be accepted by the Tribunal. The evidences retrieved from the archives were only a tiny fraction of the Japanese government records. The records were a log of the important decisions and initiatives taken by the Japanese government (including the Emperor, the Cabinet, the Diet, the Imperial General Headquarters, and the War Ministry) in the political, military, economic and diplomatic domains over many decades. The Tribunal only required evidences from the 18-year period (from the Huanggutun Incident in 1928 to the Japanese surrender in 1945), which depicted Japan's scheme of expansion, waging of aggressive wars, aggressions against humanity and violation of international laws and customs, directly related to the 28 defendants. Since the required evidences comprised only a small portion of the available archives, a substantial portion of the Japanese archives was left unused by the Tribunal. Although the Tribunal could not use these documents as evidences, they were of particular interest to students of modern Japanese history who explored Japan's aggressive policies and foreign relations.

The Archives Office of the Tribunal also stored records from the secret archives of Nazi Germany about Japanese conspiracies and the Germany-Japan collusion. It also had documents sent by some Allied Powers, about Japanese aggression and the atrocities committed by Japanese armies in

'expedition'. Once the 'secret basement' was uncovered, the GHQ excavated all the safes buried there, and found each safe having a seal reading 'no opening without cabinet resolution'. This not only meant that the archives preserved in those safes were confidential and important for the Japanese government, but also that their concealment was a systematic conspiracy collectively conducted by the highest Japanese authorities. Undoubtedly, at least several of the defendants in the Tokyo Tribunal were involved in this conspiracy; some such as Tōjō, Kido, Nagano and Doihara were its primary instigators.

different places. Some of these materials were utilized by the contesting parties and submitted as evidences to the Tribunal, but most of them remained as historical records in the Archives Office after the Tokyo Trial ended.

This is an overview of the important archives of the Tokyo Tribunal. In conclusion, the archives were not only important for the Tokyo Trial, but provided useful material for the study of Japan.

Sadly, as soon as the Tokyo Trial ended, the GHQ transported the archives to the US War Department in Washington, DC. All documents, whether they were the original evidentiary documents admitted by the Tribunal, the confidential files of the Japanese government or Nazi Germany, or the materials provided by the Allied Powers, were transported and became the exclusive property of the United States. The other Allies no longer had any right over the documents; even photocopies or printed forms of the documents were seized by the United States and kept confidential. The Chinese government had negotiated for a photocopy of Kido's Diaries, but the US government denied it. During the Tokyo Trial, in view of the significant probative and historical values of Kido's Diaries, the GHQ made more than 100 photocopies of it. China, an Allied Power that had fought Japan for the longest period, and was a major participant in the Tokyo Trial, was refused even a single photocopy of this important document. It was undoubtedly selfish of the US government to refuse China's reasonable request.

Thus, the Tokyo Tribunal's extensive archives ultimately landed in the coffers of the US Government.

CHAPTER 3

Arrest and Prosecution of Japanese Major War Criminals

3.1 FOUR ARREST WARRANTS FROM THE GENERAL HEADQUARTERS

According to the resolution of the Moscow Conference on 26 December 1945, the Supreme Commander for the Allied Powers had the authority to implement all the terms in Japan's Instrument of Surrender. One of the important conditions for Japan's surrender (see Articles 1 and 6 of the Instrument of Surrender) was 'to carry out the provisions of the Potsdam Declaration in good faith'. According to Article 6 of the Potsdam Declaration, 'there must be eliminated for all time the authority and influence of those who have deceived and misled the people of Japan into embarking on world conquest', and Article 10 proclaims: 'We do not intend that the Japanese shall be enslaved as a race or destroyed as a nation, but stern justice shall be meted out to all war criminals, including those who have visited cruelties upon our prisoners.'[1]

In order to implement these two articles, the GHQ adopted two measures at an early stage of the occupation of Japan. First, it arrested in batches more than 100 alleged major war criminals, i.e. the 'Class-A war criminals', who were politicians, warlords, financiers, diplomats or

---

[1] For the Resolution of the Moscow Conference, see *Collection of International Treaties (1945–1947)*, World Affairs Press, pp. 120–128. For the Potsdam Declaration, ibid., pp. 77–78. For Japan's Instrument of Surrender, ibid., pp. 112–114.

propagandists with primary responsibility for the Japanese war of aggression. Second, it purged in batches almost 200,000 'Japanese militarists' and also those who had held senior positions in the Japanese government, army, fascist groups or large enterprises during the war.[2]

It was necessary for the GHQ to take these measures because punishing war criminals and thwarting militarists was not only a power conferred to it by an international mandate but also an obligation it owed to the Allied Powers.

During the early period of the Allied occupation of Japan at the end of the World War II, the GHQ seriously exercised its obligatory power. This threw the Japanese reactionaries into a frenzy; it was evident that the memory of Japanese aggression was still fresh in the minds of the Allied people, and even the Americans could not forget the attack on Pearl Harbor and the hardships of warring against Japan. Consequently, there was a shared feeling of animosity against Japan among the Allies and a strong imperative to punish the prime instigators of the aggressive war and eliminate Japanese militarism. At that time, the US government had not yet demonstrated its support for Japanese militarism, although some people in Washington, DC and on Wall Street had visualized Japan as a potential ally of the United States in the Far East.

Therefore, the GHQ executed systematic and planned operations to arrest war criminals and purge militarists in the early stages of Allied occupation.

As the purging of militarists was not directly related to the Tokyo Trial, it will not be elaborated here.

The arrest of major war criminals is the focal point of our discussion. The purpose of arresting them was to subject them to trial and consequent legal sanctions. In fact, all the defendants tried by the Tokyo Tribunal were selected from those arrestees.

---

[2] 'Purge' means 'remove' or 'get rid of'. Those who had been purged were not allowed to hold any public office until the purge was lifted. They were not only barred from serving as officials or congressmen at all levels of government, but were also unable to take higher positions in social organizations or business groups, such as the positions of president, manager, director, chairman, secretary and accountant. At the beginning of the occupation, more than 190,000 Japanese militarists were purged by the GHQ. Later, they were rehabilitated batch after batch due to the US policy to protect Japan's reactionary forces. By the time the San Francisco Peace Treaty was signed in September 1952, most of the purged militarists had re-established their civil rights. After the conclusion of the Peace Treaty, the Japanese government cancelled the 'purge' for them all.

The arrest of Japanese major war criminals, or the 'Class-A war criminals', was conducted in four batches between September and December of 1945.

The *First Arrest Warrant* was issued by the GHQ on 11 September 1945, less than ten days after Japan signed the Instrument of Surrender (2 September) and the US military landed in Japan (3 September).

Thirty-nine people were listed in the first arrest warrant and Hideki Tōjō, the notorious former Prime Minister, ranked first.

This arrest warrant had two features: First, it was mostly targeted against those who had been government leaders when the Pacific War broke out and senior officers who had committed atrocities in the Pacific War. Second, apart from the Japanese war criminals, it included a number of foreign officials who had cooperated with Japan and participated in the aggression and had remained in Japan after the war ended.

Therefore, whereas the first batch of arrestees excluded many important Japanese war criminals, it comprised some foreign offenders.

Apart from Hideki Tōjō, the Japanese Prime Minister during the Pacific War, the first arrest warrant included other Japanese dignitaries such as: Shigenori Tōgō (Minister of Foreign Affairs), Shigetarō Shimada (Minister of Navy), Okinori Kaya (Minister of Finance), Nobusuke Kishi (Minister of State and Vice Minister of Munitions), Ken Terajima (Minister of Transportation, Vice Admiral), Michiyo Iwamura (Minister of Justice), Chikahiko Koizumi (Minister of Welfare), Kunihiko Hashida (Minister of Education),[3] Hiroya Ino (Minister of Agriculture and Forestry), Kenji Doihara (General, Director of Army Aviation, long engaged in espionage in China), Kingorō Hashimoto (a fascist military man, founder of the Cherry Blossom Society and the Great Japan Youth Party, later known as the Great Japan Sincerity Association), Teiichi Suzuki (President of the Cabinet Planning Board and Minister of State), Yoshitake Ueda (Vice Admiral), Masaharu Homma (Lieutenant General, Commander of the Expeditionary Force in the Philippines),[4] Shigenori Kuroda (Lieutenant General, Commander of the Expeditionary Army in the Philippines), Shozo Murata (Ambassador to the Second Philippine Republic), Akira Nagahama (Commander of

---

[3] Koizumi and Hashida committed suicide before being arrested.

[4] Homma was soon extradited to the Philippines. He was on trial and sentenced to death along with General Tomoyuki Yamashita nicknamed 'Manila Tiger', by the US Military Tribunal in the Philippines.

the Kempeitai [Military Police Corps] in the Philippines), Seiichi Ohta (Lieutenant Colonel, directly responsible for the Manila massacre), and eight other Japanese persons (27 in total). Twelve non-Japanese persons, including José P. Laurel (President of the Second Philippine Republic), Jorge B. Vargas (Laurel's ambassador to Japan), Benigno Aquino Sr. (Speaker of the National Assembly of Laurel's regime), Heinrich Georg Stahmer (German ambassador to Japan), Alfred Kreitschmer (German military attaché to Japan), Dr. Thein Maung (Burman ambassador to Japan), Luang Vichitr Vadhakar (Thai ambassador to Japan), and another German, two Australians, one Dutch and one American who had worked in the Japanese fascist government were also arrested.

Not all of the non-Japanese arrestees in the first arrest warrant could be considered as 'Class-A war criminals'; therefore, they were repatriated after the GHQ decided that the Tokyo Tribunal was a special trial against only the Japanese war criminals. Later, it was learnt that some of these non-Japanese criminals were tried and sentenced for treason by their domestic courts, whereas others were set free. Those freed, even participated in domestic campaigns in an attempt to return to the political arena.

As for the 27 Japanese war criminals listed in the first arrest warrant, 25 were detained in prison by the GHQ military police, except for Koizumi and Hashida who had committed suicide before the arrest. Some of the detainees had even voluntarily allowed themselves to be imprisoned.[5]

In this first batch of arrests, Tōjō's was undoubtedly the most dramatic. His panicky and unsuccessful suicide attempt evoked world-wide criticism, particularly by the Japanese people.

After the declaration of 'unconditional surrender', the people of Japan were more prone to commit suicides. The commoners did not wish to be 'slaves of foreign powers' and those in authority wanted to escape becoming prisoners—the three-term Prime Minister Fumimaro Konoe, former War Ministers General Anami and General Sugiyama, and the former Commander-in-chief of the Kwantung Army General

---

[5] The GHQ's arrest procedure was unclear for the first batch of war criminals. Some were taken away on the day after the arrest warrant, whereas others were kept waiting for a few days. There was no clear stipulation for their voluntary surrender. These problems, however, were sorted before the second arrest warrant. The time-limit for voluntary surrender was 10 days, and the military police could enforce the arrest warrant on the 11th day morning if the person did not voluntarily report to prison within the stipulated period.

Honjo committed suicide. Some resorted to 'seppuku' (a ritual suicide by disembowelment) and others poisoned themselves and their wives to demonstrate their integrity and allegiance to their motherland. Under the influence of many years of fascist ideology in 'Yamato-damashii' (the great Japanese spirit) and 'Bushido' (the Samurai code), they had chosen to die in both a tragic and impressive way. Tōjō's 'suicide', however, was different.

Hideki Tōjō was one of the chief instigators of the Japanese invasion against China and was the person most responsible for the Pacific War. Knowing that he would be subject to severe legal sanctions after the surrender, he locked himself in his home for about ten days after the Allied Force landed in Japan. He contemplated whether to die or continue living. If he continued to live, he would be imprisoned and eventually sentenced to death. He could escape this fate by committing suicide; however, he lacked the courage to do it.

After ten days at home, Tōjō was still unsure about whether to commit suicide. On 11 September 1945, the arrest warrant for 39 people was issued and broadcast by the GHQ; he was the first on the list. When the military police arrived in jeeps and surrounded his house, he tried to escape arrest by shooting himself in the chest; he was, however, only mildly injured. He was then captured by the military police. This was the farcical suicidal attempt by Tōjō which provoked ridicule all around the world. The Japanese people criticized his failed suicide attempt and considered it a shame to the Japanese nation. As Tōjō was a general with over forty years of military experience, they wondered how he could not even kill himself, let alone the enemies.[6]

---

[6] In order to subdue the Japanese people's attack on Tōjō and efface his gaffes, Tokisaburo Shiohara, former Minister of Communications and later a defence lawyer for Tōjō in the Tokyo Trial, made the following explanation to the press: 'The reason why Tōjō was ridiculed around the world was his failed attempt at suicide, which would not have happened if he had received prior notice of his arrest and had had sufficient time to consider it. After the defeat in the War, Tōjō had two alternatives: First, if there was liberty to express freely, he would have been eager to write a book to inform the world about his faith and the truths of the War. Second, as he was afraid of the impending foreign arrest, he could escape it by committing suicide. Therefore, he always kept a pistol with him. He had asked the doctor to draw a circle in ink around his heart, and he redrew it after taking a bath. Tōjō not only kept his sabre beside him all day long, but also filled his favourite tobacco pipe with potassium cyanide to commit suicide. His sudden arrest on 11 September gave him no time to reflect. Only after he heard the sound of the approaching jeep, did he realize that he was formally being arrested. He took a bath, changed into a

A comment from the reporters of *Asahi Shimbun* in the Tribunal best portrays the reaction of the Japanese people at that time:

> The failed suicide of Hideki Tōjō has become a mockery around the world. The Minister of War, Tōjō had ironically issued 'War Instructions' that 'men should not drag out an ignoble existence as prisoners of war'. He has, however, exhibited an entirely different and disgraceful behaviour in his reluctance to commit suicide. Even the War Ministers General Anami and the Sugiyamas had the courage to commit suicide; Tōjō is perhaps laughed at by their buried corpses. In a conversation with an American journalist, Tōjō had remarked that he had long been aware of his impending death. He, however, lacked courage, so he panicked during the arrest process by the US military police. Why was he as timid as a hare when he had been so reckless in the past? His suicide could have been a fitting tribute to the true image of our defeated Japan![7]

As the Minister of Navy during the Pacific War, Shigetarō Shimada was listed second in the first arrest warrant. His attitude was more sincere and frank; he made a clear-headed statement to the press after being arrested:

> Since my transfer to the reserve force and as an inactive officer, I longed for victory in the final battle. But after the Instrument of Surrender was issued by the Emperor, I have pondered over my faults and contemplated committing seppuku to appease public indignation. However, considering the edict from the Emperor to carry out in good faith the Potsdam Declaration, I have continued living to this day. I being identified and arrested as a war criminal has long been anticipated. I apologize to the Emperor and the people of our nation.[8]

Shimada's words perhaps expressed the feelings of most Japanese Class-A war criminals arrested at that time.

Except for the foolery by Tōjō and the early suicides of Koizumi and Hashida, the rest of the 39 people listed in the first arrest warrant were duly arrested or had voluntarily reported themselves to prison. They were

---

new uniform, went to the study and shot himself in the ink circle. He collapsed but did not die. Now that he has revived, he would like to publicize these facts.' His reasoning was flawed and failed to persuade the Japanese people to forgive Tōjō.

[7] *The Tokyo Trial* by the Journalist Team of *Asahi Shimbun* in the Tokyo Tribunal, Vol. 1, p. 12.

[8] Ibid., pp. 13–14.

at first detained at the Yokohama Detention Centre, but shortly moved to Omori Prison, and later transferred to Sugamo Prison.[9]

Out of the 37 prisoners, including Tōjō, 12 non-Japanese arrestees were released and repatriated by the GHQ. Masaharu Homma was extradited and subsequently sentenced to death along with Tomoyuki Yamashita by the US Military Tribunal in the Philippines. Therefore, only Tōjō and 23 other Japanese prisoners in this batch were in long-term detention at Sugamo Prison.

The *Second Arrest Warrant* was issued by the GHQ on 19 November 1945, more than two months after the first one. Eleven important Japanese war criminals were listed as follows (biographical notes in parentheses were added by Japanese Central Liaison Office):

Araki, Sadao (General, Baron, successively Ministers of War and Minister of Education, extreme militarist)
Honjo, Shigeru (General, Baron, member of the Privy Council, responsible for staging the Mukden Incident without respecting the will of the upper political circles when serving as Commander of the Kwantung Army)
Kanokogi, Kazunobu (former President of Japanese Journalism Patriotic Association, participated in secret societies for many years, advocating militarism. Close Comrade of the late Mitsuru Toyama [right-wing fascist leader])
Koiso, Kuniaki (General, Prime Minister, initiator of the Northern Expansion Doctrine and the Southern Expansion Doctrine)
Kuhara, Fusanosuke (former Secretary-General of the Constitutional Association of Political Friendship, intimate friend of the late Prime

---

[9] The first batch of the arrest was not only confusing in procedure and the self-reporting deadline, but the place of detention was also relocated twice. Therefore, most of the war criminals listed in the first warrant were panic-stricken, but some of them voluntarily surrendered themselves to prison: Iwamura in the morning of 14 September 1945; Kaya, Ino, Suzuki and Murata, on the afternoon of the same day; Hashimoto and Ueda in the morning of 15 September, Homma and Kuroda, on the afternoon of the same day; Terajima on 16 September; Kishi on 17 September; Doihara on 23 September; Tōgō on 30 September (his surrender was late as he was allowed to stay home for medical treatment for a few days). All the arrest warrants that followed the first warrant clearly stipulated that the time-limit for voluntary surrender was 10 days and the place of reporting was Sugamo Prison, which became the fixed place for the detention of Japanese war criminals of all the three classes.

Minister Giichi Tanaka and General Sadao Araki, conspired to stage the February 26 Incident)

Kuzu, Yoshihisa (leader of the former fascist group Black Dragon Society and trusted fellow of the late Mitsuru Toyama)

Matsuoka, Yōsuke (former Minister of Foreign Affairs, during his term, Japan entered into alliance with Germany and Italy; he won the favour of Ministry of War and the militaristic groups for his anti-American proposition)

Matsui, Iwane (General, responsible for the Nanking Massacre and the bombing of USS Panay and British HMS Ladybird as Commander of the Expeditionary Force; later served as head of the Asia Promotion Section of the Imperial Rule Assistance Association)

Masaki, Jinzaburo (General, a staff officer in the Inspectorate General of Military Training, instigating young officers to launch reform and usurpation)

Minami, Jirō (General, Minister of War at the time of the Mukden Incident, and served as Governor-General of Korea and President of the Political Association of Great Japan, a fascist group)

Shiratori, Toshio (former Ambassador to Italy, one of the most stubborn fascist militarists)

These 11 arrestees qualified for 'Class-A war criminals' or 'major war criminals' due to their status and responsibilities. Apparently, the list was more meticulously prepared than the first, omitting the earlier mistake of including non-Japanese and Japanese persons who could not be termed as 'Class-A war criminals'.

Except for Honjo who had committed suicide and Matsuoka who was seriously ill, the remaining nine on the list voluntarily surrendered themselves. They went with their luggage to the prison within 10 days after the arrest warrant was issued.

At this juncture, it is worth discussing the suicide of Shigeru Honjo.

General Honjo was a Japanese fascist military leader and an active promoter of the aggressive policy. In 1931, he was the commander of the Kwantung Army, which made him the man directly responsible for the Mukden Incident.

After Japan's surrender, Honjo knew that he was liable to be tried as a war criminal. He was upset with the news of Marshal Sugiyama (the then Minister of War) and his wife's suicide by poison and the criticism directed at Tōjō for his failed suicide attempt. These circumstances prompted Honjo to commit suicide at 10:30 a.m. on 20 November 1945, immediately after he heard about his arrest warrant, at the director's office in Aoyama Gakuin Army University.

His suicide was considered heroic by the Japanese people. He left behind two suicide notes prepared long before his death, titled as 'Sincerity Forever'.[10]

Yōsuke Matsuoka was another prominent figure in the second batch of arrestees. As a Japanese growing up in the United States, he was fluent in English. He served as Minister of Foreign Affairs, Japan's chief delegate to the League of Nations, and President of the South Manchurian Railway. He was favoured by the young fascist officers for advocating withdrawal from the League of Nations and formation of the Axis military alliance among Germany, Japan and Italy. By the time of the Pacific War, he had already withdrawn from the political arena because of lung disease. He had been sick and living in his old residence in Kitaazumi District of Nagano Prefecture from the time of surrender to arrest. After the arrest warrant was issued on 19 November 1945, Matsuoka, with his head wrapped in a blanket, made the following remarks to the press on the next day:

> Although I have been ordered to report myself to Sugamo Prison, I am unable to walk for even half a kilometre because of systemic sclerosis. At my age of 66, I can do nothing much. Japan forged the three-country alliance to promote peace, and therefore, after the establishment of the Soviet–Japanese Neutrality Pact, I proposed to go to the United States and negotiate on a Pacific Agreement. Prime Minister Fumimaro Konoe and I reached an agreement on this. Unfortunately, his cabinet disintegrated soon after, and that opportunity was lost. We had never dreamt about warring with the United States; it was an unavoidable circumstance. The situation was grave until our defeat. Of late, I have even lost my enthusiasm for my favourite Haiku.

Matsuoka's statement was an attempt to hide his faults, but it also expressed his deep sorrow. It portrayed manners that were very unlike

---

[10] During the Tokyo Trial, Honjo's suicide notes were read out by his son who was the witness. Honjo wrote them with the intention to reduce the criminal liability of the Japanese emperor and other war criminals by himself bearing the sole responsibility for the Mukden Incident and the continued encroach on Northeast China.

him; he was formerly known for his heroism and arrogance at the League of Nations and as he bid adieu to Stalin in Moscow.[11]

Despite his poor health, Matsuoka was arrested by the GHQ as per schedule. He was given treatment in prison. In May 1946, when the Tokyo Tribunal officially opened, he was tried as one of the 28 major war criminals, but he died in prison within the next four months, and his name was removed from the list of defendants.

The *Third Arrest Warrant* was issued on 2 December 1945, just 13 days after the second warrant. Of the 59 war criminals enlisted in it, the majority were 'celebrities' who had long oppressed the Japanese people, and their alleged war crimes were severe enough to categorize them as 'Class-A war criminals'.

Among this batch of arrestees, there were two former Prime Ministers (Kōki Hirota and Kiichirō Hiranuma), one veteran of the press industry (Iichiro Tokutomi, aged 83) and one prince (Morimasa Nashimoto, aged 72).

Following are the 59 war criminals listed in the third arrest warrant (biographical notes in parentheses were added by the Japanese Central Liaison Office):

> Aikawa, Yoshisuke (member of the House of Peers, former Chairman of Manchurian Industrial Development Company and Nissan)
> Amau, Eiji (successively Vice Minister of Foreign Affairs and head of the Intelligence Bureau)
> Ando, Kisaburo (Home Minister)
> Aoki, Kazuo (successively President of the Cabinet Planning Board and Minister of Greater East Asia)

---

[11] Matsuoka was one of the boldest Japanese politicians. Growing up in Oregon, the United States, he had once been a bus-boy there, and so was often called as 'Oregonian bus-boy' by the Western newspapers. After returning to Japan, he gradually ascended to the Japanese political arena because he spoke fluent English and was good at gratifying the warlords and getting acquainted with the young officers. When Japan withdrew from the League of Nations in 1933, he was Japan's chief delegate. At the League of Nations General Assembly, he tried to discredit China by saying: 'China is not a country, but only a geographical term.' In April 1941, Matsuoka signed the Soviet–Japanese Neutrality Pact with the Soviet Union. As he left for Japan, Stalin bid him farewell at the Moscow train station. After they embraced, he said to Stalin threateningly, 'If you violate this pact, I must behead you.' Then he pretended to wring Stalin's neck. His arrogance and savagery were obvious.

Arima, Yoriyasu (successively President of Asia Promotion Federation and Chief Secretary of the Imperial Rule Assistance Association)
Fujiwara, Ginjiro (successively Minister of Commerce, Minister of State, and Minister of Munitions)
Furuno, Inosuke (President of Domei News Agency)
Goko, Kiyoshi (Chairman of Mitsubishi Heavy Industries)
Goto, Fumio (successively Minister of Agriculture and Forestry, Home Minister, Minister of State, and head of the Youth Corps of the Imperial Rule Assistance Association)
Hata, Hikosaburo (Lieutenant General, successively Vice Chief of the Army General Staff, President of the Army War College, and Chief of Staff of the Kwantung Army)
Hata, Shunroku (Field Marshal, successively Commander of the China Expeditionary Force, and Minister of War)
Hiranuma, Kiichirō (President of the Privy Council, successively Prime Minister and Minister of State)
Hirota, Kōki (successively Minister of Foreign Affairs and Prime Minister)
Honda, Kumataro (diplomat, former Ambassador to Wang Ching-wei's puppet regime in Nanking)
Hoshino, Naoki (successively Chief Cabinet Secretary and Minister of State, closely connected with Manchukuo)
Ida, Bannon (member of the House of Peers, former Chief Secretary of the Imperial Rule Assistance Association)
Ikeda, Shigeaki (successively Governor of the Bank of Japan, Minister of Finance, member of the Privy Council, and President of Mitsui Zaibatsu)
Ikesaki, Tadataka (member of the House of Representatives, Counsellor of the Ministry of Education, author of several books on the Far East)
Ishida, Otogoro (Major General, former Commander of the Kempeitai)
Ishihara, Koichiro (President of Ishihara Sangyo Kaisha)
Kamisago, Shoshichi (Major General, former Commander of the Kempeitai in the Taiwan Army of Japan)
Kawabe, Masakazu (General, Commander of the Northern China Area Army following the Marco Polo Bridge Incident, later served as Commander of the Burma Area Army)

Kikuchi, Takeo (Lieutenant General, well-known for refuting the 'emperor organ theory')

Kinoshita, Eiichi (Major General, Captain of the Kempeitai in the Eastern Military Area)

Kobayashi, Junichiro (Colonel, Secretary of the Imperial Rule Assistance Association)

Kobayashi, Seizo (Admiral, successively Vice Minister of Navy, Commander of the Combined Fleet, Governor-General of Taiwan, President of the Imperial Rule Assistance Association, the Minister of State in Koiso's cabinet)

Kodama, Yoshio (engaged in wartime espionage in China, author of *Sugamo Diary* and *I Was Defeated*)

Matsuzaka, Hiromasa (former Minister of Justice and chief procurator)

Mizuno, Rentaro (former Minister of Justice, successively adviser to the Imperial Rule Assistance Association and President of the Asia Promotion Federation, and participated in activities organized by other political groups)

Mutaguchi, Renya (retired Lieutenant General, fought actively in Burma)

Nagatomo, Tsugio (Major General, Commander of the Kempeitai in the Central Area)

Nakajima, Chikuhei (founder of Nakajima Aircraft Company, successively Minister of Commerce, Minister of Railways, adviser to the Cabinet, and Minister of Munitions in Higashikuni's cabinet)

Nakamura, Aketo (Lieutenant General, successively Commander of the Kempeitai and Commander of the Area Army in Thailand)

Prince Nashimoto, Morimasa (Field Marshal, member of the Supreme War Council, and the chief priest of the shrine)

Nishio, Toshizo (General, successively Commander of the China Expeditionary Force and Governor of the Tokyo Metropolis)

Nomi, Toshiro (Major General, former Commander of the Kempeitai in the Taiwan Army of Japan)

Okabe, Nagakage (member of the House of Peers, successively General Secretary to the Lord Keeper of the Privy Seal, Vice Minister of War, and Minister of Education in Tōjō's cabinet)

Ōkawa, Shūmei (professor at Hosei University, published various works on national movement in the Far East, such as *Some Issues in Re-emerging Asia*, a fanatic follower of Pan-Asianism)

Okura, Kunihiko (founder of the Okura Institute for the Study of Spiritual Culture, successively President of Toyo University and Principal of the Tung Wen College)
Ono, Hiroichi (Major General, once served at the Kempeitai, former Commander of the 11th Army Division)
Ota, Kozo (professor at Hosei University, successively Minister of Education and Chief Secretary of the Imperial Rule Assistance Association)
Ota, Masataka (successively President of the Hochi Shimbun, Vice Minister of Finance, and Secretary of the Imperial Rule Assistance Association)
Sakurai, Hyougoro (former Secretary-General of the Constitutional Democratic Party and Chief Counselor of the Burmese military government)
Sasakawa, Ryoichi (President of the Patriotic People's Party, ultra-nationalist)
Satō, Kenryō (Lieutenant General, successively Chief of the Military Affairs Bureau of the Ministry of War and Secretary-General of the Supreme Council for the Direction of the War)
Shimomura, Hiroshi (successively Vice President of the Asahi Shimbun and President of the Intelligence Bureau)
Shinto, Kazuma (President of the Dark Ocean Society)
Shiono, Suehiko (former Chief Procurator and Minister of Justice)
Shioden, Nobutaka (Lieutenant General, President of Anti-Semitism Association in Japan)
Shoriki, Matsutaro (President of the Yomiuri Hochi Shimbun)
Tada, Hayao (General, successively Vice Chief of the Army General Staff and Commander of the Northern China Area Army)
Takachi, Shigeto (Commander of the Kempeitai in Korea)
Takahashi, Sankichi (Admiral, successively Commander of the Combined Fleet, member of the Supreme War Council, and adviser to the Asia Promotion Section of the Imperial Rule Assistance Association)
Tani, Masayuki (Minister of Foreign Affairs)
Tokutomi, Iichiro (veteran of the press industry)
Toyoda, Soemu (Admiral, successively Commander of the Combined Fleet and Chief of the Navy General Staff)
Tsuda, Shingo (President of Kanebo company and former Counsellor of the Ministry of Finance)

Ushiroku, Jun (General, successively Vice Chief of the Army General Staff and member of the Supreme War Council, and was long active in the Vietnamese area)

Yokoyama, Yui (came into prominence during the wartime, suspected by the Japanese and foreigners)

It is evident that the third batch of arrests was extensive and representative; the list covered not only military personnel, politicians and diplomats, but also entrepreneurs, plutocrats, publishers, opinion leaders, and even royal aristocrats who were thought to be inviolable.

The release of the list agitated the upper classes in Japan. Prominent personalities who had abused the masses were imperilled because they were somehow connected to the war crimes. They were afraid that they would be arrested someday, but their fears were unfounded. The United States began to display a protective stance towards Japan's reactionary forces and the arrest of war criminals reduced. After the fourth arrest warrant, the arrests ceased and many Japanese war criminals were shielded from arrest; many prior arrestees were also released.

As in the previous batches, many of the enlisted suspects voluntarily reported at Sugamo Prison within the stipulated ten days.[12] While surrendering, some of them confessed and others justified their crimes to foreign journalists. For instance, Marshal Shunroki Hata told the foreign press, 'What happened today was anticipated. I am keenly aware of my involvement in the war, so there is no room for me to defend my deeds with sophistry.' Senior Admiral Sankichi Takahashi said, 'What's done is done. I had better report myself in and accept the punishment.' The former Prime Minister Kiichirō Hiranuma, however, told the foreign journalists, 'People in the world misunderstand me as a Japanese fascist mentor, but

---

[12] The GHQ required that the persons in the arrest warrant should report themselves to prison within ten days, which proved to be an effective and plausible directive in postwar Japan. Although it appeared impractical to many foreigners, the order was sensible under the circumstances. Japan as an island country was isolated and enveloped by the Allied navy, from which nobody could escape abroad. In addition, Japan had always been known as a 'police country', where households' transfers and residents' moves were strictly registered and monitored, making it difficult for anyone to hide within the country. For these reasons, most of those listed by the GHQ as war criminals preferred to voluntarily surrender themselves at a convenient time before the deadline, in an unhurried manner instead of being handcuffed and shoved disgracefully into the prison van by the military police.

they do not know that I am actually against fascist ideology.' Matsutaro Shoriki, President of the Yomiuri Shimbun Company, said, 'It could be a mistake that I am listed for arrest as a war criminal.'

Iichiro Tokutomi (also known as Soho Tokutomi), a respectable pressmen of 83 years, also surrendered voluntarily. When the arrest warrant was released, he was recuperating from an illness at Izusan-Horai. He staggered into the prison with great difficulty and expressed his feelings in a short Chinese poem, which was widely circulated by the Japanese. It read, 'For whom did I shed blood and tears? Broken is my heart and flying are my white hairs. Having experienced the vicissitudes of life, nothing seems right in my entire 83 years.'

In the third batch of Class-A war criminals on the arrest list, there was another noted personality, Yoshio Kodama, who caused a sensation in the Japanese society. Yoshio Kodama was the head of the notorious espionage agency 'Kodama Kikan' when Shanghai was occupied by Japan. As an 'inexperienced young scholar', he could not be qualified as a 'Class-A war criminals' on account of his age and status, but he was anyway included in the warrant because of the nature and gravity of his crimes.

On the day of the third arrest warrant (2 December), a shocking story about Kodama's corrupt practices was reported by the Japanese newspapers. He was thought to have blackmailed some Chinese person and extracted over 300,000 yuan when he had presided over Kodama Kikan in Shanghai. Three hundred thousand yuan was not a huge amount as compared to the treasures plundered from China by the Japanese invaders. It still drew attention from the Japanese people as the report surfaced at the time of his arrest warrant.[13]

Despite this minor episode, Kodama was not one among the first group of defendants standing trial before the Tokyo Tribunal. On the contrary, he spent less than three years at Sugamo Prison and was then released by GHQ without authorization. His once sensational 'corruption case' was completely forgotten.

The _Fourth Arrest Warrant_ of Class-A war criminals was issued by the GHQ on 6 December 1945, only four days after the third. It was the last batch of arrests of the major war criminals in Japan. Only nine persons were listed, of whom two (Konoe and Kido) were particularly important in the Japanese political circle. The list was as follows:

---

[13] See _The Tokyo Trial_ by the Journalist Team of _Asahi Shimbun_ in the Tokyo Tribunal, Vol. 1, pp. 23–25.

Konoe, Fumimaro (Duke, three-term Prime Minister, the person most responsible for the aggression of China)
Kido, Kōichi (Marquis, Lord Keeper of the Privy Seal, successively Minister of Education, Home Minister, Minister of Welfare, and chief confidential adviser to the Emperor; presided over the Elder Statesmen meetings)
Sakai, Tadamasa (Count, Vice President of the House of Peers)
Ōshima, Hiroshi (Lieutenant General, Ambassador to Germany)
Okochi, Masatoshi (President of the Institute of Physical and Chemical Research)
Ogata, Taketora (successively Minister of State and President of the Intelligence Bureau)
Odachi, Shigeo (member of the House of Peers, and once Home Minister)
Godo, Takuo (successively Minister of Commerce and Minister of Railways)
Suma, Yakichiro (successively Consul General in Nanking and Ambassador to Spain)

Among the nine war criminals, Fumimaro Konoe and Kōichi Kido were the most important. Kido served as the head of the royal affairs (Lord Keeper of the Privy Seal) and was the closest adviser to the Emperor. He was an intermediary between the cabinet and royal family and a key figure in Japanese politics for more than a decade. He had a close relationship with the upper-class politicians, especially with Konoe.

In the last warrant, the inclusion of Fumimaro Konoe was followed by the shocking event of his death by suicide.

Konoe was an influential man in Japanese politics. He was an aristocrat who often called himself 'the beloved of the fate', implying that he was an unusually fortunate person, or 'God's favoured one' in Chinese language. He ascended to the top ranks of the Japanese government with the encouragement and favouritism of Kinmochi Saionji, the last surviving senior statesman and three-term Prime Minister. Like Saionji, Konoe also served as Prime Minister thrice during the period between the launch of an aggressive war against China and the start of the Pacific War, that is, four years from the Marco Polo Bridge Incident in 1937 to the eve of the Pearl Harbor Incident in 1941. Konoe had to bear the major responsibility for the expansion and persistence of Japan's full-scale aggressive war against China. During his terms as the Prime Minister, he repeatedly declared that Japan would not end the war until China 'bows the knees and sues for peace'.

Contrary to the expectations of Saionji, Konoe not only failed to constrain the exploits of aggressive warlords, but also supported them in a bid to gain their favour.

Konoe was not a warlord, although he strongly supported the invasion of China. However, he could neither win the confidence of the militarists nor muster the courage to expand the war to the Pacific region and risk Japan. He was overthrown from his position as the Prime Minister just before Japan's stealthy attack on Pearl Harbor and the launch of the Pacific War. He was replaced by Hideki Tōjō, a pure warlord chieftain.

As Konoe was not directly involved in the initiation of the Pacific War, he thought that the United States might not be inimical to him, and he tried to re-enter the political arena as an aristocrat after Japan's defeat. He served as a Minister of State without Portfolio in the surrender cabinet headed by Prince Naruhiko Higashikuni as the Prime Minister. The cabinet dissolved in less than two months and he resigned from it on 5 October 1945, a month after Japan's surrender. It was replaced by the cabinet of Kijuro Shidehara, who had lived in seclusion since the Mukden Incident. In Shidehara's cabinet, Konoe was appointed as Lord Keeper of the Privy Seal. During that period, he constantly visited his Japanese mentor Soichi Sasaki, who was an emeritus professor of Kyoto Imperial University and an authority on constitutional law. Konoe apparently intended to participate in the amendment of the Japanese Constitution. When public criticism on aristocrats intensified in Japan and abroad, Konoe relinquished his honorary title by submitting his decision to do so to the Emperor on 24 October 1945; however, he continued to pursue his political ambitions. After relinquishing his title, he proceeded to meet the Minister of State and Chairman of the Committee of Investigation on Constitutional Issues, Jōji Matsumoto, to discuss the political system of Japan and initiate constitutional reforms. Around that time, it was rumoured that Konoe would organize a new party in opposition to participate in the future elections.

Konoe's personal ambitions did not materialize; his unscrupulous activities and immoderate ambitions were attacked by the press services of the Allied Powers. An editorial of *The New York Times* alleged that he was not fit for assisting in the amendment of the Japanese Constitution, and that he ought to be listed as a war criminal.

The GHQ operated by the Americans usually paid little attention to the remarks of the other Allied Powers, but it could not ignore the public opinion from the United States voiced by a reputed newspaper such as *The New York Times*.

The onslaught on Konoe by *The New York Times* and other sources forced the GHQ to intervene and clarify its stance. On 1 November 1945, the GHQ spokesman informed the journalists that Konoe was only an intermediary between the GHQ and the royal family and would not be involved in the amendment of the Japanese Constitution. This statement by the GHQ was a blow to Konoe's hopes of participating in the constitution's amendment.

The 89th extraordinary session of the Diet was then organized towards the end of November 1945. During the session, Diet Member Takao Saito questioned Konoe and accused him as the chief instigator of the comprehensive war of aggression against China. Saito claimed that Konoe bore the highest responsibility for World War II and the consequences of the Japanese defeat. This further disillusioned Konoe, and although no resolution was passed against him in the session, he was disgraced.

On the evening of 6 December 1945, a radio announcement of the arrest warrant was made by the GHQ; Konoe, at that time, was receiving some guests at his magnificent villa in Karuizawa. The news was a major blow to his political fantasies.

As a rule, the arrest warrant stipulated a time limit of ten days for their voluntary surrender; the military police were to arrest them if they did not report themselves at Sugamo Prison by 15 December 1945.

Konoe was greatly tormented; he spent five days in his villa in Karuizawa, refusing visitors and wandering around in mental dereliction. He was in a dilemma whether to follow the dictate and 'muddle along' or commit suicide. He either had to commit a heroic suicide like Sugiyama and Honjo, or live shamefully like Tōjō and Shimada.

On 11 December 1945, Konoe returned from Karuizawa to his duke mansion in Tokyo. He continued to grapple with the question of life and death, although he was outwardly relaxed. He often chatted with his wife Chiyoko, his brother Hidemaro Konoe (a famous Japanese musician), his married sister, and his children. After five days, when the time for voluntary surrender came to a close, the GHQ prepared to arrest him.

On the night of 15 December 1945, Konoe had been chatting with his family about some future plans until 1:00 a.m. After the family dispersed, he called his son, Michitaka Konoe, and had a long discussion with him about the war of aggression against China. He confessed his involvement in the China Incident for which he rightly deserved to be punished. After Michitaka left, Konoe entered a 12-tatami-mat room, changed into white clothes, drank poison and fell dead. The deed was discovered at dawn by his wife; his face had turned pale and his body was stiff. The light was on and a few drops of the fatal liquid was found in a brown vial in the brazier. The 'beloved of the fate' had finally lost his luck and the once outstanding aristocrat was dead.

Shortly after the death of Konoe, the prison van arrived and journalists from various countries came in jeeps to report the arrest of Konoe. Their trip was in vain and they had to return disappointed.

Except for Konoe who committed suicide a few hours before the arrest, all the war criminals listed in the fourth arrest warrant voluntarily reported themselves to Sugamo Prison within the stipulated period.

After the fourth batch of arrests, the GHQ stopped issuing arrest warrants against Japanese major war criminals. Contrary to the expectations of the Japanese, the arrest of war criminals did not intensify but tapered and was eventually stopped.

A total of 118 war criminals were listed in the four arrest warrants (respectively 39, 11, 59 and 9). In early 1946, only about 100 of them were imprisoned. Non-Japanese arrestees had been repatriated to their home countries. Some Japanese criminals committed suicide before the arrest (e.g. Honjo, Konoe, Hashida and Koizumi); some were extradited abroad to stand trial (e.g. Homma). Some others were released by the GHQ shortly after their arrest because of insufficient evidence (e.g. Prince Nashimoto, Goko and Ueda).[14]

It can be argued that there were more than 100 major war criminals or Class-A war criminals from the Japanese upper classes in the wartime; but those 100 arrestees were genuine major war criminals or Class-A war criminals because they were all responsible for thrusting Japan into a war

---

[14] Yoshitake Ueda was one of the first 39 arrestees and the first person to be released from Sugamo Prison. Kiyoshi Goko, a magnate from Mitsubishi, was set free on 13 April 1946. His release indicated that the GHQ would not pursue the responsibility of the Japanese monopoly capitalists. As expected, all those plutocrats, arms dealers and entrepreneurs were shortly released. Chief Prosecutor Keenan stated that the Japanese capitalists were forced by the military to participate in the war of aggression and they did so not out of their own free will.

of aggression through their influential status. Since not all major war criminals were arrested, the arrest and trial of those few could be considered as a symbolic effort to punish those guilty for the Japanese war crimes.

After the arrests of war criminals in late 1945, there were two urgent tasks for the GHQ: first, to organize an international tribunal for the trial of Japanese Class-A war criminals; second, to investigate the arrestees and select the first group to be prosecuted in the tribunal. The first task has been discussed in the previous chapter; the second task will be discussed now in the following two sections.

3.2 Investigation and Preparation for Prosecution by the IPS

The International Prosecution Section (IPS) was an important part of the GHQ which had the primary responsibility for dealing with Japanese Class-A war criminals. This was a responsible and demanding portfolio.

In the early days of the occupation of Japan, the IPS was involved in preparing a list of Class-A war criminals and arresting them in batches. Under special circumstances, it had to decide whether some arrestees could be released without prosecution or be repatriated or extradited to other countries. For example, the repatriation of all the non-Japanese war criminals; the release without prosecution of Morimasa Nashimoto, Kiyoshi Goko and Yoshitake Ueda; and the extradition of Masaharu Homma to the Philippines were all decided by the IPS.

The head of the IPS was Joseph B. Keenan, an American politician. Keenan's domineering personality and whimsical mannerisms (refer Chapter 2, Sect. 2.4) have already been discussed. Nevertheless, Keenan contributed much to the prosecution of Japanese major war criminals and the establishment of the Tokyo Tribunal. He played a key role in the organization of the Tokyo Trial.

Since Keenan was a legal adviser and a trustworthy comrade of the Supreme Commander MacArthur, he was assigned many important tasks. Towards the end of 1945, when the arrest of war criminals came to a halt, he was involved in drafting the Charter of International Military Tribunal for the Far East (the 'Tokyo Charter'), choosing the Tribunal's location, and renovating the chosen building for the Tribunal. These tasks were necessary because the arrested war criminals had to be tried and convicted as mandated by the Potsdam Declaration. Although Keenan had the assistance of his staff for these tasks, he bore the responsibility for their completion.

On 19 January 1946, the Supreme Commander for the Allied Powers issued the Tokyo Charter and subsequently appointed the judges of the Tribunal. Joseph B. Keenan was designated as the Chief of Counsel (Chief Prosecutor) of the Tribunal. He also held two other positions: legal counsel of the GHQ and head of the IPS. It was evident that Keenan was appointed as the Chief Prosecutor of the Tokyo Tribunal to utilize the resources of the IPS which he headed and carry out the prosecution work of the Tribunal.

According to the provisions of the Tokyo Charter, the Chief Prosecutor was fully responsible for the 'investigation' and 'prosecution' of charges against the defendants, while the associate prosecutors dispatched by the other Allied Powers could only assist him.[15] The prosecution unit of the Tokyo Tribunal adopted the 'single-head system' or 'autocracy', unlike the Nuremberg Tribunal. In Nuremberg, the prosecution was based on the 'collegiate system', that is, the functions of the chief prosecutor were performed by the committee comprising prosecutors from the four countries, who took turns as chairman of the committee and had equal rights and obligations.[16]

After the promulgation of the Tokyo Charter and the formal designation of Keenan as the Chief Prosecutor, he immediately dispatched the IPS staff to initiate a range of prosecution activities. Additionally, he recruited some experts in evidence investigation from the United States to assist in the activities. In early 1946, preparations for the prosecution were entirely managed by Americans because the Tokyo Tribunal was not established and the associate prosecutors from other countries had not yet arrived in Tokyo.

In general, the preparatory work for the prosecution by the Tokyo Tribunal was divided into the following tasks: (a) interrogating the arrestees and obtaining their statements; (b) collecting documents that could be used as evidence from voluminous Japanese government records; (c) conducting field investigations, obtaining written testimonies of any witnesses, and making appointments with them to appear in court; (d) contacting the government officials and relevant organizations of the

---

[15] See *Charter of the International Military Tribunal for the Far East*, Article 8.

[16] See *Charter of the International Military Tribunal*, Article 14.

Allied Powers for the collection of documentary evidence; (e) selecting the defendants for the first trial; (f) drafting the indictment and its appendices.

These were challenging tasks because of the wide geographical range, historical coverage, complex types of crimes and large number of defendants involved in each case.

Given below is a brief description of these tasks, the first one being the interrogation and confession of the arrestees.

In the old judicial system, a confession was usually the only evidence of a crime. Until the prisoner admitted his crime, the case could not be closed. Once the prisoner confessed his crime and authorized the report of his words by his signature or fingerprint, the matter would be dissolved. Consequently, confession was extracted by brutal force; prisoners were tortured or compelled to sign on a confession, and the brutalities employed were ignored once the case was closed.

The prisoner's confession is not regarded as the only evidence of the crime in the modern judiciary system, and a prisoner could not be forced by any means to confess his crime. Nevertheless, the confession voluntarily provided by the prisoner is a strong evidence for the court's verdict and determination of penalty; under normal circumstances a person will never admit a crime which he has not committed, and as is often the case, only the guilty person knows the exact details of the incident.

Since the IPS still regarded confession as an important evidence in the modern judicial system, it prioritized interrogation and statement-recording of nearly 100 alleged Class-A war criminals detained at Sugamo Prison as part of its preparatory work. In fact, it had begun its work in the last three months of 1945 when the war criminals were being sent to prison in batches. The interrogation at that time was rudimentary because of insufficient manpower and background information in the IPS.

Several prisoners who had committed big crimes were released during this superficial, preliminary investigation process. For example, after a hasty interrogation, Yoshitake Ueda was released by the IPS because of 'insufficient evidence'; later, Kiyoshi Goko was also released. Neither of them had a detailed interrogation. This hasty procedure was sometimes adopted for political purposes.

Nevertheless, most of the Class-A war criminals under custody underwent a serious and thorough interrogation. During the first three months of 1946, from the publication of the Tokyo Charter to the finalization of the indictment, the IPS was mostly involved in questioning the prisoners and taking down their statements. This was primarily because the IPS had by then received additional manpower. A group of highly skilled and experienced investigators recruited by the IPS had arrived in Tokyo from the United States. Most of them were professional investigators of the FBI, and they were skilled at understanding the psychology of prisoners through interrogation techniques. On analysing criminal records and investigating, they could easily decipher the truth. Second, as a result of the preparation and preliminary efforts over the last few months, the IPS team members were better versed with the background information of the cases. Those involved in the interrogation had a fairly good understanding of Japanese history, society and politics. They were familiar with the past experiences and dispositions of the prisoners through personal correspondence and information gathered from government records. Third, the associate prosecutors and their assistants from other Allied Powers also arrived in Tokyo. Although they did not directly participate in the interrogation process, they could provide relevant resources and answer questions. As the prosecutors were overseeing the interrogation process, the American interrogators were compelled to work harder. Fourth, as the organization of the Tribunal was almost complete, the indictment needed to be written soon; therefore, the first group of defendants had to be selected from among the prisoners. A prerequisite to the selection was a thorough interrogation of Class-A suspects that were detained at Sugamo Prison.

Owing to the urgency of the task, the IPS mobilized more staff members to interrogate the prisoners and record their statements. The main investigators, however, were still the FBI experts from the United States and the henchmen of Chief Prosecutor Keenan.

The IPS had a unique manner of interrogation.

Generally, in the common law system there is no interrogation but a 'pre-trial' procedure performed in court instead of prison. Although the Tokyo Tribunal predominantly followed the common law system in trial procedures, it sometimes used its own methods for investigation.

The interrogation of the Japanese war criminals took place at Sugamo Prison where they were detained. If anyone was on bail for medical reasons, the interrogation was conducted at his house.[17]

The interrogation was not as formal as the pre-trial procedure in the common law system. Apart from the prisoner to be interrogated, there was the interrogator, the interpreter, a clerk and a stenographer present at each interrogation. Before the process began, the interrogator would exact an oath from the prisoner, clerk, interpreter and stenographer. After the interrogation, the stenographer would translate the shorthand notes into a formal 'interrogation record' which would be ratified by the interrogator, interpreter and clerk. Neither the shorthand draft nor the finalized interrogation record was shown to the prisoner; this was a major drawback in the interrogation process because eventually, when the prosecutor submitted an interrogation record as documentary evidence, the defendant and his lawyer would often raise objections and question its accuracy. Sometimes, they even denied the confession made by the defendant at the time of interrogation. In this case, the interrogator or other staff present during interrogation had to be summoned to court to register their testimony. Such unforeseen events disrupted and delayed the trial process of the Tribunal.

As observed earlier, the interrogation was an arduous task. The cases handled by the Tokyo Tribunal covered a wide geographical area, had a long history, and pertained to a variety of crimes, especially because most of the prisoners were important persons who were involved in complex political activities for almost two decades. A competent interrogator must first examine sociopolitical and economic scenarios, military affairs and diplomacy in Japan in the last 20 years, and second, he should investigate the crimes committed and the important positions held by his interrogatee. This data enabled him to ask important and relevant questions during the interrogation process.

An interrogator could always refer to the exhaustive material obtained from the Japanese government or retrieve details from the Japanese

---

[17] For example, the interrogation of Kiichirō Hiranuma, former Prime Minister, was conducted at his home. At the age of 80, Hiranuma was released on bail because of his sickness. Therefore, every interrogation of his was conducted at his home by the interrogator, an interpreter and a stenographer. Using his old age to his advantage, Hiranuma did not answer many questions with the excuse that he could not recall their answers. At that time, his wife would provide him with some clues to 'help him recall' things.

people associated with the IPS, but it was his job to meticulously sort and scrutinize the information to determine their relevance to the case. He also had to grasp the mentality of the prisoners and strategically extract details from them. This was imperative to ensure the credibility of the obtained statements and confessions so that they may be used as strong evidences by the prosecution in court.

The interrogations by the IPS yielded reasonably good results. Many of the statements and confessions from the prisoners were effectively used by the prosecution as supporting evidence for criminal charges.

The interrogation was most intense after the arrests of major war criminals in late 1945, and before the official opening of the Tribunal in May 1946. Initially, all the arrested Class-A suspects were being interrogated, so it was difficult to do a detailed, in-depth interrogation. However, after the first 28 defendants were identified for trial, the interrogation became focused. Defendants with a complicated history were interrogated as many as six times, and scores of statement pages were obtained from them. On an average, each defendant was interrogated at least twice. The interrogations became more serious towards the Tribunal's opening; this was because, according to the common law system, the prosecutor could note down the results of the interrogation process only before the court's acceptance of the indictment. Once the court had accepted an indictment and scheduled a trial date, the opposing parties (the prosecution and defence, the latter including the defendants and their lawyers) could not interact with each other without the consent of the court. The prosecutor is forbidden to interact not only with the defendants but also with the witnesses for the defence, else he can be charged with 'tempting the witness of the other party'.[18] The same is true for the defence in relation to the prosecution's witnesses. In short, the two parties are strictly separated and barred from communicating with each other, once the trial begins.

---

[18] This offense, 'tempting the witness' means to confuse, soften, entice or bribe the other side's witness, making him less capable to testify for the other side. In the common law practice, each side to the legal proceedings can consult with its own witnesses and guide them on what and how to speak. The party cannot, however, contact a witness from the other side; violating which, it can be charged with 'tempting the witness'. The witness is thus treated like a 'private property'. The only solution for either party is to adequately 'cross-examine' the other side's witness and his testimony, and bring to notice the discrepancies therein, thus reducing the probative value of such witness' testimony.

This principle of strict separation between opposite parties was not expressly stated in the Tokyo Charter, or the Rules of Procedure of the Tokyo Tribunal, but it was an undisputable practice, traditionally followed in the common law system and adopted by the Tribunal. This principle is a proof of the influence of common law traditions over the Tokyo Trial. It also explains why the IPS had to hastily complete its interrogation and statement-recording before the Tribunal's formal acceptance of the indictment on 29 April 1946.[19]

The second major task of the IPS in its preparation for the trial was to find resources related to the crimes committed by the defendants from the Japanese government archives. The resources were used both as background information for interrogation before trial and as supportive evidence for the prosecution during trial. Since the materials were sourced from government archives, their probative value was indisputably high.

However, the task presented some difficulties:

1. The Japanese government archives were stacked separately in the Archives Office on the third floor of the Tribunal's building. Many documents had been destroyed during the Allied air strikes or by Japanese officials before the surrender. It was a daunting task for the prosecution team to consolidate the relevant documents and arrive at an understanding of each defendant's crimes. Fortunately, the Japanese government had hidden the most essential documents (detailed minutes of the Imperial Conferences, the Cabinet meetings, the 'Five-Minister' meetings, the Privy Council meetings, and the Elder Statesmen meetings) in metal cabinets and buried them in the basement of a destroyed building. They were remarkably

---

[19] Itagaki and Kimura were two defendants who were not interrogated before the opening of the Tokyo Tribunal. At the time of Japan's surrender, both of them were stationed overseas as commanders of the Japanese troops (Itagaki in Singapore, and Kimura in Burma). They were escorted to Tokyo just before the Tribunal opened, and it was too late for the prosecution to interrogate them and record their statements. Two other defendants, Shigemitsu and Umezu, were also in a similar situation. For reasons to be mentioned in the next section of this chapter, these two defendants were arrested only shortly before the submission of the Indictment, so there was no time for the prosecution to interrogate and take their statements. As mentioned, the prosecution and defence were not allowed to contact each other once the indictment was filed.

discovered by the occupation army.[20] The retrieved documents were displayed in the Archives Office of the Tribunal. They provided valuable information about the formation of the government's aggressive policy and the launch of the war of aggression, as well as the proposals and speeches made, and roles played by defendants who were in the political fray. This evidence would undoubtedly be admitted by the Tribunal and hence was used by the prosecution to the fullest extent in cases concerning primary war criminals.

2. The archival resources of the Japanese government were numerous and dispersed. The Japanese often used Chinese expressions meaning 'as vast as a misty sea' and 'so many as to fill a house to the rafters' to describe them. Adequate and efficient workforce was required to optimally use these resources.
3. The resources presented language challenges. The documents of the Japanese government were in Japanese, but most of the IPS staff did not know Japanese. Therefore, they had to hire Japanese personnel to peruse the documents and translate the relevant parts; but the quality and fidelity of their translations could not always be relied upon.

These difficulties delayed the IPS in their task of retrieving relevant documents from the archives. By the time the indictment was drafted and the Tribunal's session commenced, they had obtained only a few documents to support the indictment. Most of the strong evidences against the defendants were discovered and presented later in the trial. By then, the IPS staff had become more experienced in their searches, and their knowledge of Japan's sociopolitical conditions had enhanced. Moreover, the prosecutors from the other Allied Powers such as China and the Soviet Union, had arrived for assistance. Strong evidences against Shigemitsu and Umezu were discovered by the Soviet prosecution team, and criminal evidences for Doihara and Itagaki were retrieved by the Chinese prosecutors Ni Zhengyu, Wu Xueyi, and Liu Zijian. As these documents were presented in court as evidences much later in the trial proceedings, they were considered as supplementary evidences at the cross-examination of the defence witnesses and at the rebuttal stage by the prosecution.

---

[20] For the legendary discovery of the secret files of the Japanese government in those cabinets, see Chapter 2, Sect. 2.6 of this book.

It must be noted that the presentation of evidence was a major step in the trial proceedings. If the party obtained a suitable evidence, it could manage to present it at any stage of the trial. Therefore, unlike the task of interrogating war criminals which had to be stopped before the trial began, evidence procurement was done all through the trial.

In addition, there are two noteworthy points: First, in addition to the numerous Japanese government archives displayed in the Tribunal's Archives Office, there were a few confidential documents and manuscripts such as 'Manchuria Memorandum', 'The Diary of Marquis Kido', and 'Saionji Notes'. These limited materials were also merited for their probative value. Second, to ensure fairness, the Tribunal allowed the prosecutors as well as the defence lawyers to visit the Archives Office to reference materials. Consequently, the Archives Office became an arsenal to both parties, and groups from both parties worked every day to gather relevant information. Prosecution and defence lawyers from opposite parties worked harmoniously and refrained from interfering in the activities of the opposite party; this was a unique feature of the Tokyo Tribunal.

The third task of the IPS in its preparation for the trial was to conduct on-the-spot interviews of the victims and eye-witnesses and investigate the crimes of the defendants. As crimes were committed across East Asia and the Pacific, only selective investigations could be performed. Field investigation proved effective for certain types of crimes but were useless for other types. For example, evidence on the formation of Japan's policy of aggression and the launch of aggressive wars charged under Crimes against Peace could only be found in the Japanese government archives and the statements of major war criminals; it was thus futile to conduct interviews and investigations in other places. Interviews and field investigations, however, provided evidences on inhumane atrocities committed in Asia, such as the mass murder of civilians, maltreatment of prisoners, plunder and rape which was organized by major war criminals. The investigators interviewed the local people who had witnessed or experienced an atrocity and took down their statements. These statements that were authorized by their narrators served as testimonies in court. The testimonies were first-hand accounts of the experiences of victims and had a high probative value. The investigators could also schedule meetings with some key witnesses who would be called to testify later in the trial, so that they could make their allegations against the defendants in person.

As field investigation was particularly suitable for massacres and other mass atrocities, it was performed many times before the trial began. For example, for the atrocities committed by the Japanese army in Manila and other places, the 'Bataan Death March', forced labour in the Burma-Thailand Railway, and arbitrary killing in the concentration camps of Southeast Asia, the IPS sent its staff to conduct field investigations and collect written testimonies in Indonesia, Burma, Southeast Asia, and the Philippines. The best investigation was performed on the Nanking Massacre, and conducted by Chief Prosecutor Keenan himself.

The Nanking Massacre was one of the biggest disasters of World War II. The scale, duration, and death toll of this catastrophe was unprecedented in history and it evoked universal condemnation. The IPS which was responsible for prosecuting the Japanese war criminals, seriously dealt with this crime because the main instigator of the massacre was General Iwane Matsui who had been arrested and detained in prison. In early March of 1946, Chief Prosecutor Joseph B. Keenan, accompanied by the Chinese associate prosecutor and a team of about seven efficient assistant prosecutors, chartered a flight from the GHQ to China, to personally investigate the case and collect evidence to support the prosecution. They stayed for two weeks in Nanking, Shanghai, Peking and other places in China.

Keenan and his team also intended to tour China during their short stay.[21] Keenan had often remarked, 'China is a country with an ancient civilization. It has the greatest number of historic sites and scenic spots in the world. It would be a great pity to traverse the Far East without visiting China.' The predominant aim, however, for Keenan and his companions was to gather evidence. They managed to collect some important documents and interview witnesses.

---

[21] Touring and sightseeing were other important reasons for Keenan and his retinue to visit China. After Keenan returned to Tokyo, someone asked him how was his trip, and he replied, 'If you see the Temple of Heaven in Peking, it will be a worthwhile trip.' It was evident that he thought highly of Chinese historic sites and scenic spots. Keenan was a rich lawyer in the United States for many years. He had purchased many antiques, calligraphy and paintings, brocade and jewellery during that trip to China. He was disgusted with the bargaining system ('the seller can ask for a sky-high price, while the buyer can make a down-to-earth counter-offer') prevalent in China at that time, and he had often complained that the price he had paid for an object was much more than that paid by his entourage.

During their visit to China, they visited many official organs and charities, collected statistical data on the Nanking Massacre, conversed with Chinese and foreign eye-witnesses, and gathered many written testimonies. They also made appointments with a dozen witnesses who were to testify at the trial in Tokyo. They identified the first person who opened fire in the 1937 Marco Polo Bridge Incident and invited a few key personalities (such as the Wanping Administrative Commissioner and County Chief, and the 29th Army Deputy Commander and Mayor of Peking) to take the witness stand in Tokyo. All through the Tokyo Trial, the IPS did an excellent job of procuring evidences on the Nanking Massacre and the Marco Polo Bridge Incident. Therefore, although the field investigations required a huge amount of financial and human resources, they were useful.

The manpower and funding constraints made it difficult to conduct field investigation and interviews, and they were stopped entirely after the submission of indictment and the commencement of trial sessions. The field surveys depleted much of IPS's resources. The majority of staff from the FBI returned to the United States as they had only been temporarily deported to assist in the interrogation process, and the remaining members of the IPS exerted their best efforts. The solicitation of evidentiary documents and written testimonies from the Allied Powers were to be done by the associate prosecutors of the respective countries, who took up the task of obtaining them from the organizations or individuals of their own countries. The IPS formally contacted the Allied Powers for evidence, but primarily, the associate prosecutors sent by the Allies handled the process. The prosecutors understood the legislations of their own countries and knew how to procure the required documents. Hence, their efforts brought better results than written requests by the IPS.

Various materials provided by the Allied Powers, such as government documents, investigation reports, and written testimonies, were useful for prosecution by the IPS. Many of them were presented to the Tribunal as evidence during the Tokyo Trial. In this respect, China and the Soviet Union made more contribution than the other Allies. Some documents, however, were not presented to the Tribunal because the American Chief Prosecutor had them concealed for his own selfish reasons.[22]

---

[22] Some of the materials provided by China and the Soviet Union to the IPS were related to the Japanese royal family, the economic aggression or the responsibilities of the plutocrats, many of which were not disclosed by Keenan. For example, the materials on

3.3 Selection and Bibliographic Information of the 28 Defendants

From the above two sections, we can infer that the IPS arrested more than 100 alleged major war criminals (the 'Class-A war criminals') by the end of 1945, conducted extensive interrogations, and obtained a large number of their statements and confessions. Some prisoners were released at its own discretion, under the excuse of 'insufficient evidence'. The IPS then engaged itself in retrieving crime information of the detained prisoners from the Japanese government archives and documents received from the Allied Powers. In addition, the IPS allocated staff to conduct field investigations and witness interviews on crimes committed by specific war criminals.

By the early spring of 1946, the IPS had a fair understanding of the past records of all alleged Class-A war criminals under detention, and the complex political relations among them. The information collected was sufficient for drafting the indictment.

Before the drafting of the indictment, the IPS had to resolve the question of whom and how many Class-A arrestees were to be prosecuted as the first group of defendants to stand trial. It was not feasible to prosecute all war criminals under one case. At the Nuremberg Trial which was simultaneously being conducted, only 22 German major war criminals were tried and the cases were simpler and shorter than those at the Tokyo Tribunal. The IPS chose to emulate the operation of the Nuremberg Tribunal by restricting the number of defendants to 30.

Another prerequisite issue to be addressed before drafting the indictment was the determination of the starting and ending dates of war crimes. The prosecutors were in agreement about the ending date of war crimes, that is, on Japan's surrender in 1945, but they disputed about the starting date. Some were of the opinion that 7 December 1941, the day Japan attacked Pearl Harbor, should be considered as the beginning of the war because the event prompted wars against many other countries and changed the course of World War II—Japanese expansion became a new aspect of World War II. Some others argued that 7 July 1937, when the all-out war of aggression against China that was triggered by the Marco

the approval of the bacteriological war by the Japanese emperor, and the crimes of Araki during the Japanese invasion of Siberia were withheld by Keenan and not presented to the Tribunal as evidence.

Polo Bridge Incident broke out, should be regarded as the starting point of war crimes. They rationalized that the attack on Pearl Harbor and subsequent wars against countries in the Pacific region were launched for the sole purpose of winning its aggressive war in China and were simply an extension of this primary objective. Some prosecutors considered the Mukden Incident on 18 September 1931 as the beginning of war crimes because the Imperial Japanese Army had invaded Shenyang, occupied Manchuria (the four North-eastern provinces in China), and thereby set the stage for its comprehensive war of aggression against China in 1937. Some proposed an even earlier date in 1928, the year in which the Huanggutun Incident which killed Chang Tso-Lin took place; this is because this incident fanned the flames of hostility between Japan and China and led to the Mukden Incident in 1931. Japan's intention to encroach the whole territory of China was thus revealed.

Undoubtedly, the last proposition reflected a knowledgeable stance, and was especially satisfactory to the Chinese. The date could be traced back to an even earlier time, but it would be difficult to verify the facts.

After considerable deliberation, the IPS decided to adopt the final proposition that the war crimes charged against the defendants started from 1928 (the Huanggutun Incident) and ended in 1945 (Japan's surrender), spanning for about 17 years.

Having ascertained the number of defendants (about 20–30) and the period in which the chargeable crimes had been committed (approximately 17 years), the IPS was confronted with another difficult question: who should be prosecuted first? In other words, which of the 20–30 Class-A war crime suspects should be selected as the defendants of the first trial and be prosecuted at the Tokyo Tribunal?

This question triggered many debates; the IPS staff unanimously agreed about the culpability of notorious personalities like Hideki Tōjō, but differed in their opinions of less known offenders. For instance, the associate prosecutor from the Soviet Union insisted on the inclusion of Yoshisuke Aikawa (member of the House of Peers, Chairman of Manchurian Industrial Development Company) and Chikuhei Nakajima (founder of Nakajima Aircraft Company, successively Minister of Commerce, Minister of Railways and Minister of Munitions), but Chief Prosecutor Joseph B. Keenan did not agree; both Aikawa and Nakajima were successful entrepreneurs and capitalists, and it was a long-established US policy to favour magnates and capitalists. As mentioned earlier, the sudden release of Kiyoshi Goko (former President of Mitsubishi Heavy Industries) was a case in point.[23]

After much deliberation, Keenan chose the following 28 persons as the first group of defendants (in alphabetical order of their surnames in English):

1. ARAKI, Sadao
2. DOHIHARA, Kenji
3. HASHIMOTO, Kingorō
4. HATA, Shunroku
5. HIRANUMA, Kiichirō
6. HIROTA, Kōki
7. HOSHINO, Naoki
8. ITAGAKI, Seishirō
9. KAYA, Okinori
10. KIDO, Kōichi
11. KIMURA, Heitarō
12. KOISO, Kuniaki
13. MATSUI, Iwane
14. MATSUOKA, Yōsuke
15. MINAMI, Jirō
16. MUTŌ, Akira
17. NAGANO, Osami
18. OKA, Takazumi
19. ŌKAWA, Shūmei
20. ŌSHIMA, Hiroshi
21. SATŌ, Kenryō
22. SHIGEMITSU, Mamoru
23. SHIMADA, Shigetarō
24. SHIRATORI, Toshio
25. SUZUKI, Teiichi
26. TŌGŌ, Shigenori
27. TŌJŌ, Hideki
28. UMEZU, Yoshijirō.

---

[23] For Goko's release, see Footnote 14 under Sect. 3.1 of this chapter.

The majority of these 28 war criminals were arrested towards the end of 1945 and were detained in Sugamo Prison, with the exception of four: Mamoru Shigemitsu, Yoshijirō Umezu, Seishirō Itagaki and Heitarō Kimura.

Mamoru Shigemitsu and Yoshijirō Umezu were the Japanese representatives for the surrender. On behalf of the Emperor of Japan, the Japanese Government and the Japanese Imperial General Headquarters, they signed the Instrument of Surrender on 2 September 1945, at the surrender ceremony held by the representatives of the Allied Powers in Tokyo Bay, aboard the battleship, USS Missouri. The GHQ had a good opinion of the Japanese representatives, and thought that they deserved preferential treatment. Therefore, neither of them was listed in the four arrest warrants. Nevertheless, on account of their status and notoriety, they qualified as 'Class-A war criminals', suitable to be enlisted in the first group of major war criminals to stand trial.

The IPS had listed these two in the indictment when deciding on the first batch of defendants, but did not arrest them until the indictment was presented to the Tribunal. Therefore, their detention began only after formal prosecution. As mentioned before, the prosecutors and defendants formed opposite parties after the indictment was filed, and were not allowed to interact with each other. Therefore, the IPS did not have an opportunity to interrogate these two war criminals and take their statements. Consequently, there was no interrogation report or confession statement in the prosecution material against Shigemitsu and Umezu.

Seishirō Itagaki and Heitarō Kimura were faced with a similar situation. Their exclusion from the four arrest warrants in 1945, was not because of any preferential treatment, but because both of them were not in Japan at that time. When Japan surrendered, General Itagaki and General Kimura had important postings abroad (Itagaki as Commander of the Seventh Area Army in Singapore, and Kimura as Commander of the Expeditionary Force in Burma). After Japan's surrender, they were arrested by the local governments. They were also included in the first batch of defendants by the IPS for their flagrant actions. They were, however, not escorted to Sugamo Prison in Tokyo until the eve of the trial, and there was no time for their interrogation and statement-taking by the IPS.

Apart from the above four, the rest of the accused, that is, 24 of them who had been detained for long at Sugamo Prison, were carefully interrogated by the IPS. The interrogation records and their detailed statements were put on file and utilized as evidence by the IPS during the trial.

A final list of 28 major war criminals as the first batch of defendants was prepared. It was, however, regretted that the IPS did not include any important financial magnates or capitalists such as Yoshisuke Aikawa, Fusanosuke Kuhara and Chikuhei Nakajima. Overall, the list was satisfactory and included ambitious and notorious fascist aggressors who had for years misused their power and also ill-treated the Japanese. They had risen to prominence and were key players in Japanese politics, military affairs, diplomacy and propaganda for many years.

In analysing the war crimes of these 28 defendants, we identify the following types:

1. Former prime ministers: Tōjō (initiator of the Pacific War), Hirota (veteran diplomat), Hiranuma and Koiso (long-serving fascist militarists); these four prime ministers had enjoyed a high status in Japanese politics and were ringleaders of Japan's aggressive wars throughout the period of prosecution (1928–1945).
2. Typical long-serving militarists who actively preached aggression: Araki and Minami.
3. The most active criminals in the long-term aggression against China: Doihara, Itagaki and Umezu; and the most notorious criminals who had committed atrocities against Chinese people: Matsui and Hata.
4. Financiers, and major initiators and executors of Japan's wartime economic mobilization and the economic exploration in China: Kaya and Hoshino.
5. Major schemers and participants of Pacific War in the Tōjō cabinet: Nagano, Shimada, Kido, Suzuki, Satō and Oka.
6. Principal criminals who had committed atrocities in the Philippines, Burma and other places during the Pacific War: Kimura and Mutō.
7. Veteran diplomats who actively spread the idea of aggression: Shigemitsu, Tōgō and Matsuoka; and diplomats who actively collaborated with the Axis Powers—Germany and Italy, and organized an anti-communist military alliance: Ōshima and Shiratori.
8. Theorists, propagandists and agitators for fascism and policies of aggression: Ōkawa and Hashimoto.

It is, however, inaccurate to group the defendants into rigid categories because they were involved in various activities; it was only a convenient classification based on their predominant preoccupations. These defendants were selected for being major and representative figures in the Japanese wars of aggression.[24]

On the other hand, these 28 defendants were not perfectly representative of Japanese war crimes because many typical offenders were excluded from the list. The IPS had declared that this was only the first batch of criminals on trial, and there would be a second, third, and even fourth batch which would include other important personalities. This assurance, however, proved to be false. As the intention of the United States to shield Japan's reactionary forces became more pronounced, the IPS released many of the detained Class-A suspects, individually or in batches, during the first trial. Shortly after the judgement of the first trial, the IPS released the remaining alleged Class-A war criminals detained at Sugamo Prison. Consequently, the Tokyo Tribunal was bereft of cases and was dissolved without any formal announcement; the judges, eager to return home, were happy with the Tribunal's premature dissolution. This anticlimactic finish, stirred dissatisfaction among the Japanese people. They asked: why were some war criminals sentenced to death penalty or life imprisonment, whereas others who had committed equivalent crimes were at large with no legal punishment or trial?

It was difficult to find a reasonable answer to this question. It could only be admitted that the Tokyo Trial, like the Nuremberg Trial, was only a symbolic attempt to punish war criminals.

Given below are the biographical notes of the 28 Class-A war criminals prosecuted at the Tokyo Tribunal as the first, and the only, group of defendants, their ages being those at the beginning of the trial in 1946, and their experiences from 1928 to 1945 (the period of prosecution) being compiled based on Appendix E to the Indictment (Fig. 3.1).

---

[24] Golunsky, academician in the Soviet Academy of Sciences and the associate prosecutor from the Soviet Union, in a speech entitled 'The Trial of Japanese Major War Criminals' on 27 March 1947, categorized the defendants into five groups: (a) prime ministers; (b) military dignitaries; (c) important diplomats; (d) financial and economic dignitaries; (e) imperialist philosophers. He assigned a separate class to the elder statesman, Marquis Kido. Golunsky's categorization was also passable but had some defects: the groups were odd-sized; the 'military dignitaries' were more than a half of the total, whereas each of the remaining categories had only two or three defendants. In addition, the grouping of 'military dignitaries' was generalized and did not show the particular characteristics and criminal responsibilities of the criminals. Therefore, we do not adopt his categorization in this book.

3 ARREST AND PROSECUTION OF JAPANESE MAJOR WAR CRIMINALS 155

Fig. 3.1 The Class-A war criminals

Fig. 3.1 (continued)

Sadao Araki (70 years old): Araki graduated from the Imperial Japanese Army Academy and the Army War College and served as a military attaché in Russia, Commander of the Kwantung Army, Bureau Chief of the Army General Staff, President of the Army War College, and Commander of the 6th Division.

Araki held the following posts from 1928 to 1945: Chief of General Affairs Department of the Office of Inspector General of Military Training (1931); Minister of War in the Inukai cabinet and the Saito cabinet (December 1931–July 1934); promoted to the rank of full General (1933); member of the Supreme War Council (1934–1936); member of the Cabinet Advisory Council on China (1937); Minister of Education in the Konoe cabinet and the Hiranuma cabinet (May 1938–August 1939); and member of the Cabinet Advisory Council (from 1940 to the surrender of Japan).

Araki was the archetypal aggressive fascist militarist. He was ennobled with the title of baron for successfully occupying the four provinces in Northeast China. He exerted his influence on the Ministry of Foreign Affairs to withdraw from the League of Nations. After the May 15 Incident in 1932, he and Jinzaburo Masaki (Vice Chief of the General Staff) and Senjuro Hayashi (Inspector General of Military Training) eventually became the three central figures of the army.[25] Earlier, during the March

---

[25] The 'May 15 Incident' refers to the event in 1932 when the Prime Minister Tsuyoshi Inukai was murdered. After the Mukden Incident, when Japan occupied the four provinces of Northeast China and established 'Manchukuo', the Japanese government was divided into two rival factions: one advocated reopening negotiations with China, so that the situation could be temporarily alleviated, and the other argued for seizing the opportunity to continue expanding the force of aggression against China. Inukai supported the former, whereas Araki belonged to the latter. At the end of 1931, Inukai was instructed to set up a cabinet. Despite his intention to appoint Nobuyuki Abe as Minister of War, this position was taken by Araki because of the pressure from the army. Araki was supported by the fascist military men of the Imperial Way Faction. Consequently, disputes often occurred between the Prime Minister and the Minister of War. The conflict reached a pinnacle on 8 May 1932, when Inukai delivered a speech in Yokohama opposing military interference and praising democratic politics. On 15 May 1932, Inukai was assassinated by several junior officers of the Imperial Way Faction when resting in his official residence alone. The defendant Ōkawa provided pistols for this assassination, and another defendant Hashimoto also admitted his involvement in his book *The Way of Reconstruction of the World*.

Incident and the October Incident of 1931, junior officers of the Imperial Way Faction and fascists had tried in vain to help the three generals organize a cabinet of military dictatorship headed by Araki.[26]

Kenji Doihara (64 years old): Doihara graduated from the Imperial Japanese Army Academy and the Army War College; he had long been engaged in espionage and sabotage in China, and was well-known to the Chinese as a Japanese spy. He commanded the 30th Infantry Regiment, headed the Houten Special Agency in Mukden (Shenyang in Liaoning Province) and commanded the 9th Infantry Brigade.

Doihara held the following posts from 1928 to 1945: Commander of the Special Service Section in Northeast China (September 1931, the time of the Mukden Incident); Mayor of Shenyang (September–October 1931, for the Japanese occupation); served at the headquarters of the Kwantung Army (1933); Chief Adviser to the 'North China Autonomous Government', Commander of the 5th Army Division in Northeast China (1938–1940); member of the Supreme War Council (1940–1943); Inspector General of Army Aviation (1941); promoted to

---

[26] The 'March Incident' and 'October Incident' refer to two unsuccessful 'coups' before and after the 1931 Mukden Incident. The March Incident was plotted by the defendants Hashimoto and Ōkawa. Originally, it was organized so that Ōkawa could initiate and lead a mass demonstration of his dissatisfaction with the Diet and political parties, in which he could provoke and magnify a confrontation between the demonstrators and the police, and create a terrible chaos so that the army could declare martial law and achieve the goal of dissolving the Diet and establishing a military dictatorship. Hashimoto handed over 300 bombs meant for the army's manoeuvre to Ōkawa, who wanted to use them to cause panic and chaos among the demonstrators and give the appearance of a riot. But because of Ōkawa's over-enthusiasm, he disclosed the plan in advance to the then Minister of War Kazushige Ugaki, who then realized the whole conspiracy, and immediately used all his powers to thwart it. Therefore, the March Incident was prevented. The October Incident was also an unsuccessful 'coup' attempted by some junior officers. By then, the Mukden Incident had already occurred, and there were some fierce young officers who were dissatisfied with the government's misgivings and hesitations; so they advocated that the Japanese army should simply occupy and develop the whole of 'Manchuria' and further expand to the rest of China. Moreover, they believed that to implement this idea, they had to first of all dissolve the Diet, abolish all political parties, and organize the regime of military dictatorship by the officers. Their plan was 'to clarify the ideological and political atmosphere by assassinating the head of government'. Hashimoto and his Sakurakai (Cherry Blossom Society) were at the centre of this conspiracy. Hashimoto himself confessed that in order to swiftly establish a government headed by Araki, he intended to implement the plan in early October of 1931; but because Lieutenant Colonel Hiroshi Nemoto disclosed the secret, the plot was sabotaged before its implementation, and its organizers, including Hashimoto were arrested.

full General (April 1941); Commander-in-Chief of the Eastern District Army in Japan (1943); Commander of the 7th Area Army in Singapore (1944–1945); and Inspector General of Military Training (April 1945).

Doihara was known for being a 'China hand' among the Japanese officers, for he had been a prominent disciple of Toshihachiro Sakanishi, President Yuan Shikai's Japanese adviser. Before the Mukden Incident on 18 September 1931, he had stayed in China for more than 20 years, during which he became acquainted with Chinese officers and politicians, because of his excellent command of the Chinese language. Having been in espionage for long, he collected information for the Japanese government and tried his best to set one Chinese warlord against another. Owing to this reason, he intervened in almost every civil war or coup d'état (e.g. the Zhili-Anhui War, the first and the second Zhili-Fengtian Wars and the Manchu Restoration) in a period of regional division ushered by the Northern Warlords. The Huanggutun Incident, the Mukden Incident, the Marco Polo Bridge Incident and the founding of the Manchukuo, were his carefully orchestrated 'masterpieces'. He was merely a colonel in 1931, but in 1941, he was promoted to the rank of full General for his contributions in the Japanese invasion of China—a rare occurrence in the history of the Japanese army. He and his notorious classmates, Seishirō Itagaki, Rensuki Isogai and Yasuji Okamura, graduated from the 16th class of the Imperial Japanese Army Academy. All of them were determined to dedicate themselves to the invasion of China.[27] Among the

---

[27] The names and crimes of these four ringleaders of the Japanese invasion were familiar to the Chinese people. However, their fates were not the same. Doihara and Itagaki were two of the defendants prosecuted and finally sentenced to death by the Tokyo Tribunal. Isogai was not accused by the IPS because of his lower status. He was extradited to China for trial in the summer of 1946, as required by the Chinese government, and was soon sentenced to death. Okamura was the luckiest among the four. He not only escaped a death sentence, but was set free without any punishment. As the last commander-in-chief of the China Expeditionary Force, Okamura was well-known to Chinese people for his notorious 'Three Alls Policy' (to kill all, burn all, loot all). When Japan surrendered, he was ordered to handle matters concerning the surrender and expatriation, and thus established a closer relationship with the Chiang Kai-shek government. As a result, although Okamura was also listed as a war criminal in name, he was acquitted and released on 26 January 1949, before the Chiang Kai-shek government fled to Taiwan. In less than five days after the release, he was taken by an American warship to Japan, along with 260 Japanese war criminals who had been sentenced and were serving their terms in China. After returning to Japan, he continued to engage in activities hostile to the Chinese people with impunity.

four of them, Doihara was most active, cruel and ruthless and committed countless crimes against the Chinese people.

Kingorō Hashimoto (57 years old): As a graduate of the Imperial Japanese Army Academy and the Army War College, he was the military attaché to the Japanese Embassy in Turkey and the Japanese Embassy in Russia. Inspired by his admiration for President Kemal and the Turkish National Movement in Turkey, he created the Cherry Blossom Society (Sakurakai) with young officers in Japan to establish a new cabinet based on the ideology of 'supremacy of the Emperor'. Although he was only a lieutenant colonel at that time, he could manipulate the minds of people and persuade a great number of young officers to follow him.

During the period between 1928 and 1945, Hashimoto served at the Army General Staff Office (1933); retired from military service (February 1936); wrote *Declaration of Kingorō Hashimoto* (1936); re-entered the army's active service (1937); commanded an artillery regiment during the Nanking Massacre (1937); commanded the Japanese forces which shelled the British HMS Ladybird and the American USS Panay (1937); authored a large number of books, articles in the magazine *The Sun Dai Nippon* and other publications, and public speeches, all advocating aggressive warfare; was member of a number of societies for the instigation of army control over politics and furtherance of aggressive warfare; was promoter of a number of plots designed to remove politicians and officers whom he did not consider adequately aggressive; was one of the founders of the Imperial Rule Assistance Association (1940); and was elected as a member of the House of Representatives (1942).

As a supporter of extreme nationalism and fascism, Hashimoto had been feverishly advocating 'great-nation chauvinism' and military dictatorship. Shūmei Ōkawa (another fascist extremist) and he were the principle conspirators of the March Incident and the October Incident in 1931. They attempted to overthrow the cabinet by coups d'état and establish a military dictatorship. Having failed in the coups, he tried gathering some young officers to set up a fascist group—Great Japan Youth Party. After the outbreak of the full-scale war of aggression against China in 1937, the Japanese army fought successively in the Hangzhou Bay, Wuhu, Songjiang, Lushan in Jiujiang, and other places in China, under his leadership. In addition, he caused diplomatic troubles for Japan by savagely attacking and sinking the gunboats USS Panay and HMS

Ladybird.[28] After he returned to Japan on transfer, he reorganized and renamed the Great Japan Youth Party as the Great Japan Sincerity Association. Later, he joined the newly established Imperial Rule Assistance Association as a representative of the Great Japan Sincerity Association and held the prestigious post of executive secretary until Japan's surrender.

Shunroku Hata (68 years old): As a graduate of the Imperial Japanese Army Academy and the Army War College, he was a typical Japanese fascist officer and well-known for advocating the mechanization of arms. In the Russo-Japanese War from 1904 to 1905, he was a first lieutenant in the artillery. A bullet wound in his chest from the Battle of Mount Song had left him thin and weak for the rest of his life.

Hata held the following posts from 1928 to 1945: field command of the 14th Army Division (1933); Chief of Army Aviation Department (1935); Commander of the Taiwan Army (1936–1937); Inspector General of Military Training and member of the Supreme War Council (August 1937); a full General on promotion (February 1937); Commander-in-Chief of the Central China Expeditionary Army (February 1938); member of the Supreme War Council (January 1939); Minister of War in the Abe cabinet (August 1939–January 1940); Commander-in-Chief of the Central China Expeditionary Army, appointed twice (July 1940–1944); Field Marshal on promotion, member of the Board of Marshals and Admirals (June 1944); Inspector General of Military Training (November 1944 to the surrender of Japan).

Having served in the army for over 40 years, Hata was popular among tactical, modern Japanese officers. He was frequently involved in the political plots and fights of the young fascist officers. Hata was directly responsible for innumerable atrocities committed against Chinese people because he had twice been the commanding general of the Central China

---

[28] While attacking Nanking, the Japanese army shelled and sunk the American and British gunboats, Panay and Ladybird, respectively, in the Yangtze River, shocking the Western world. It was not an accident but a deliberate attempt to gauge the reaction of the Western countries to their ghastly deed. On facing their tough stance, Japan relented and expressed its 'deep regret' and 'sincere apologies', and promised to 'repay all the losses', 'punish those responsible', and 'issue necessary orders to prevent similar events from happening again'. After the matter was resolved through the diplomatic channel, Hashimoto, the principal trouble-maker, was dismissed from active military service. He returned home from China to engage in political activities in Japan.

Expeditionary Army and had fought in different regions of the Yangtze Valley for about five years.

Kiichirō Hiranuma (former Prime Minister, 80 years old): He graduated with a law degree from Tokyo Imperial University. He was the oldest among the 28 major criminals in the Tokyo Trial. Before starting his political activities in 1923, Hiranuma had for many years served as a professional judge, and as the chief procurator since 1911. Hiranuma's initiation into politics happened in the second cabinet of Yamamoto in 1923, when he was appointed as Minister of Justice. He gave up his judicial career and involved himself entirely in politics. Eventually, he forsook Shintoism for fascism and founded and presided over the National Foundation Society (Kokuhonsha)—Japan's earliest fascist group.

Hiranuma held the following posts from 1928 to 1945: Founder and President of the National Foundation Society (Kokuhonsha) (1926–1936), Vice President of the Privy Council (1930–1936); President of the Privy Council (1936–1939); Prime Minister (January–August 1939); Minister of State and for a period, Home Minister and Vice Prime Minister in the second and third Konoe cabinets, respectively (July 1940–October 1941); member of the Thought Control Council (August 1941); and President of the Privy Council (1945).

Hiranuma's political career was smooth because his doctrines of 'Great Japan' and fascist theories appealed to the young radical officers and he won their trust and support. He was a political acrobat who closely colluded with Araki and Masaki in the army, and Kato and Heizo in the navy. For many years, he used his status as a judge to influence people in the judicial circles and spread fascism. Although he appeared to be a respectable old gentleman, he was an insidious schemer who instigated almost every coup d'état in Japan.

Kōki Hirota (former Prime Minister, 69 years old): Hirota graduated from Tokyo Imperial University with a law degree. He dedicated all his life to the Japanese diplomatic services, as a career diplomat and a fascist. Having served in the Ministry of Foreign Affairs for several years, he was quickly promoted to the position of minister at the Netherlands. Later, he was recalled to become the Director of Europe and America Department of Foreign Ministry.

Hirota held the following posts from 1928 to 1945: Ambassador to the Soviet Union (1930); Minister of Foreign Affairs in the Saito cabinet (September 1933–July 1934) and in the Okada cabinet (July 1934–March

1936); Prime Minister and for a time, Minister of Foreign Affairs concurrently (March 1936–February 1937); Minister of Foreign Affairs in the Konoe cabinet (June 1937–May 1938); and member of the Cabinet Advisory Council (1940).

When serving as the Prime Minister in 1936, Hirota signed the Anti-Comintern Pact with Nazi Germany. This directly revealed his support for the fascist Axis Powers. Later, as Minister of Foreign Affairs in the Konoe cabinet, he signed the Tripartite Pact with Germany and Italy, and formally initiated Japan into the Axis Powers. From 1937 onwards, Japan's aggression against China steadily rose and reached a crescendo. Although Prime Minister Konoe was the first to be blamed, the Foreign Minister, Hirota, was also held responsible. Hirota had flattered the warlords and blindly followed their directives. His political strategy, like Hiranuma's, was to win the favour of reactionary officers by colluding with them to spread aggression and fascist ideology. He was the backbone of the militarist group, Dark Ocean Society (Gen'yosha), and a prominent official of its fascist offshoot, the Black Dragon Society (Kokuryu-kai).

Naoki Hoshino (55 years old): Hoshino graduated from the Law School of Tokyo Imperial University in 1917 and was employed by the Ministry of Finance for many years. He was a man of great experience and skill. He had managed finances for many years and was known as a promising financial expert in Japanese circles.

Hoshino held the following posts from 1928 to 1945: Chief of the General Bureau in the Finance Department of the 'puppet' state, Manchukuo (1932); Chief of General Affairs in the Finance Ministry of Manchukuo (1934); Vice Minister of Finance of Manchukuo (1936); Chief of General Affairs Bureau in the National Affairs Office of Manchukuo (December 1936); Chief of General Affairs in Manchukuo (July 1938),[29] President of the Cabinet Planning Board, and later, Minister of State in the Konoe Cabinet (July 1940–April 1941); Chief

---

[29] In the puppet 'Manchukuo' government structure, each ministry had a minister; the puppet post of the minister was held by a Chinese officer, but the vice minister who was a Japanese official, had the real authority. Therefore, in actuality, the vice minister was the highest official in that ministry. The Japanese vice ministers held a weekly meeting and handed over the passed resolutions to the State Council for their unaltered adoption. This was also true in case of the Prime Minister; although the position of Prime Minister was held by a senior Chinese traitor such as Zheng Xiaoxu or Zhang Jinghui, the real authority rested with the Chief of General Affairs, a Japanese, who was the de facto prime minister having a retinue of officials at different levels. As Hoshino had long served as

Cabinet Secretary and Minister of State in the Tōjō cabinet (16 October 1941–July 1944); and Adviser to the Finance Ministry (December 1944).

Hoshino was initially only an efficient staff member in Japan's Ministry of Finance, but after arriving in Manchukuo, he gradually changed into a proficient aggressor. He colluded with erstwhile magnates of the Kwantung Army in Manchuria such as Hishikari, Honjo, Miyake, Okamura, and Tōjō and won their favour and trust. In Manchukuo, he used his financial powers to exploit resources, plunder and extort money from people in Northeast China. He employed local resources and manpower to further Japan's aggressive war policies. After eight years of his evil exploits, Hoshino returned to Japan to hold prominent posts in the Konoe and the Tōjō cabinets. He ensured that the aggression against China continued and promoted the Pacific War against the United States, Britain and other countries. The Japanese people considered Hoshino as Tōjō's right-hand man.

Seishirō Itagaki (62 years old): He graduated from Japanese Army Cadet School at Sendai and the Imperial Japanese Army Academy. Itagaki, along with Doihara—the notorious 'China hand', Okamura and Isogai, graduated from the 16th class of the Imperial Japanese Army Academy.

Itagaki fought in the Russo-Japanese War from 1904 to 1905. Later, he joined the Kwantung Army and committed atrocities in Northeast China for a long period. He was one of the most hated Japanese criminals by the Chinese people.

Itagaki held the following posts from 1928 to 1945: Colonel in the Kwantung Army (1929); Major General in the Kwantung Army (1932); Vice Chief of Staff of the Kwantung Army (1934); Commander of the 5th Army Division in China (March 1937); Chief of Staff of the Kwantung Army (1936–1937); an officer in the General Staff Office (May 1937); Minister of War in the Konoe cabinet and the Hiranuma cabinet and concurrently, President of the Manchurian Affairs Bureau of the Cabinet (June 1938–August 1939); Chief of Staff of the China Expeditionary Force (September 1939); Commander of the Japanese Army in Korea (July 1941–1943); member of the Supreme War Council (1943); and Commander of the 7th Area Army in Singapore (April 1945). He was promoted to the rank of full General in July 1941.

Manchukuo's Chief of General Affairs, he was certainly responsible for the various criminal measures adopted there.

In 1929, Itagaki was merely a colonel in the Kwantung Army, but he was appointed as Minister of War in 1938 and promoted as a full General in 1941. His 'tremendous contributions' to the invasion of China led to his rapid rise in status at an unprecedented speed. When serving in the Kwantung Army, he was the major initiator and executor of a series of historical actions, such as occupying Northeast China, forcing Northeast China to separate itself from China, and establishing the puppet state, Manchukuo. He was believed to have dreamt of becoming the 'emperor of Manchukuo'. After the launch of the full-scale war of aggression against China in 1937, he led the army to fight in various parts of China, successively in Shanxi, Shandong and Subei regions where he committed countless crimes and atrocities. Itagaki's name and atrocities, just like Doihara's, were not unknown to any woman or child of those regions. When Japan surrendered, he was serving as Commander of the Expeditionary Force in Singapore and was escorted to Tokyo only the day before the Tokyo Tribunal officially opened its first session.

Okinori Kaya (58 years old): He was the preeminent expert in managing money matters in wartime Japan and was often called as a 'financial magician'.

Kaya held the following posts from 1928 to 1945: Chief Secretary of the Finance Ministry (1934); Minister of Finance in the Konoe cabinet (June 1937–May 1938); member of the Advisory Committee of the China Affairs Board (1939); President of the North China Development Company (1939–1941); Minister of Finance in the Tōjō cabinet (June 1941–February 1944) and Director of the Imperial Rule Assistance Association (1944).

Kaya acquired financial power because he could pander to the aggressive policy and war strategy in his political proposals and win the favour of fascist officers. In both the crucial periods of Japan's aggressive war (the full-scale invasion of China and the Pacific War), he headed the Ministry of Finance, which was an office equivalent to the commander-in-chief in wartime Japan. He was in charge of domestic banking, monetary practices and foreign trade and strongly supported the warlords in the aggressive wars by mobilizing the country's financial resources. While serving as the President of the 'North China Development Company', he exploited and plundered resources in China. Shortly before Japan's surrender, he was made the Chairman of a newly formed 'Inflation Control Committee', which was established by the Japanese government in an attempt to avert Japan's bankruptcy. This was the last office he held in the government;

however, even he, the 'magician' could do nothing to control inflation and stop Japan's economy from worsening.

Kōichi Kido (58 years old): He was a marquis and the grand nephew of Takayoshi Kido, one of the leaders of the Meiji Restoration. He graduated from the Law School of Kyoto University. He was close friends with his schoolmate Fumimaro Konoe; both were noblemen who shared similar interests and aspirations. During their long careers, they worked together, supported each other, and were both celebrated in Japanese politics. Kido entered politics upon graduation, and he held numerous minor bureaucratic posts in the Ministry of Agriculture and Commerce, followed by the Ministry of Commerce and Industry and the Industrial Rationality Bureau.

Kido held the following posts from 1928 to 1945: Chief Secretary to the Lord Keeper of the Privy Seal (1930); Minister of Education in the Konoe cabinet (1937); Minister of Health and Welfare in the Konoe cabinet (1938); Home Minister in the Hiranuma cabinet (1939); Lord Keeper of the Privy Seal (1940–1945); chief confidential adviser to the Emperor and often presided over the Elder Statesmen meetings.

Having served in the Office of Lord Keeper of the Privy Seal, and later himself holding the post of Lord Keeper of the Privy Seal for many years, Kido exerted a great influence on the ever-changing situations of Japanese politics. Apart from being the closest adviser to Emperor Showa, he was also an important intermediary between the Emperor and the cabinet. Kido sought approval from the Emperor for every cabinet reshuffle and replacement of Prime Minister.[30] At the time of Kido's appointment as Lord Keeper of the Privy Seal, the cabinet was being reorganized, and the military men were plotting the launch of the Pacific War and staunchly supporting Hideki Tōjō's ascendency. Kido not only refrained

---

[30] The 'Lord Keeper of the Privy Seal' (Naidaijin, sometimes referred to as 'Minister of the Imperial Household') and his office had important political status in pre-war Japan. The office of Lord Keeper of the Privy Seal was not a subsidiary organ of the cabinet, but a supreme agency looking after the Emperor and all matters in the imperial court; the Lord Keeper of the Privy Seal of Japan was not a member of the cabinet, but the medium between the cabinet and the Emperor, and the most trusted political adviser and assistant to the Emperor. Every time there was a government's or cabinet's reorganization, and succession of the prime minister or ministries, the Emperor's approval had to be obtained through him, which made him not only a key figure in Japanese politics, but also the one most familiar with the various internal changes. As Kido held the post for many years, great importance was attached to his private diary by the Tokyo Tribunal.

from thwarting their motives, but also supported them. It was believed that Kido's encouragement influenced the formation of Tōjō's 'Adventure Cabinet'. Like Konoe, Kido was an aristocrat employed by fascist warlords.

Kido kept a diary and wrote his thoughts on it regularly for decades. After the surrender of Japan, his diary was found by the GHQ and immediately sent to the Tokyo Tribunal to be preserved in its Archives Office. Kido had always been a central figure in the Japanese government. Therefore, his personal notes were integral to an understanding of Japan's history of political evolution and helped formed a clear picture of the gradual formulation of war policies, escalation of the war of aggression, changes in personnel in successive cabinets, and the overt and covert struggles between different factions and parties. Both the prosecution and the defence searched the diary entries for suitable material that could be presented to the Tribunal as evidence. The Tribunal, however, did not easily confirm their probative value because Kido demonstrated fascist ideology and feudalistic prejudice. Notwithstanding, *The Diary of Marquis Kido* was still the most detailed, systematic and accurate personal record of the private activities of Japan's top political, economic, military and diplomatic circles over the past two decades.[31]

Heitarō Kimura (58 years old): He graduated from the artillery unit of the Imperial Japanese Army Academy and the Army War College. Kimura had been the Chief of Staff in an army division. He was dispatched to fight in the Japanese Siberian Intervention and subsequently sent as a military attaché to Germany. After returning to Japan, he served in the Army General Staff Office and concurrently taught in the Army War College.

Kimura held the following posts from 1928 to 1945: Chief of Staff of the Kwangtung Army (1940); Vice Minister of War in the Konoe cabinet

---

[31] From the comprehensive *The Diary of Marquis Kido*, only the portions relating to the defendants' criminal responsibilities were extracted by the litigant parties and submitted to the Tribunal as evidence. The prosecution used information that was against the defendants, whereas the defence used information that was favourable to the defendants. These records comprised only a small part of the diary; the diary itself was an excellent reference for the study of Japan's political and diplomatic history of more than two decades. For this reason, the GHQ made 100 copies of the diary. The original diary along with its copies were shipped to Washington, DC and seized by the US Army Department for sole ownership. The US government shamefully would not share even one set of copies with its Allies who had fought alongside the United States.

and the Tōjō cabinet (1941–February 1944); member of the Supreme War Council (1943); Commander-in-Chief of the Japanese Army in Burma (1944) and the full General on promotion (1945).

Kimura used to be an efficient career military officer before assuming the post of Chief of Staff of the Kwangtung Army. However, after being appointed twice as the Vice Minister of War, he became an important member of the Japanese fascist group for expansion and aggression. In the latter part of the Pacific War, he was deputed to Burma as the Commander-in-Chief. Consequently, he was directly responsible for the atrocities committed in Burma, and thereby the Tokyo Tribunal sentenced him to death-by-hanging.

Kimura was detained in Burma when Japan surrendered and escorted to Tokyo only on the eve of the first open session of the Tokyo Trial.

Kuniaki Koiso (former Prime Minister, 67 years old): Koiso graduated from the Imperial Japanese Army Academy and the Army War College, and he fought in the Russo-Japanese War from 1904 to 1905. Later, he became the leader of the Special Services Agency in Northeast China and served in the General Staff Office and the army; he was commissioned as Battalion Commander of the 2nd Infantry Regiment, Commander of the 51st Division and other posts. He was promoted to be a Major General in 1926 and a Lieutenant General in 1931.

Koiso held the following posts from 1928 to 1945: Director of the Military Affairs Bureau of the War Ministry (1930); Vice Minister of War in the Inukai cabinet (1932); Chief of Staff of the Kwantung Army (1932–1934); Commander of the Army in Korea (1935–1936); Minister of Colonial Affairs in the Hiranuma cabinet (1939); Minister of Colonial Affairs in the Yonai cabinet (1940); Governor-General of Korea (May 1942) and Prime Minister (July 1944–April 1945). Koiso was promoted to the rank of full General in 1937.

Koiso and Hata graduated from the Imperial Japanese Army Academy in the same year. Both were key figures in the Japanese fascist clique for the expansion and aggression and colluded with modern minds adept in military strategy and tactics. In 1925, as the monitor of the Military Mapping and Surveys Section in the General Staff Office, he proposed that a tunnel be dug between Shimonoseki and Moji-ku; he obtained approval for the project by personally presenting his working drawings to every competent authority. On completion of this project, he was acknowledged for his contribution and eventually he rose to a high political position in the ensuing two decades. However, Japan was doomed to failure when he succeeded Tōjō as the Prime Minister. He made no achievement during the nine months of his term, but only maintained the status quo in a lost game.

Iwane Matsui (69 years old): Matsui graduated from the Imperial Japanese Army Academy and the Army War College. He served in the Army General Staff Office and subsequently held the posts of Chief of the Intelligence Division of the Kwantung Army, and the Commander of the 11th Division. While preparing for the launch of a full-scale invasion of China, Matsui made a thorough study of the geographic features of China, especially of the coastal provinces in Southeast China; this made him win the laudatory title, 'China hand'.

Matsui held the following posts from 1928 to 1945: the army plenipotentiary at the World Disarmament Conference in Geneva (1931); member of the Supreme War Council (March 1933); Commander-in-Chief of the Central China Area Army (October 1937–February 1938); member of the Cabinet Advisory Council (July. 1938–January 1940); adviser to the Asia Promotion Federation (1940); adviser to the Greater East Asia Affairs Section of the Imperial Rule Assistance Association (1943) and President of the Greater East Asia Development Society (1944). He founded the Greater East Asia Society and was promoted to full General in 1933.

Matsui was known for supporting the 'Continental Policy' (i.e. Japan should first occupy China and the Asian continent) and promoting 'Pan-Asianism' (i.e. Japan should exclusively control Asia and oppose encroachment by the Europeans and Americans) among the Japanese fascist officers. After the outbreak of the comprehensive war of aggression against China in July 1937, the Japanese army suffered a setback in the Battle of Shanghai and thrice changed its Commander-in-Chief before appointing Matsui for the post. Under the leadership of Matsui, the troops advanced through Hangzhou Bay, captured Shanghai, and proceeded to attack Nanking. After Nanking fell into Japanese hands in December 1937, Matsui connived the most horrifying atrocities against Chinese civilians which were committed by his subordinates; they included indiscriminate slaughter, rape, arson and robbery. During the unprecedented 'Nanking Massacre' which lasted for six weeks, several hundred thousand civilians were killed. This tragedy shook the world and was strongly denounced by all. The universal reaction forced the Japanese government to recall Matsui to Japan. On returning home,

Matsui pretended to be repentant for his crimes and requested retirement, but in reality, he continued his fascist activities of aggression.[32] The Tokyo Tribunal sentenced him to death mainly for his involvement in the Nanking Massacre.

Yōsuke Matsuoka (66 years old): Matsuoka was raised in Oregon, the United States. After returning to Japan in 1902, he joined the Foreign Ministry. His fluency in English and doctrines of aggression helped him win the favour of fascist officers and he soon ranked among the most influential diplomats.

Matsuoka held the following posts from 1928 to 1945: Chief of the Japanese delegation to the League of Nations (1933); President of the South Manchurian Railway Company (1935–1939); member of the Cabinet Advisory Council (1940); and Minister of Foreign Affairs in the Konoe cabinet (July 1940–July 1941). Matsuoka authored *Showa Restoration* (1938) and other books and articles, and also delivered speeches advocating the Axis alliance and the war of aggression.

Matsuoka was a conceited Japanese diplomat who headed Japan's delegation to the League of Nations and announced Japan's withdrawal from it. He was also a major advocate of a Japanese alliance with Nazi Germany and Fascist Italy. His greatest achievement was signing the Soviet-Japanese Neutrality Pact. After Nazi Germany's invasion of the Soviet Union and the downfall of Konoe's third cabinet, Matsuoka's political career also came to an end. He then suffered a relapse of pneumonia and spent a long period resting and recuperating in his hometown. At the time of

---

[32] Matsui, in his defence in court, presented a photograph of an altar in honour of the officers and soldiers sacrificed in Nanking which was installed at his residence, in an attempt to prove that he repented in all sincerity. He said that he had returned to Japan after the 'Nanking Massacre', feeling the gravity of his sins and determining to withdraw from politics. He also had resolved to become a vegetarian and live a religious life. He built an altar and performed religious service every morning and evening. However, his statements were false. The photo of the supposed 'altar' showed two memorial tablets placed thereon, one reading 'To the Japanese officers and soldiers killed in action', and the other 'To the Chinese officers and soldiers killed in action'. Matsui had treated the aggressors and the victims of aggression on par. Besides, those honoured were restricted to the officers and soldiers; it was absurd that the hundreds of thousands of Chinese civilians massacred were ignored. Meanwhile, it was also hypocritical of Matsui to pledge 'retirement', because according to records, after he was ordered to return to Japan in early 1938, he continued to hold important posts in the cabinet and fascist groups such as the Asia Promotion Federation, and the Imperial Rule Assistance Association. From 1944 onwards, he served as the President of an aggressive group, the Greater East Asia Development Society.

arrest, he was very sick; he died within four months after the trial began. His name was then taken off the list of defendants and excluded from final judgement.

Jirō Minami (73 years old): Minami graduated from the cavalry unit of the Imperial Japanese Army Academy. He served as Commander of the 3rd Cavalry Brigade, Governor-General of the Kwantung Leased Territory, Commandant of the Cavalry School, Commandant of the Imperial Japanese Army Academy, Chief of the Cavalry Section of the Ministry of War, Commander of the Army 16th Division and Vice Chief of General Staff. He was promoted to the rank of full General in 1930, and was one of the most senior Japanese officers.

Minami held the following posts from 1928 to 1945: Commander-in-Chief of the Army in Korea (1929), Minister of War in the Wakatsuki cabinet (April–December 1931), member of the Supreme War Council (1931–1934), Commander-in-Chief of the Kwangtung Army (1934–1936), Governor-General of Korea (1936–1942), member of the Privy Council (1942–1945) and President of the Political Association of Great Japan (1945).

Just like Araki, Minami was a long-serving fascist officer who believed in Shintoism and military aggression. Both of them became role models for the young army men. When the Mukden Incident took place in 1931, Minami, as the Minister of War, shielded the trouble-making officers instead of punishing them. He avoided any peaceful resolution of the conflict by duping the Prime Minister Wakatsuki and subjugating other ministers in the cabinet. The war thus spread to all four provinces in Northeast China. Minami had plotted Japan's expansion into the entire territory of Northeast China and the establishment of Manchukuo, which brought many disastrous effects. He was a hypocritical Governor-General of Korea for many years who resorted to every conceivable means of exploiting, enslaving and suppressing the Korean people and was therefore one of the most hated Japanese criminals in Korea.

Akira Mutō (55 years old): On graduating from the Imperial Japanese Army Academy and the Army War College, Mutō was given the title of Captain and assigned to Europe and America, and later to Germany to study army tactics. After returning to Japan, he served in the Ministry of War and the Army General Staff Office.

Mutō held the following posts from 1928 to 1945: Instructor at the Army War College (1930–1932); Senior Officer of the Military Affairs Bureau of the War Ministry (1935–1936); section chief in the General

Staff Office (1937); Director of the Military Affairs Bureau of the War Ministry (October 1939–April 1942); Commander of the 2nd Guards Division in Sumatra (1943) and Chief of Staff of the 14th Area Army in the Philippines under General Tomoyuki Yamashita (1944). From August 1937 onwards, Mutō also served in the General Staff Office of the Central China Area Army, and later in the Commander's Office of the Kwantung Army.

Mutō was one of the youngest defendants. He was known as an able and resourceful fascist officer with a good knowledge of army tactics. Although he was of a lower rank, he had been given much authority. Having served for long in the Military Affairs Bureau of the War Ministry, he was made the Director of the Bureau and acted in that capacity for a few years. The Military Affairs Bureau was a central force in the War Ministry. As the Director of the Bureau, he significantly influenced historical decisions to: intensify aggression against China, found the puppet regime in Nanking, collude with the Axis Powers of Germany and Italy, forcibly occupy Vietnam, break negotiations with the United States, launch the Pacific War, and declare war against Britain, the United States and other countries. When commanding Japanese troops in Sumatra and serving as Chief of Staff under General Yamashita in the Philippines, he directed his subordinates to commit countless atrocities against the local people.[33] His high criminal responsibility in the atrocities led to him being awarded the death sentence by the Tokyo Tribunal.

Osami Nagano (67 years old): Nagano was a career naval officer who graduated from the Imperial Japanese Naval Academy and the Naval War College. He was the commander of a land-based, heavy naval gun unit during the Russo-Japanese War from 1904 to 1905. By successfully bombarding Lüshun Harbor, he gained the reputation of an officer skilled in battle command. In 1920, Nagano as a naval attaché to the United States attended the Washington Naval Conference accompanied by General Kato, the Japanese naval representative. After returning to Japan, he became a section chief of the Navy General Staff and commanded the 3rd Battleship Division. Later, he commanded the

---

[33] General Tomoyuki Yamashita was the Commander-in-Chief of the Japanese Army in the Philippines. In 1945, he was sentenced to death-by-hanging by an American military tribunal in Manila; so was General Masaharu Homma, who had been arrested in Japan and extradited to the Philippines for trial.

1st China Expeditionary Fleet and was Commandant of the Training Squadron.

Nagano held the following posts from 1928 to 1945. Vice Chief of the Naval General Staff (1930); delegate to the Geneva Naval Conference (1931); member of the Supreme War Council (1933); Chief Delegate to the London Naval Conference (1935); Minister of Navy in the Hirota cabinet (March 1936–February 1937); Commander-in-Chief of the Combined Fleet (1937); (reappointed as) member of the Supreme War Council (1940) and Chief of the Naval General Staff (April 1941–February 1944). Nagano was promoted to be a full Admiral in 1934 and Marshal Admiral in 1943.

Nagano was one of the well qualified naval officers in Japan. In addition to his involvement in fascist officers' plots to seize political power and wage aggressive wars against China, he bore major responsibility for the Pearl Harbor attack and the Pacific War. Along with the then Prime Minister Hideki Tōjō and the Commander of the Combined Fleet Isoroku Yamamoto, Nagano instigated the attack on Pearl Harbor and the war against the United States, Britain and other countries.

Nagano succumbed to heart disease on 5 January 1947, after which his name was removed from the list of defendants, and the Tokyo Tribunal did not sentence him.

Takazumi Oka (57 years old): Oka graduated from the Imperial Japanese Naval Academy and the Naval War College. He once led the Japanese fleet to fight against Germany in World War I; he was later assigned to observe navy tactics in Turkey after the war. After returning to Japan, he served in the Ministry of Navy and the Navy General Staff.

Oka held the following posts from 1928 to 1945: section chief of the General and Military Affairs Bureau of the Navy Ministry (1938); Chief of the General and Military Affairs Bureau of the Navy Ministry (1940–1944); Vice Minister of Navy in the Koiso cabinet (July 1944) and Commander-in-Chief of the Chinkai (Korea) Naval Station (September 1944–June 1945). Oka was promoted to the rank of Vice Admiral in 1942.

Oka devoted all his life to the Japanese Navy, and was noted for his talent in general affairs. Although he was of a lower rank, he could influence the decisions of the higher authority. Oka's decisive role in the Navy was similar to Mutō's in the army. He served in the Navy Military Affairs Bureau and headed it during an eventful period in Japan. During his term, many important military decisions were made and he participated in the plots of aggression, and especially, the attack on Pearl Harbor, the naval war in the Pacific Ocean, and the occupation of Western colonies in Southeast Asia. Unlike Tōjō, Yamamoto and Nagano, Oka as well as his superior, Shimada, the then Minister of Navy, was believed to have proposed that they carefully implement drastic naval strategies in the Pacific Ocean. Therefore, the fascist officers taunted him as 'cowardly' and 'incompetent'. Nevertheless, his prudence did not stop him and his superior from yielding to the radical warriors and executing hazardous plans of aggression. He was thus held responsible for the consequences of those plans.

Shūmei Ōkawa (61 years old): He was the most arrogant propagandist and agitator among the Japanese fascist literati. Ōkawa graduated from the Philosophy Department of the Tokyo Imperial University, where he had studied classical Indian philosophy and later developed interest in colonialism and colonial policies. He wrote *A Study of Chartered Colonisation Companies* and was awarded the degree of Doctor of Laws in 1927. He then devoted himself to writing and lecturing and preached the doctrines of 'Great Japanism' and Pan-Asianism. He founded secretive fascist groups such as 'Rosokai' and 'Yuzonsha'. In 1924, Ōkawa founded the *Nippon* magazine along with Yasuoka Masahiro (President of the Institute of Golden Pheasant), which championed the overthrow of political parties and privileged classes, and the unification of the people discontented with the circumstances to form a right-wing group and seize political authority by force.

Ōkawa held the following posts from 1928 to 1945: Director General of the East Asia Research Institute of the South Manchurian Railroad (from 1926 onwards); an organizer of the Mukden Incident (September 1931); and author of *A Japanese History Reader* (1935) and other books, articles and speeches, advocating aggressive war for the expulsion of the white race from Asia.

Being a zealous propagandist and agitator of racism and chauvinism, Ōkawa, like the arrogant military man Hashimoto, was always instigating political events and stirring trouble. Owing to this, they both shared a close political rapport. In 1931, they schemed the unsuccessful 'March Incident' and 'October Incident'.[34] They both were also involved in planning the Mukden Incident in the same year. In 1932, that is, a year

---

[34] For details of the March Incident and October Incident of 1931 and the May 15 Incident of 1932, see Footnotes 25 and 26 above in this section.

after the successful operation of the Mukden Incident, Ōkawa founded another fascist group 'Jinmukai' to forcibly overthrow the cabinet and promote the Showa Restoration. He planned and executed the assassination of Prime Minister Tsuyoshi Inukai on 15 May 1932 (i.e. the notable 'May 15 Incident'). Ōkawa was arrested with conclusive evidence and sentenced to 15 years of imprisonment, which was later reduced to four years. After he was discharged from prison in 1937, Japanese full-scale aggression against China broke out, making it conducive for Ōkawa to spread Pan-Asianism and fascism in Japan. By then, Ōkawa had become a notable political figure and a frequent guest of Prime Minister Fumimaro Konoe, who was known as the 'main source' of Konoe's think tank. Ōkawa boldly preached Japanese fascist ideology in wartime Japan.

Ōkawa wrote many books during his life, such as *A Japanese History Reader, Some Issues in Re-emerging Asia, A study of the Japanese spirit, Japan and the Japanese way* and *2600 years of the Japanese history*. The works had little academic value as they were chauvinistic and coloured by the ideology of 'Great Japanism', but they were useful propaganda material.

Ōkawa showed symptoms of mental disorder after Japan's surrender. He was deeply upset by Konoe's suicide; his political dreams were shattered and he began hallucinating. On the first day of the Tribunal's open session, Ōkawa was sitting right behind Tōjō. When the session was about to close, he suddenly slapped Tōjō's bald head and shouted, 'I will kill Tōjō! I will kill Tōjō!'. Ōkawa was later diagnosed to be mentally ill by the medical experts designated by the Tribunal; so the Tribunal suspended the trial against him. He was still ill when the Tribunal pronounced its judgement in November 1948. As he had not been tried, Ōkawa escaped punishment.[35]

Hiroshi Ōshima (61 years old): As a graduate of the Imperial Japanese Army Academy and the Army War College, Ōshima was successively appointed as an assistant military attaché in the Japanese embassy in

---

[35] The Tokyo Tribunal declared Ōkawa to be 'temporarily suspended from the trial' and retained the right to resume his trial 'by this or another court' after his recovery. However, in less than two months after the Tribunal announced its judgement, on 24 December 1948, he was released from prison by the GHQ, together with the last batch of Japanese Class-A prisoners. Not only did he get away unpunished, but he was also subsequently elected as a member of the Diet. This was regarded as a mockery of the legal system.

Germany, military attaché in the Japanese embassy in Australia, and Commander of the 10th Field Artillery Regiment.

Ōshima held the following posts from 1928 to 1945: Military Attaché in the Japanese embassy in Germany (1936); and Ambassador to Germany (first time from October 1938 to October 1939, and again from February 1941 to May 1945 when Germany surrendered).

Ōshima, a Japanese fascist officer, was a good diplomat; having long served in the Japanese embassy in Germany, and twice being the Ambassador to Germany, he worshipped Hitler for his ambition and the achievements made by Nazi Germany. Therefore, he recommended a strong alliance with the Axis Powers to assist their motives of territorial expansion. He played a major role in the conclusion of the Anti-Comintern Pact with Germany in 1936 and the Tripartite Pact in 1940. Like Toshio Shiratori, the Ambassador to Italy, Ōshima was considered by the Japanese as a vehement promoter of collusion with the Axis Powers.

Ōshima served as the Ambassador in Berlin until Germany's surrender, after which he was arrested by the Allied Powers and escorted back to Japan. He was one of the nine Class-A war criminals in the last arrest warrant issued by GHQ on 6 December 1945.

Kenryō Satō (52 years old): After graduating from the Imperial Japanese Army Academy and the Army War College, Satō served in the Administration Bureau of the Ministry of War; later, he was appointed as an assistant to the Chief of Staff of the South China Area Army and as Vice Chief of Staff of the China Expeditionary Force. Having long served as the military attaché in the Japanese embassy in the United States, he had good knowledge of US politics, economy, military and foreign affairs and earned the title of 'America hand' in the Ministry of War.

Satō held the following posts from 1928 to 1945: Instructor at the Army War College (1935); member of the Cabinet Planning Board (1937–1938); section chief in the Military Affairs Bureau of the War Ministry (February 1941–April 1942); and Director of the Military Affairs Bureau of the War Ministry (April 1942–December 1944). Satō was promoted to the rank of Major General in October 1941, and then, Lieutenant General in March 1945.

Although Satō did not have a high position in the army, he won the favour of the authorities for his intelligence, resourcefulness and sense of responsibility. In 1938, when he presented the National General Mobilization bill to the Diet on behalf of the War Ministry, he threatened the Diet members to adopt the bill. Having served in the Military Affairs

Bureau, the most important unit in the Ministry of War, and headed it for two and a half years, he was familiar with every scheme of the Tōjō cabinet. He was responsible for the plan to block traffic lines in the north of Vietnam and occupy Vietnam.

Mamoru Shigemitsu (60 years old): Shigemitsu graduated from the Law School of Tokyo Imperial University. On winning the first place in the examination for diplomats, he was recruited by the Ministry of Foreign Affairs. He served successively as secretary at the Japanese embassies in Germany and in the United Kingdom, counsellor in the Ministry of Foreign Affairs, section chief in the Bureau of Treaties, and First Secretary at the Japanese embassy in China.

Shigemitsu held the following posts from 1928 to 1945: Minister to China (1931); Vice Minister of Foreign Affairs in the Saito cabinet and the Okada cabinet (1933–1936); Ambassador to the Soviet Union (November 1936–November 1938); Ambassador to Great Britain (1938–June 1941); Ambassador to the puppet Chinese government in Nanking (December 1941–April 1943); Minister of Foreign Affairs in the Tōjō cabinet (April 1943–July 1944); and Minister of Foreign Affairs and concurrently, Minister of Greater East Asia in the Koiso cabinet (July 1944–April 1945).

Shigemitsu was reappointed as Minister of Foreign Affairs in the cabinet of Prince Naruhiko Higashikuni when Japan surrendered. He signed the Instrument of Surrender on behalf of the Emperor and the Japanese government along with the other Japanese representative, Yoshijirō Umezu, who signed on behalf of the Imperial General Headquarters, at a ceremony on board the USS Missouri on 2 September 1945.

Shigemitsu was primarily known as a career diplomat for his superior insight and abilities. He was calm and poised even in the face of political adversity. After the full-scale invasion of China and the outbreak of the Pacific War, Shigemitsu became the Minister of Foreign Affairs in the Tōjō cabinet. He now colluded with the warlords as a key conspirator of Japan's aggressive policies. He was the Minister to China when the Battle of Shanghai took place on 28 January 1932. On 29 April, while attending an assembly to celebrate the Emperor's birthday, Shigemitsu was severely wounded and lost his leg in a bomb attack instigated by a Korean independence activist; Admiral Yoshinori Shirakawa, Commander-in-Chief of the Shanghai Expeditionary Army, was killed in the explosion.

From then onwards, he had to walk clumsily leaning on two canes. The disability was like an 'anti-aggression mark' imprinted upon an aggressor.

Shigetarō Shimada (64 years old): Shimada graduated from the Imperial Japanese Naval Academy in the same year as Marshal Admiral Isoroku Yamamoto and Admiral Koichi Shiozawa. Upon graduation, Shimada served successively as the Naval Attaché in Italy, Instructor at the Naval War College, Commander of the 7th Submarine Division, and Chief of Staff of the 3rd Fleet and 1st Fleet.

Shimada held the following posts from 1928 to 1945: Chief of Staff of the Combined Fleet (1930); Vice Chief of the Naval General Staff (1935–1937); Commander of the 2nd Fleet (December 1937); Commander of the China Area Fleet (May 1940); Minister of Navy in the Tōjō cabinet (October 1941); member of the Supreme War Council (1944); and Chief of the Naval General Staff (February–July 1944). Shimada was promoted to the rank of full Admiral in 1940.

Shimada held various important posts in the Japanese Navy for a long period. He not only knew all the strategies adopted by the Japanese fascist officers, but also participated in their exploits. As the Minister of Navy in the Tōjō cabinet, he was jointly liable for the Pacific War. However, Shimada was believed to have opposed the attack on Pearl Harbor and the war against the United States, or at least have cautioned the Government. This was a vain defence that he made in the Tokyo Trial; he had for long held a responsible position at the time of the Pacific War, and his involvement in the conspiracy of aggression could not be easily dismissed. He also could not deny his participation in the various conspiracies against China. Irrespective of his stance, he continued to bear responsibility for his crimes.

Toshio Shiratori (60 years old): After graduating from Tokyo Imperial University and while serving in the Ministry of Foreign Affairs, Shiratori was appointed successively to the Japanese embassies in China, Great Britain, the United States and Germany. Later, he was transferred back to Japan and became Director of the Information Bureau of the Foreign Ministry.

Shiratori held the following posts from 1928 to 1945: Director of the Information Bureau of the Foreign Ministry (1930); Minister to Sweden, Norway, Denmark and Finland (1936); Ambassador to Italy (1939); adviser to the Foreign Ministry (1940); and Director of the Imperial Rule Assistance Association (1943). Shiratori published an article in *Contemporary Japan* which asserted the need of a world conflict for the establishment of the 'New Order in Asia' (16 April 1941).

As a young officer in the Japanese diplomatic circle, Shiratori was admired for his political ideas and fluency in English; he advocated collusion with Germany and Italy and was antagonistic towards the United States and Britain. Shiratori was a chauvinist, and in his early career he collaborated with fascist Ōkawa to support the invasion of China; join the Axis Powers; and confront Britain, the United States, and the Soviet Union. During the Mukden Incident in 1931, he was the Director of the Information Bureau under the Foreign Ministry. He took pains to slander China in his propaganda; subsequently, with the support of the Ministry of War, he insisted that Japan withdraw from the League of Nations. He also promoted the ideologies of 'Japanese Monroe Doctrine for Asia' and 'Japanese Imperial Way'. While serving as the Ambassador to Italy and as an adviser to Foreign Minister Matsuoka, he tried his best to promote an anti-communist alliance between Nazi Germany, Italy and Japan, without which the 'New World Order' could not be established. The Japanese media befittingly called Matsuoka, Ōshima and Shiratori 'the Three Men for Axis Diplomacy'.

Teiichi Suzuki (59 years old): Suzuki graduated from the Imperial Japanese Army Academy and the Army War College. He served in the General Staff Office as its staff member and media monitor.

Suzuki held the following posts from 1928 to 1945: staff member of the Military Affairs Bureau of the War Ministry (1931); official of the Investigation Bureau of the Cabinet (1935); Commander of the 14th Regiment (1936); Chief of the Political Affairs Division of the China Affairs Board (December 1938–April 1941); acting President of the China Affairs Board (1940); President of the Cabinet Planning Board and Minister without Portfolio in the Konoe cabinet and the Tōjō cabinet (April 1941–October 1943)[36]; member of the Cabinet Advisory Council (November 1943–September 1944); and Director of the Imperial Rule Assistance Association (1944).

---

[36] The supposed 'minister without portfolio' was a minister who was not in charge of any of the government ministries; he was also called as the 'Minister of State without Portfolio' or just 'Minister of State'. He would attend all cabinet meetings and decision-making processes like one of the cabinet members. In terms of political status, he was on par with cabinet heads of other ministries.

Suzuki was an 'upcoming fascist' among the warlords. In terms of qualification and experience, he was very inferior to Araki, Minami, Hata, Matsui and Koiso; he could not be compared to even Tōjō, Itagaki, Umezu or Doihara. He was approximately of the same status as Mutō and Satō among the military men. However, Suzuki advanced more quickly and reached a higher position than the latter two because of his political acumen. During the Mukden Incident in 1931, he was merely a staff member in the General Staff Office. He won acclaim from the authorities in the Ministry of War by staunchly supporting Japan's withdrawal from the League of Nations. Suzuki further distinguished himself after Japan's full-scale invasion of China in 1937. He served in the China Affairs Board (the main organization which planned aggression against China) and became its Acting President.[37] When the Pacific War took place in 1941, he was President of the Cabinet Planning Board and a Minister without Portfolio in the Konoe cabinet and the Tōjō cabinet. He made outstanding contributions to the aggressive war by mobilizing the nation's human and financial resources and strengthening the production of military supplies. By that time, Suzuki had become an important member of the Japanese militaristic clique.

Shigenori Tōgō (65 years old): Tōgō was a graduate of the Literature Department of Tokyo Imperial University. He was admitted into the Ministry of Foreign Affairs on passing the examination for diplomats in his fifth attempt. Despite his multiple failed attempts, he was an astute diplomat who successively served as the Chief of the First Section of the European and American Affairs Bureau in Foreign Ministry, First Secretary of the Japanese embassy in the United States, Counsellor at the Japanese embassy in Germany, and Director of the European and American Affairs Bureau of the Foreign Ministry.

Tōgō held the following posts from 1928 to 1945: Ambassador to Germany (October 1937); Ambassador to the Soviet Union (October 1938); Minister of Foreign Affairs and concurrently, Minister of Colonial Affairs in the Tōjō cabinet (October 1941–March 1942); and Minister

---

[37] The name 'Ko-A-In' (phonetic translation) literally meant 'Asia Development Board', but was referred to as the 'China Affairs Board' in the English version of the Tribunal's records. This was an acceptable alternative because, although this institution apparently aimed at Asia's development, it was actually a specialized agency under the Japanese government. The organization was established to plan the invasion of China, especially the economic aggression against China, that is, the exploitation of China's resources to support Japan's 'Greater East Asia War'.

of Foreign Affairs and concurrently, Minister of Greater East Asia in the Suzuki cabinet (April 1945).

Compared to other diplomats, Tōgō was simple and unassuming. While serving as an Ambassador to the Soviet Union, he calmly handled the 'Nomonhan Incident' and the fishery problems between Japan and the Soviet Union. However, he bore joint responsibility for the Pacific War since it was waged during his term as the Foreign Minister in the Tōjō cabinet; he was also responsible for the cabinet's decision to continue and intensify aggression against China. At a crucial moment, when the Japanese navy was about to attack Pearl Harbor, Tōgō withheld the telegram, a final extension of peace from President Roosevelt to Japanese Emperor, thus eliminating the possibility of reconciliation. Therefore, apart from his official liability, Tōgō's endorsement of the war made him one of its major conspirators. His subsequent actions could never fully acquit him of his responsibility for the war. He had indignantly resigned from office and following a disagreement with Tōjō, long disappeared from the political arena. On the eve of Japan's breakdown, as the Foreign Minister in the Suzuki cabinet, he had sent a proposal of peace and appealed to the Soviet Union for mediation.

Tōgō's wife was German. She attended every one of the 818 open sessions which lasted for about two years. She would sit on a particular seat on the second floor and listen to the trial proceedings with headphones. She would often glance at her husband and smile bitterly when their eyes met. People spoke approvingly of these warm exchanges.

Hedeki Tōjō (former Prime Minister, 63 years old): Tōjō was a graduate of the Imperial Japanese Army Academy and the Army War College; he served for many years in the Ministry of War, the Army General Staff Office and the Kwantung Army. He was the most radical leader of the fascist clique for the Japanese expansion and aggression.

Tōjō held the following posts from 1928 to 1945: Chief of the First Section of the General Staff Office (1931–1932); Chief of the Investigation Section of the Army Communications School (1932); Commander of the Military Police of the Kwantung Army (1935); Chief of Staff of the Kwantung Army (1937); Vice Minister of War in the Konoe cabinet (May to December 1938); Director General of Army Aviation (1938–1939); Minister of War in the Konoe cabinet (July 1940–December 1941); and Prime Minister and concurrently, Minister of War (2 December 1941–July 1944), during which period he was intermittently, Home Minister,

Minister of Munitions and Chief of General Staff. Tōjō was promoted to a full General in October 1940.

Tōjō was the most noted Japanese major war criminal among the 28 defendants in the Tokyo Tribunal. Western press often referred to the Tokyo Trial as 'the trial of Tōjō and 27 other Japanese major war criminals'. Tōjō was a participator in the aggressive attacks against China and the chief instigator of the Pacific War. During Tōjō's tenure, Japan's attack on Pearl Harbor, declaration of war on the United States, and spates of violence and brutalities against the United States, Britain, France, the Netherlands, Australia and other Western countries took place. He was considered as the most notorious leader of the Japanese militaristic clique. Tōjō was obviously the defendant most despised by the Western countries. In terms of qualifications and experience, he was less than Araki and Minami, and even less than Hata, Koiso and Matsui. However, Tōjō was more aggressive and audacious than them and bravely executed conspiracies of aggression. Tōjō was known as 'razor' among his colleagues for his razor-sharp mind and physical agility which were superior to most people. When the Pacific onslaught failed and Japan was about to collapse, he was forced to relinquish power and withdraw from politics, and also earn the wrath of the Japanese people. Soon after Japan's surrender and right before being arrested, he orchestrated a suicide attempt which provoked much ridicule.

He was one of the seven criminal defendants sentenced to death by the Tokyo Tribunal, and also one of the two former Prime Ministers sentenced to death, the other one being Kōki Hirota.

Yoshijirō Umezu (65 years old): After graduating from the Imperial Japanese Army Academy and the Army War College, Umezu was sent to Europe for observing and investigating military affairs in various countries. He returned to Japan to serve as a section chief in the Military Affairs Bureau of the War Ministry and Commander of the 1st Army.

Umezu held the following posts from 1928 to 1945: Chief of the General Affairs Department of the War Ministry (1931); Commander of the China Garrison Army (1934–1936); Vice Minister of War in the Hirota cabinet, the Hayashi cabinet and the Konoe cabinet (March 1936–May 1938); Commander of the Kwantung Army and 'Ambassador' to Manchukuo (1939–1944) and Chief of General Staff (July 1944–1945 until Japan's surrender). Umezu was promoted as a full General in 1940.

Umezu was an efficient and respected Japanese fascist officer. He was often the backbone of Japan's various aggressive plots and was nicknamed as the 'Treasure of Army' by the Japanese. In his term as the Commander of the China Garrison Army he tried his best to collude with the North China military and popularize 'North China autonomy'. This he did with the intention to realize Japan's aggressive policy of annexing more of China's territory after the occupation of Northeast China. He tried to isolate North China from the rest of China and establish in it a puppet regime controlled by Japan. The notorious Ho-Umezu Agreement signed in 1935 was a consequence of Umezu's coercion upon the then weak Chinese government.[38] In 1938, Umezu led the Japanese army to fight in North China and commit atrocities against the Chinese people. During his five years as the Commander of the Kwantung Army and the 'Ambassador' to Manchukuo, when Japanese aggression was at its peak, Umezu devised all ways to plunder Northeast China and fleece its people to promote Japan's sinister plans. For these reasons, the notoriety of Umezu was known to every household in China.

When Umezu served in his last, but most important office, as Chief of the General Staff, Japan was on the brink of surrender. Within a year, Japan formally announced its defeat. At the surrender ceremony, on board the American warship USS Missouri, Umezu was one of the two representatives of Japan. He signed the Instrument of Surrender on behalf of the Imperial General Headquarters, whereas the other representative, Mamoru Shigemitsu, signed on behalf of the Emperor and the Japanese government.

The GHQ felt that Umezu and Shigemitsu ought to be given special treatment as they were Japanese representatives who had officially participated in the ceremony of Japan's surrender. Therefore, their arrests were delayed until the eve of the prosecution, unlike those of the other Class-A war criminals who were detained several months before the Tribunal opened.

---

[38] The 'Ho-Umezu Agreement' was a typical document of Japan's harsh interference with China's internal affairs and violation of China's sovereignty. It stipulated that the Chinese central government's army must withdraw from Hebei Province; the Hebei provincial head office of Kuomintang must be closed and prohibit all activities; and all anti-Japanese behaviour must be prohibited in Hebei Province. This agreement was solely signed for the 'Hebei Incident', but there were numerous such 'incidents' instigated by the Japanese in North China. This agreement portrayed the extent to which Japan had violated China's sovereignty, and the Chinese government had yielded to Japan's despotic power.

This completes the brief biographies of the 28 Japanese Class-A war criminals tried before the Tokyo Tribunal. As mentioned earlier, there were two defendants (Matsuoka and Nagano) who died of illness during the course of the trial, and another (Ōkawa) who was suspended from trial because of his mental disorder. Therefore, although the Tribunal commenced with 28 defendants in May 1946, only 25 of them were sentenced in November 1948.

3.4 Eleven Countries' Indictment Against Japanese Major War Criminals

3.4.1 Presentation and Acceptance of the Indictment

'Indictment' is the first and most important step taken by any party (the plaintiff or prosecution) for the filing of a case. A case is registered and the trial proceedings commence only after the indictment is presented to the court and accepted by it.

There are two ways of interpreting the nature of indictment in criminal cases in jurisprudence as well as in judicial practice. One school considers the indictment as part of the trial proceedings because it comes into force only after court's approval of it. In practice, the Anglo-American courts usually undergo a preliminary trial by the grand jury or a 'pre-trial' to decide whether the prosecution is sufficiently tenable, and then the court decides whether to accept the case in accordance with the findings of the grand jury.[39] Therefore, the acceptance of the case is usually considered as the court's approval of the indictment, and a part of the trial proceedings. Another thought process is that, the court need not conduct a preliminary examination or pre-trial procedure for the mere validation of a case within its jurisdiction. Accordingly, an indictment is considered as the

---

[39] 'Grand jury' is an ancient system in the common law tradition. Unlike the ordinary jury (or 'petit jury'), which is usually composed of 12 citizens, it has 12–24 jurors and is therefore called 'grand jury'. In some criminal cases, the court must convene a grand jury composed of impartial local citizens for a 'pre-trial' before commencing a substantive trial. In the pre-trial, the grand jury has the right to accept the evidence and hear statements of the witnesses and of both parties, and finally decides whether there is considerable evidence to comprise a case for trial. The grand jury's opinion and decision are submitted to the court by its foreman in the form of a presentment. The court then decides accordingly whether or not to try the case. This system is still largely maintained in the common law system, with only slight differences in the scope, authority and organization of the grand jury due to subsequent legislation in different countries.

act of one party (the plaintiff or prosecution) alone, and apart from the court proceedings. The courts under the civil law system usually do not have a grand jury or pre-trial procedure, and the indictment of a party is unquestioningly accepted. Moreover, the interrogation, investigation and statement-taking, were certainly not a part of the court procedures, but comprised the preparatory work done by the prosecution.

There were varied opinions on the nature of the indictment filed by the IPS to the Tokyo Tribunal. For example, Soviet jurists Raginsky (М. Ю. Рагинский) and Rozenblit (С. Я. Розенблит) firmly believed that it was the act of the Tribunal that had approved it rather than of any party (the prosecution).[40]

Raginsky and Rozenblit's opinion was wrong because it runs contrary to the facts. The process of the Tribunal's acceptance of the Indictment was as follows[41]:

At 4 p.m. on 29 April 1946, all eleven judges of the Tokyo Tribunal gathered in the judges' conference room with Walbridge, the General Secretary, and Dell, the Clerk who was in charge of document registration.

Chief Prosecutor Keenan then joined the conference. He sat down and said, 'I have the original Indictment signed by the chief of counsel and each of the Allied prosecutors, or his proxy, which Indictment I will leave with Dell, the Clerk.'

President Webb asked, 'You propose to file that?'

Keenan answered, 'Yes, that is being forwarded.'

The President said, 'That is the original. It will be read, if required, at the arraignment.'

When Keenan was about to leave after the above conversation, the President said to Keenan, 'We direct you to serve copies of the Indictment and the Charter on each of the accused forthwith.' The President's direction to the Chief Prosecutor was based on the Tokyo Charter. Item (a) of Article 9 provided: 'Each accused shall be furnished, in adequate time for defence, a copy of the indictment, including any amendment, and of this Charter, in a language understood by the accused.'

---

[40] М. Ю. Рагинский and С. Я. Розенблит, *International Trial of the Japanese Major War Criminals* (Chinese Translation), World Affairs Press, pp. 91–92.

[41] *Transcripts of Proceedings and Documents of the International Military Tribunal for the Far East* (29 April 1946), pp. 116–119.

Chief Prosecutor Keenan understood and nodded in agreement and then left the conference room. The President immediately declared the meeting closed.

The entire process of the Indictment submission took less than ten minutes. The judges had not read the Indictment beforehand, let alone investigate and discuss it. How could such a simple procedure be described as the 'approval' of the Indictment by the Tribunal? Theoretically, any act of the Tribunal would have to go through a collective discussion at the judges' conference where a resolution was made. The Tribunal did not take such steps at all for the Indictment of the IPS. On the contrary, it simply accepted the Indictment and ordered the Clerk to register and file it.

It can be inferred from the above proceedings that the Tribunal's 'approval' of the Indictment presented by the IPS, as posited by Raginsky and Rozenblit, is not only baseless, but opposes facts.

From the very beginning, the Tribunal had been dissatisfied with the precision and logical rigour of the Indictment. For example, the Indictment categorized crimes of the defendants into 55 counts, but it was reduced to ten in the Judgement rendered after the court hearings. This omission of crimes by the Tribunal will be elaborated later. It is now mentioned only to prove the proposition that the Indictment had not been approved by the Tribunal.

3.4.2 Format and Preamble of the Indictment

The Indictment from the IPS to the Tribunal was titled 'INTERNATIONAL MILITARY TRIBUNAL FOR THE FAR EAST, INDICTMENT No. 1'. The presence of the word 'No. 1' indicated that the IPS had envisaged further indictments after the trial of the 28 war criminals accused in Indictment No. 1. However, as mentioned earlier, there were no more indictments after the first, due to the United States' clear policy to shield Japanese war criminals.

The opening words of the Indictment were:

THE UNITED STATES OF AMERICA, THE REPUBLIC OF CHINA, THE UNITED KINGDOM OF GREAT BRITAIN AND NORTHERN IRELAND, THE UNION OF SOVIET SOCIALIST REPUBLICS, THE COMMONWEALTH OF AUSTRALIA, CANADA, THE REPUBLIC OF FRANCE, THE KINGDOM OF THE NETHERLANDS, NEW

ZEALAND, INDIA, AND THE COMMONWEALTH OF THE PHILIPPINES

AGAINST

ARAKI, Sadao... [Note: A list of 28 defendants, in alphabetical order of their surnames in English is omitted here.]

From the above words, it can be inferred that the plaintiffs who instituted the prosecution were undoubtedly the eleven major Allied Powers who fought against Japan, and not the IPS or the GHQ. However, according to the provisions of the Tokyo Charter, it was the Chief Prosecutor who had the responsibility to prosecute the defendants.[42] At first glance, these two standpoints seem contradictory. If the eleven countries were listed as the plaintiffs, the responsibility of prosecution ought not to be devolved upon the Chief Prosecutor; conversely, if the Chief Prosecutor was responsible for the prosecution, the Indictment ought not to list the eleven countries as the plaintiffs. This is a valid argument; a reasonable explanation is that, given the unprecedented importance of the case, the prosecution had to be conducted in the name of the eleven countries, and the responsibility of the Chief Prosecutor for the prosecution was only obligatory. The Chief Prosecutor had to assume the role of a head lawyer acting on behalf of the plaintiffs in the trial, but the actual plaintiffs were the eleven Allied Powers. It is perhaps for this reason that the Tribunal referred to the Chief Prosecutor as 'the Chief of Counsel of the prosecution', or 'the Chief Counsel for the prosecution'.

The Tokyo Charter's stipulation for the contents of the Indictment is simple and clear: 'The indictment shall consist of a plain, concise and adequate statement of each offense charged.'[43]

Despite some serious drawbacks, the Indictment filed to the Tokyo Tribunal by the IPS on behalf of the 11 countries, mostly complied with the Charter and was satisfactory.

The Indictment charged the defendants for a total of 55 counts (alleged crimes). Before presenting those counts sequentially, the 'Preamble' gave a brief account of the political significance and nature of the

---

[42] See *Charter of the International Military Tribunal for the Far East*, Article 8(a).
[43] See *Charter of the International Military Tribunal for the Far East*, Article 9(a).

criminal activities committed by the Japanese imperialist ruling group. The Preamble was as follows:

> In the years hereinafter referred to in this Indictment, the internal and foreign policies of Japan were dominated and directed by a criminal militaristic clique and such policies were the cause of serious world troubles, aggressive wars, and great damage to the interests of peace-loving peoples, as well as the interests of the Japanese people themselves. The mind of the Japanese people was systematically poisoned with harmful ideas of the alleged racial superiority of Japan over other peoples of Asia and even of the whole world. Such parliamentary institutions as existed in Japan were used as implements for widespread aggression, and a system similar to those then established by Hitler and the Nazi party in Germany and by the Fascist party in Italy was introduced. The economic and financial resources of Japan were to a large extent mobilized for war aims, to the detriment of the welfare of the Japanese people.
>
> A conspiracy between the defendants, joined in by the rulers of other aggressive countries, namely Nazi Germany and Fascist Italy, was entered into. The main objects of this conspiracy was to secure the domination and exploitation by the aggressive States of the rest of the world, and to this end to commit, or encourage the commission of crimes against peace, war crimes, and crimes against humanity as defined in the Charter of this Tribunal, thus threatening and injuring the basic principles of liberty and respect for the human personality.
>
> In the promotion and accomplishment of that scheme, these defendants, taking advantage of their power and their official positions and their own personal prestige and influence, intended to and did plan, prepare, initiate or wage aggressive war against the United States of America, the Republic of China, the United Kingdom of Great Britain and Northern Ireland, the Union of Soviet Socialist Republics, the Commonwealth of Australia, Canada, the Republic of France, the Kingdom of the Netherlands, New Zealand, India, the Commonwealth of the Philippines, and other peaceful nations, in violation of international law, as well as in violation of sacred treaty commitments, obligations and assurances; such plan contemplated and carried out the violation of recognized customs and conventions of war by murdering, maiming and ill-treating prisoners of war, civilian internees, and persons on the high seas, denying them adequate food, shelter, clothing, medical care or other appropriate attention, forcing them to labour under inhumane conditions, and subjecting them to indignities; exploit to Japan's benefit the manpower and economic

resources of the vanquished nations, plundering public and private property, wantonly destroying cities, towns and villages beyond any justification of military necessity; perpetrate mass murder, rape, pillage, brigandage, torture, and other barbaric cruelties upon the helpless civilian population of the over-run countries; increase the influence and control of the military and naval groups over Japanese government officials and agencies; psychologically prepare Japanese public opinion for aggressive warfare by establishing so-called Assistance Societies, teaching nationalistic policies of expansion, disseminating war propaganda, and exercising strict control over the press and radio; set up 'puppet' governments in conquered countries; conclude military alliances with Germany and Italy to enhance by military might Japan's programme of expansion.

The last paragraph of the Preamble of the Indictment states:

Therefore, the above-named Nations by their undersigned representatives, duly appointed to represent their respective Governments in the investigation of the charges against and the prosecution of the Major War Criminals, pursuant to the Potsdam Declaration of the 20 July 1945, and the Instrument of Surrender of the 2 September 1945, and the Charter of the Tribunal, hereby accuse as guilty, in the respects hereinafter set forth, of Crimes against Peace, War Crimes, and Crimes against Humanity, and of Common Plans or Conspiracies to commit those Crimes, all as defined in the Charter of the Tribunal, and accordingly name as Defendants in this cause and as indicated on the Counts hereinafter set out in which their names, respectively appear, all the above-named individuals.

3.4.3 *Fifty-Five Counts Charged Against the Defendants*

The Indictment presents a total of 55 counts of the charges against the defendants following the Preamble, some of which are against all the defendants, others against a section of them; this is the main part of the Indictment. The 55 counts are divided into three groups; the first was 'Crimes against Peace (i.e. the Crime of Aggression)', the second, 'Murder', and the third, 'Other Conventional War Crimes and Crimes against Humanity'. The content of each group is described below:

3.4.3.1 Group One: Crimes Against Peace (Counts 1–36)
Group One was the longest group of charges in the Indictment, and listed 36 counts which covered the various types of Crimes against Peace:

COUNT 1. All the Defendants together with divers other persons, between the 1st January, 1928 and the 2nd September, 1945, participated as leaders, organizers, instigators, or accomplices in the formulation or execution of a common plan or conspiracy, and are responsible for all acts performed by themselves or by any person in execution of such plan.

The object of such plan or conspiracy was that Japan should secure the military, naval, political and economic domination of East Asia and of the Pacific and Indian Oceans, and of all countries and islands therein and bordering thereon and for that purpose should alone or in combination with other countries having similar objects, or who could be induced or coerced to join therein, wage declared or undeclared war or wars of aggression, and war or wars in violation of international law, treaties, agreements and assurances, against any country or countries which might oppose that purpose. [Note: References to the Appendices are hereby omitted; the same applies to the following Counts 2–36.]

COUNT 2. All the Defendants together with divers other persons, between…, participated as… in execution of such plan.

The object of such plan or conspiracy was that Japan should secure the military, naval, political and economic domination of the provinces of Liaoning, Kirin, Heilungkiang and Jehol, being parts of the Republic of China, either directly or by establishing a separate state under the control of Japan, and for that purpose should wage declared or undeclared war or wars of aggression, and war or wars… against the Republic of China. [Note: '…' represents the same wording as that in Count 1, which is hereby omitted. The same applies to the following Counts 3–5.]

COUNT 3. All the Defendants together with divers other persons, between…, participated as… in execution of such plan.

The object of such plan or conspiracy was that Japan should secure the military, naval, political and economic domination of the Republic of China, either directly or by establishing a separate state under the control of Japan, and for that purpose should wage declared or undeclared war or wars of aggression, and war or wars… against the Republic of China.

COUNT 4. All the Defendants together with divers other persons, between…, participated as… in execution of such plan.

The object of such plan or conspiracy was that Japan should secure the military, naval, political and economic domination of East Asia and of the Pacific and Indian Oceans, and of all countries and islands therein or bordering thereon, and for that purpose should wage declared or undeclared war or wars of aggression, and war or wars... against the United States of America, the British Commonwealth of Nations (which expression wherever used in the Indictment includes the United Kingdom of Great Britain and Northern Ireland, the Commonwealth of Australia, Canada, New Zealand, South Africa, India, Burma, the Malay States and all other parts of the British Empire not separately represented in the League of Nations), the Republic of France, the Kingdom of the Netherlands, the Republic of China, the Republic of Portugal, the Kingdom of Thailand, the Commonwealth of the Philippines, and the Union of Soviet Socialist Republics, or such of them as might oppose that purpose.

COUNT 5. All the Defendants together with divers other persons, between..., participated as... in execution of such plan.

The object of such plan or conspiracy was that Germany, Italy and Japan should secure the military, navel, political and economic domination of the whole world, each having special domination in its own share, the sphere of Japan covering East Asia, the Pacific and Indian Oceans and all countries and islands therein or bordering thereon, and for that purpose should mutually assist one another to wage declared or undeclared war or wars of aggression, and war or wars... against any countries which might oppose that purpose, and particularly against the United States of America, the British Commonwealth of Nations, the Republic of France, the Kingdom of the Netherlands, the Republic of China, the Republic of Portugal, the Kingdom of Thailand, the Commonwealth of the Philippines and the Union of Soviet Socialist Republics.

The above five counts (1–5) are accusations against all the defendants for the <u>common plan or conspiracy</u> to wage wars of aggression.

COUNT 6. All the Defendants between the 1st January, 1928 and the 2nd September, 1945, planned and prepared a war of aggression and a war in violation of international law, treaties, agreements and assurances, against the Republic of China.

COUNT 7. All the Defendants between…, planned and prepared a war of aggression and a war…, against the United States of America. [Note: '…' represents the same wording as that in Count 6, which is hereby omitted. The same applies to the following Counts 8–17.]
COUNT 8. All the Defendants between…, planned and prepared a war of aggression and a war…, against the United Kingdom of Great Britain and Northern Ireland and all parts of the British Commonwealth of Nations not the subject of separate counts in this Indictment.
COUNT 9. All the Defendants between…, planned and prepared a war of aggression and a war…, against the Commonwealth of Australia.
COUNT 10. All the Defendants between…, planned and prepared a war of aggression and a war…, against New Zealand.
COUNT 11. All the Defendants between…, planned and prepared a war of aggression and a war…, against Canada.
COUNT 12. All the Defendants between…, planned and prepared a war of aggression and a war…, against India.
COUNT 13. All the Defendants between…, planned and prepared a war of aggression and a war…, against the Commonwealth of the Philippines.
COUNT 14. All the Defendants between…, planned and prepared a war of aggression and a war…, against the Kingdom of the Netherlands.
COUNT 15. All the Defendants between…, planned and prepared a war of aggression and a war…, against the Republic of France.
COUNT 16. All the Defendants between…, planned and prepared a war of aggression and a war…, against the Kingdom of Thailand.
COUNT 17. All the Defendants between…, planned and prepared a war of aggression and a war…, against the Union of Soviet Socialist Republics.

The above twelve counts (6–17) are accusations against all the defendants for the planning and preparation of aggressive wars.

COUNT 18. The Defendants ARAKI, DOHIHARA, HASHIMOTO, HIRANUMA, ITAGAKI, KOISO, MINAMI, OKAWA, SHIGEMITSU, TOJO and UMEZU, on or about the

18th September, 1931, initiated a war of aggression and a war in violation of international law, treaties, agreements and assurances, against the Republic of China. [Note: 'the Republic of China' refers to the four Northeast Provinces of Liaoning, Kirin, Heilungkiang and Jehol.]

COUNT 19. The Defendants ARAKI, DOHIHARA, HASHIMOTO, HATA, HIRANUMA, HIROTA, HOSHINO, ITAGAKI, KAYA, KIDO, MATSUI, MUTO, SUZUKI, TOJO and UMEZU, on or about the 7th July, 1937, initiated a war of aggression and a war..., against the Republic of China. [Note: 'the Republic of China' refers to the whole of China. '...' represents the same wording as that in Count 18, which is hereby omitted. The same applies to the following Counts 20–26.]

COUNT 20. The Defendants DOHIHARA, HIRANUMA, HIROTA, HOSHINO, KAYA, KIDO, KIMURA, MUTO, NAGANO, OKA, OSHIMA, SATO, SHIMADA, SUZUKI, TOGO and TOJO, on or about the 7th December, 1941, initiated a war of aggression and a war..., against the United States of America.

COUNT 21. The same Defendants as in Count 20, on or about the 7th December, 1941, initiated a war of aggression and a war..., against the Commonwealth of the Philippines.

COUNT 22. The same Defendants as in Count 20, on or about the 7th December, 1941, initiated a war of aggression and a war..., against the British Commonwealth of Nations.

COUNT 23. The Defendants ARAKI, DOHIHARA, HIRANUMA, HIROTA, HOSHINO, ITAGAKI, KIDO, MATSUOKA, MUTO, NAGANO, SHIGEMITSU and TOJO, on or about the 22nd September, 1940, initiated a war of aggression and a war..., against the Republic of France.

COUNT 24. The same Defendants as in Count 20, on or about the 7th December, 1941, initiated a war of aggression and a war..., against the Kingdom of Thailand.

COUNT 25. The Defendants ARAKI, DOHIHARA, HATA, HIRANUMA, HIROTA, HOSHINO, ITAGAKI, KIDO, MATSUOKA, MATSUI, SHIGEMITSU, SUZUKI and TOGO, during July and August, 1938, initiated a war of aggression and a war..., by attacking the Union of Soviet Socialist Republics in the area of Lake Khasan.

COUNT 26. The Defendants ARAKI, DOHIHARA, HATA, HIRANUMA, ITAGAKI, KIDO, KOISO, MATSUI, MATSUOKA, MUTO, SUZUKI, TOGO, TOJO and UMEZU, during the summer of 1939, initiated a war of aggression and a war..., by attacking the territory of the Mongolian People's Republic in the area of the Khalkhin-Gol River.

The above nine counts (18–26) are accusations against certain defendants for the initiation of aggressive wars.

COUNT 27. All the Defendants between the 18th September, 1931 and the 2nd September, 1945, waged a war of aggression and a war in violation of international law, treaties, agreements and assurances, against the Republic of China.[44]
COUNT 28. All the Defendants between the 7th July, 1937 and the 2nd September, 1945, waged a war of aggression and a war..., against the Republic of China.[45] [Note: '...' represents the same wording as that in Count 27, which is hereby omitted. The same applies to the following Counts 29–36.]
COUNT 29. All the Defendants between the 7th December, 1941 and the 2nd September, 1945, waged a war of aggression and a war..., against the United States of America.
COUNT 30. All the Defendants between the 7th December, 1941 and the 2nd September, 1945, waged a war of aggression and a war..., against the Commonwealth of the Philippines.

---

[44] From this Count 27 to Count 36, the accusation is that the defendants 'waged' aggressive wars against various Allied countries. The previous counts (from Count 1 to Count 26) accuse that they 'co-planned or conspired' to wage such wars, and 'planned and prepared' and 'initiated' such wars. The logic of such a narrow classification will be discussed in Sect. 3.5 of this chapter.

[45] The wording of Count 28 was almost the same as the preceding Count 27, except that the period of crime mentioned in Count 27 was from 18 September 1931 (the 'Mukden Incident') to 2 September 1945 (Japan's surrender), whereas in Count 28 it was from 7 July 1937 (the 'Marco Polo Bridge Incident') to 2 September 1945. Logically, the period for Count 28 was included in Count 27; therefore, it was unnecessary to classify it as a separate count. This is an evidence of the superfluous wording and lack of logical rigour of the Indictment.

COUNT 31. All the Defendants between the 7th December, 1941 and the 2nd September, 1945, waged a war of aggression and a war..., against the British Commonwealth of Nations.
COUNT 32. All the Defendants between the 7th December, 1941 and the 2nd September, 1945, waged a war of aggression and a war..., against the Kingdom of the Netherlands.
COUNT 33. The Defendants ARAKI, DOHIHARA, HIRANUMA, HIROTA, HOSHINO, ITAGAKI, KIDO, MATSUOKA, MUTO, NAGANO, SHIGEMITSU and TOJO, on and after the 22nd September, 1940, waged a war of aggression and a war..., against the Republic of France.
COUNT 34. All the Defendants between the 7th December, 1941 and the 2nd September, 1945, waged a war of aggression and a war..., against the Kingdom of Thailand.
COUNT 35. The same Defendants as in Count 25, during the summer of 1938, waged a war of aggression and a war..., against the Union of Soviet Socialist Republics.
COUNT 36. The same Defendants as in Count 26, during the summer of 1939, waged a war of aggression..., against the Mongolian People's Republic and the Union of Soviet Socialist Republics.[46]

The above ten counts (27–36) are accusations against all or part of the defendants for the <u>waging</u> of aggressive wars. Along with the accusations of conspiracy (5 counts), planning and preparation of aggressive wars (12 counts) and initiation of aggressive wars (9 counts), Group One 'Crimes against Peace' in the Indictment thus comprises these 36 counts.

3.4.3.2 Group Two: Murder (Counts 37–52)

Murder is generally classified as a conventional war crime, but is treated exclusively in this Indictment, probably with the intention to attract the

---

[46] The lack of logical rigour in the Indictment is also evident in Count 36. The 'Mongolian People's Republic' was originally a part of China's territory. Although in June 1924, it unilaterally declared independence with the aid of the Soviet Union, China did not grant it formal recognition until after its referendum in 1946. Thus, in actuality, the invasion of Mongolia in 1939 was not a war of aggression against 'Mongolian People's Republic'. It was said that the Chinese associate prosecutor alerted the Chief Prosecutor about the ambiguity concerning the name, but Keenan considered it a matter of little importance and staunchly refused to revise the Indictment.

Tribunal's special attention. This group contains 16 counts as described below:

COUNT 37. The Defendants DOHIHARA, HIRANUMA, HIROTA, HOSHINO, KAYA, KIDO, KIMURA, MUTO, NAGANO, OKA, OSHIMA, SATO, SHIMADA, SUZUKI, TOGO and TOJO, together with divers other persons between the 1st June, 1940 and the 8th December, 1941, participated as leaders, organizers, instigators, or accomplices in the formulation or execution of a common plan or conspiracy, and are responsible for all acts performed by themselves or by any person in execution of such plan.

The object of such plan or conspiracy was unlawfully to kill and murder the persons described below, by initiating unlawful hostilities against the United States of America, the Commonwealth of the Philippines, the British Commonwealth of Nations, the Kingdom of the Netherlands and the Kingdom of Thailand, and unlawfully ordering, causing and permitting the armed forces of Japan to attack the territory, ships and airplanes of the said nations or some of them at times when Japan would be at peace with the said nations.

The persons intended to be killed and murdered were all such persons, both members of the armed forces of the said nations and civilians, as might happen to be in the places at the times of such attacks.

The said hostilities and attacks were unlawful because they were breaches of Treaty Article 5 in Appendix B,[47] and the accused and the said armed forces of Japan could not therefore, acquire the rights of lawful belligerents.

The accused and each of them intended that such hostilities should be initiated in breach of such Treaty Article, or were reckless whether such Treaty Article would be violated or not.

COUNT 38. The Defendants DOHIHARA, HIRANUMA, HIROTA, HOSHINO, KAYA, KIDO, KIMURA, MATSUOKA, MUTO, NAGANO, OKA, OSHIMA, SATO, SHIMADA,

---

[47] It refers to Article 1 of the Hague Convention III signed on 18 October 1907, concerning the commencement of war.

SUZUKI, TOGO and TOJO, together with divers other persons between..., participated as... in execution of such plan.

The object of such plan or conspiracy was unlawfully to kill and murder... to attack the territory, ships and airplanes of the said nations or some of them.

The persons intended to be killed and murdered... in the places at the times of such attacks.

The said hostilities and attacks were unlawful because they were breaches of Treaty Articles 6, 7, 19, 33, 34 and 36 in Appendix B,[48] and the accused and... the rights of lawful belligerents.

The accused and... in breach of such Treaty Articles, or were reckless whether such Treaty Articles or any of them would be violated or not.[49] [Note: '...' represents the same wording as that in Count 37, which is hereby omitted.]

COUNT 39. The same Defendants as in Count 38, under the circumstances alleged in Counts 37 and 38, by ordering, causing and permitting the armed forces of Japan to attack the territory, ships and airplanes of the United States of America, with which nation Japan was then at peace, at Pearl Harbor, Territory of Hawaii, on the 7th December, 1941, at about 0755 hours (Pearl Harbor time), unlawfully killed and murdered Admiral Kidd and about 4000 other members of the naval and military forces of the United States of America and certain civilians whose names and number are at present unknown.

COUNT 40. The same Defendants as in Count 38, under the circumstances alleged in Counts 37 and 38, by ordering, causing and permitting the armed forces of Japan to attack the territory

---

[48] It refers to the Exchange of Notes between the United States and Japan signed on 30 November 1908 declaring their policy in the Far East (Articles 2 and 3); the 'Four-Power Treaty' between Britain, France, Japan and the United States relating to their Insular Possessions and Insular Dominions in the Pacific Ocean signed on 13 December 1921 (Article 1); the 'Pact of Paris', or the 'Kellogg-Briand Pact', signed on 27 August 1928 by 15 countries and subsequently adhered to by most (48) other countries (Articles 1 and 2); and the Treaty between Thailand and Japan signed 12 June 1940 (Article 1).

[49] The essence of Count 38 is similar to the preceding Count 37, with only the following differences: they refer to different treaties that were violated by the defendants; Count 38 has an additional defendant Matsuoka; and Count 38 does not contain the phrase 'at times when Japan would be at peace with the said nations' at the end of the second paragraph.

and airplanes of the British Commonwealth of Nations, with which nations Japan was then at peace, at Kota Bahru, Kelantan, on the 8th December, 1941, at about 0025 hours (Singapore time), unlawfully killed and murdered certain members of the armed force of the British Commonwealth of Nations whose names and number are at present unknown.

COUNT 41. The same Defendants as in Count 38, under the circumstances alleged in Counts 37 and 38, by ordering, causing and permitting the armed forces of Japan to attack the territory, ships and airplanes of the British Commonwealth of Nations, with which nations Japan was then at peace, at Hong Kong, on the 8th December, 1941, at about 0800 hours (Hong Kong time), unlawfully killed and murdered certain members of the armed forces of the British Commonwealth of Nations, whose names and number are at present unknown.

COUNT 42. The same Defendants as in Count 38, under the circumstances alleged in Counts 37 and 38, by ordering, causing and permitting the armed forces of Japan to attach H. M. S. PETREL, a ship of the British Commonwealth of Nations, with which nations Japan was then at peace, at Shanghai on the 8th December, 1941, at about 0300 hours (Shanghai time), unlawfully killed and murdered three members of the naval forces of the British Commonwealth of Nations, whose names are at present unknown.

COUNT 43. The same Defendants as in Count 38, under the circumstances alleged in Counts 37 and 38, by ordering, causing and permitting the armed forces of Japan to attack the territory of the Commonwealth of the Philippines, with which nation Japan was then at peace, at Davao, on the 8th December, 1941, at about 1000 hours (Manila time), unlawfully killed and murdered certain members of the armed forces of the United States of America and of the armed forces and civilians of the Commonwealth of the Philippines, whose names and number are at present unknown.

COUNT 44. All the Defendants together with divers other persons, between the 18th September, 1931 and the 2nd September, 1945, participated as leaders, organizers, instigators, or accomplices in the formulation or execution of a common plan or conspiracy, and are responsible for all acts performed by themselves or by any persons in execution of such plan.

The object of such plan or conspiracy was to procure and permit the murder on a wholesale scale of prisoners of war, members of the armed forces of countries opposed to Japan who might lay down their arms, and civilians, who might be in the power of Japan, on land or sea, in territories occupied by Japan, and crews of ships destroyed by Japanese forces, in ruthless pursuit of victory in the unlawful wars in which Japan was, or would, during the said period be engaged.

COUNT 45. The Defendants ARAKI, HASHIMOTO, HATA, HIRANUMA, HIROTA, ITAGAKI, KAYA, KIDO, MATSUI, MUTO, SUZUKI and UMEZU, on the 12th December, 1937 and succeeding days, by unlawfully ordering, causing and permitting the armed forces of Japan to attack the City of Nanking in breach of the Treaty Articles mentioned in Count 2 hereof[50] and to slaughter the inhabitants contrary to international law, unlawfully killed and murdered many thousands of civilians and disarmed soldiers of the Republic of China, whose names and number are at present unknown.

COUNT 46. The same Defendants as in Count 45, on the 21st October, 1938 and succeeding days, by unlawfully ordering, causing and permitting the armed forces of Japan to attack the City of Canton in breach of..., unlawfully killed and murdered large numbers of civilians and disarmed soldiers of the Republic of China, whose names and number are at present unknown. [Note: '...' represents the same wording as that in Count 45, which is hereby omitted. The same applies to the following Counts 47–50.]

COUNT 47. The same Defendants as in Count 45, prior to the 27th October, 1938, and on succeeding days, by unlawfully ordering, causing and permitting the armed forces of Japan to attack the City of Hankow in breach of..., unlawfully killed and murdered large numbers of civilians and disarmed soldiers of the Republic of China, whose names and number are at present unknown.

---

[50] It refers to the following Treaty Articles: the Convention for the Pacific Settlement of International Disputes, 29 July 1899 (Articles 1 and 2); the Convention for the Pacific Settlement of International Disputes, 18 October 1907 (Articles 1 and 2); the Hague Convention III, 18 October 1907 (Article 1); the Exchange of Notes between the United States and Japan, 30 November 1908 (Articles 2, 4 and 5); the Convention for the Suppression of the Abuse of Opium and other Drugs, 23 January 1912; the 'Versailles Treaty', 28 June 1919 (Articles 10, 12, 13, and 15 of the Covenant of the League of Nations); the 'Nine-Power Treaty', 6 February 1922 (Articles 1, 2, 3, 4, and 7); the League of Nations Second Opium Conference Convention, 19 February 1925; the 'Pact of Paris', or the 'Kellogg-Briand Pact', 27 August 1928 (Articles 1 and 2); and the Convention relating to Narcotic Drugs, 13 July 1931.

COUNT 48. The Defendants HATA, KIDO, KOISO, SATO, SHIGEMITSU, TOJO and UMEZU, prior to the 18th June, 1944, and on succeeding days, by unlawfully ordering, causing and permitting the armed forces of Japan to attack the City of Changsha in breach of..., unlawfully killed and murdered many thousands of civilians and disarmed soldiers of the Republic of China, whose names and number are at present unknown.

COUNT 49. The same Defendants as in Count 48, prior to the 8th August, 1944, and on succeeding days, by unlawfully ordering, causing and permitting the armed forces of Japan to attack the City of Hengyang in the Province of Hunan in breach of..., unlawfully killed and murdered large numbers of civilians and disarmed soldiers of the Republic of China, whose names and number are at present unknown.

COUNT 50. The same Defendants as in Count 48, prior to the 10th November, 1944, and on succeeding days, by unlawfully ordering, causing and permitting the armed forces of Japan to attack the Cities of Kweilin and Liuchow in the Province of Kwangsi in breach of..., unlawfully killed and murdered large numbers of civilians and disarmed soldiers of the Republic of China, whose names and number are at present unknown.

COUNT 51. The Defendants ARAKI, DOHIHARA, HATA, HIRANUMA, ITAGAKI, KIDO, KOISO, MATSUI, MATSHOKA, MUTO, SUZUKI, TOGO, TOJO and UMEZU, by ordering, causing and permitting the armed forces of Japan to attack the territories of Mongoloa and the Union of Soviet Socialist Republics, with which nations Japan was then at peace, in the region of the Khalkhin-Gol River in the summer of 1939, unlawfully killed and murdered certain members of the armed forces of Mongolia and the Union of Soviet Socialist Republics, whose names and number are at present unknown.

COUNT 52. The Defendants ARAKI, DOHIHARA, HATA, HIRANUMA, HIROTA, HOSHINO, ITAGAKI, KIDO, MATSUOKA, MATSUI, SHIGEMITSU, SUZUKI and TOJO, by ordering, causing and permitting the armed forces of Japan to attack the territory of the Union of Soviet Socialist Republics, with which nation Japan was then at peace, (in the region of Lake Khasan in the months of July and August 1938) unlawfully killed and murdered certain members of the armed forces of the Union of Soviet Socialist Republics, whose names and number are at present unknown.

The above 16 counts (37–52) are accusations against all the defendants for the common plan or conspiracy to kill and murder, and against certain defendants for ordering, causing and permitting the Japanese armed forces to kill and murder on a large scale, the civilians and disarmed soldiers when capturing certain cities. Thus, Group Two 'Murder' in the Indictment comprises these 16 counts.

*3.4.3.3   Group Three: Conventional War Crimes and Crimes
             Against Humanity (Counts 53–55)*
This group contains only three counts and combines two crime categories specified in the Tokyo Charter: Conventional War Crimes (other than 'Murder' under Group Two) and Crimes against Humanity:

COUNT 53. The Defendants DOHIHARA, HATA, HOSHINO, ITAGAKI, KAYA, KIDO, KIMURA, KOISO, MUTO, NAGANO, OKA, OSHIMA, SATO, SHIGEMITSU, SHIMADE, SUZUKI, TOGO, TOJO and UMEZU, together with divers other persons, between the 7th December, 1941 and the 2nd September, 1945, participated as leaders, organizers, instigators, or accomplices in the formulation or execution of a common plan or conspiracy, and are responsible for all acts performed by themselves or by any person in execution of such plan.
The object of such plan or conspiracy was to order, authorize and permit the Commanders-in-Chief of the several Japanese navel and military forces in each of the several theatres of war in which Japan was then engaged, and the officials of the Japanese War Ministry, and the persons in charge of each of the camps and labour units for prisoners of war and civilian internees in territories of or occupied by Japan and the military and civil police of Japan, and their respective subordinates frequently and habitually to commit the breaches of the Laws and Customs of War, as contained in and proved by the Conventions, assurances and practices referred to in Appendix D, against the armed forces of the countries hereinafter named and against many thousands of prisoners of war and civilians then in the power of Japan belonging to the United States of America, the British Commonwealth of Nations, the Republic of France, the Kingdom of the Netherlands, the Commonwealth of the Philippines, the Republic of China, the Republic of Portugal and the Union of Soviet Socialist Republics and that the Government of Japan

should abstain from taking adequate steps in accordance with the said Conventions and assurances and Laws and Customs of War, in order to secure observance and prevent breaches thereof.

In the case of the Republic of China, the said plan or conspiracy began on the 18th September, 1931, and the following Defendants participated therein in addition to those above-named: ARAKI, HASHIMOTO, HIRANUMA, HIROTA, MATSUI, MATSUOKA, MINAMI.

COUNT 54. The Defendants DOHIHARA, HATA, HOSHINO, ITAGAKI, KAYA, KIDO, KIMURA, KOISO, MUTO, NAGANO, OKA, OSHIMA, SATO, SHIGEMITSU, SHIMADA, SUZUKI, TOGO, TOJO and UMEZU, between the 7th December, 1941 and the 2nd September, 1945, ordered, authorized and permitted the same persons as mentioned in Count 53 to commit the offences therein mentioned and thereby violated the laws of War.

In the case of the Republic of China, the said orders, authorities and permissions were given in a period beginning on the 18th September, 1931, and the following Defendants were responsible for the same in addition to those named above: ARAKI, HASHIMOTO, HIRANUMA, HIROTA, MATSUI, MATSUOKA, MINAMI.

COUNT 55. The Defendants DOHIHARA, HATA, HOSHINO, ITAGAKI, KAYA, KIDO, KIMURA, KOISO, MUTO, NAGANO, OKA, OSHIMA, SATO, SHIGEMITSU, SHIMADA, SUZUKI, TOGO, TOJO and UMEZU, between the 7th December, 1941 and the 2nd September, 1945, being by virtue of their respective offices responsible for securing the observance of the said Conventions and assurances and the Laws and Customs of War in respect of the armed forces in the countries hereinafter named and in respect of many thousands of prisoners of war and civilians then in the power of Japan belonging to the United States of America, the British Commonwealth of Nations, the Republic of France, the Kingdom of the Netherlands, the Commonwealth of the Philippines, the Republic of China, the Republic of Portugal and the Union of Soviet Socialist Republics, deliberately and recklessly disregarded their legal duty to take adequate steps to secure the observance and prevent breaches thereof, and thereby violated the laws of War.

In the case of the Republic of China, the said offence began on the 18th September, 1931, and the following Defendants were responsible for the same in addition to those named above: ARAKI, HASHIMOTO, HIRANUMA, HIROTA, MATSUI, MATSUOKA, MINAMI.

The above three counts (53–55) are accusations against certain defendants of the common plan or conspiracy to violate the laws of war, and of their violations of the laws of war through positive 'acts' (order, authorization or permission) or negative 'omissions' (deliberate disregard of their legal duty, failure to stop their subordinates), which led to their subordinates' wanton violations of the laws of war. Thus, Group Three 'Other Conventional War Crimes and Crimes against Humanity' in the Indictment comprises these three counts. In fact, all these counts are accusations of Conventional War Crimes apart from murder, and not accusations of Crimes against Humanity as defined in the Tokyo Charter. It can be said that an exclusive and independent accusation against the defendants for Crimes against Humanity does not exist in the Tokyo Indictment. This presents an ambiguity in the counts. Section 3.5 of this chapter offers a criticism of the Indictment.

3.4.4 Summary of the Five Appendices in the Indictment

In addition to the 55 counts against the defendants, there are five Appendices after the main text of the Indictment, provided as important references for the explanation and substantiation of the charges.

Appendix A is titled 'Summarized Particulars showing the principal Matters and Events upon which the Prosecution will rely in support of the several Counts of the Indictment in Group One' (Crimes against Peace, or the Crime of Aggression). This appendix has the following ten sections:

1. Military aggression in Manchuria;
2. Military aggression in the rest of China;
3. Economic aggression in China and Greater East Asia;
4. Methods of corruption and coercion in China and other occupied territories;
5. General preparation for war;
6. The organization of Japanese politics and public opinion for war;

7. Collaboration between Japan, Germany and Italy, aggression against French Indo-China and Thailand;
8. Aggression against the Soviet Union;
9. Japan, the United States of America, the commonwealth of the Philippines and the British Commonwealth of Nations;
10. Japan, the Kingdom of the Netherlands and the Republic of Portugal.

Each section, in a few hundred words, narrates the facts of the Japanese aggression.

Appendix B lists the articles of 20 treaties violated by the Japanese aggressors and incorporated in Groups One and Two of the Indictment:

1. The Convention for the Pacific Settlement of International Disputes, signed at The Hague on 29 July 1899 (Article 1 and Article 2);
2. The Convention for the Pacific Settlement of International Disputes, signed at The Hague on 18 October 1907 (Article 1 and Article 2);
3. The Hague Convention No. III Relative to the Opening of Hostilities, signed on 18 October 1907 (Article 1);
4. Agreement effected by exchange of notes between the United States and Japan, signed on 30 November 1908, declaring their policy in the Far East (Articles 2, 3, 4 and 5);
5. The Convention and Final Protocol for the Suppression of the Abuse of Opium and other Drugs, signed at The Hague, on 23 January 1912 and 9 July 1913;
6. The Treaty of Peace between the Allied and Associate Powers and Germany, signed at Versailles on 28 June 1919, known as the Versailles Treaty (especially Articles 10, 12, 13, 15, 22 and 23 of the Covenant of the League of Nations);
7. The Mandate from the League of Nations pursuant to the Versailles Treaty made at Geneva on 17 December 1920 (Article 3 and Article 4);
8. Treaty between the British Commonwealth of Nations, France, Japan and the United States of America relating to their Insular Possessions and Insular Dominions in the Pacific Ocean on 13 December 1921 (Article 1);

9. Identic Communication made to the Netherlands Government on 4 February 1922 on behalf of the British Commonwealth of Nations and also 'mutatis mutandis' on behalf of Japan and the other Powers signatory to the Quadruple Pacific Treaty of 13 December 1921;
10. Identic Communication made to the Portuguese Government on 6 February 1922 on behalf of the British Commonwealth of Nations and also 'mutatis mutandis' on behalf of Japan and the other Powers signatory to the Quadruple Pacific Treaty of 13 December 1921;
11. The Treaty between the United States of America, the British Commonwealth of Nations, Belgium, China, France, Italy, Japan, the Netherlands and Portugal, concluded and signed at Washington on 6 February 1922, known as the Nine-Power Treaty (Articles 1, 2, 3, 4 and 7);
12. Treaty between the United States and Japan, signed at Washington on 11 February 1922 (Article 2);
13. Treaty between the President of the United States of America, the President of the German Reich, His Majesty the King of the Belgians, the President of the French Republic, His Majesty the King of Great Britain, Ireland and the British Dominions beyond the Seas, Emperor of India, His Majesty the King of Italy, His Majesty the Emperor of Japan, the President of the Republic of Poland, and the President of the Czechoslovak Republic (15 countries), concluded and signed at Paris on 27 August 1928, known as the Kellogg-Briand Pact and as the Pact of Paris, subsequently adhered to by most countries in the world (48 countries) (Article 1 and Article 2);
14. Declaration of Imperial Japanese Government on 27 June 1929, concerning Article 1 of the Kellogg-Briand Pact of 27 August 1928;
15. The League of Nations Second Opium Conference Convention, signed at Geneva on 19 February 1925, and the Convention relating to Narcotic Drugs, signed at Geneva on 13 July 1931;
16. Treaty between Thailand and Japan concerning the continuance of friendly relations and the mutual respect of each other's territorial integrity, signed at Tokyo on 12 June 1940 (Article 1);

17. Convention respecting the Rights and Duties of Neutral Powers and Persons in War on Land, signed at The Hague on 18 October 1907 (Article 1 and Article 2);
18. Treaty of Portsmouth between Russia and Japan, signed on 5 September 1905 (Articles 2, 3, 4, 7 and 9);
19. The Convention on Embodying Basic Rules of the Relations between Japan and the Union of Soviet Socialist Republics, signed on 20 January 1925 in Peking (Article 5);
20. The Neutrality Pact between the Union of Soviet Socialist Republics and Japan, signed on 13 April 1941 in Moscow (Article 1 and Article 2).

All of these treaties were solemnly signed and ratified by the Japanese government, and were therefore absolutely binding upon Japan. However, instead of complying with them, the defendants wantonly breached the terms of the treaties during the period as stated in the Indictment.

Appendix C lists 15 statements or assurances made by the Japanese government on non-aggression or no expansion of aggression, and incorporated in Group One of the Indictment. When the defendants were in power, they broke their promises and disregarded those terms of agreement. Given below is the list of such assurances and statements:

1. 25 September 1931: Japan had no territorial designs in Manchuria;
2. 25 November 1931: There was no truth in the report of a Japanese advance on Chinchow;
3. 22 December 1931: Chinese sovereignty would be accepted and the open-door policy would be maintained;
4. 5 January 1933: Japan had no territorial ambitions south of the Great Wall in China;
5. 25 April 1934: Japan had no intention whatsoever of seeking special privileges in China, of encroaching upon the territorial and administrative integrity of China, or of creating difficulties for the bona fide trade of other countries with China;
6. 15 August 1937: Japan harboured no territorial designs on China and would spare no efforts in safeguarding foreign interest and rights in China;

7. September 1937: Japan had peaceful intentions and a lack of territorial designs in North China;
8. 17 February 1939: Japan had no territorial designs in China and the occupation would not go beyond military necessity;
9. 26 August 1939: Japan had decided to abandon any further negotiations with Germany and Italy relative to closer relations under the Anti-Comintern Pact;
10. 15 April 1940: Japan desired status quo of the Netherlands East Indies;
11. 16 May 1940: Japan had no plans nor purpose to attack the Netherlands East Indies;
12. 24 March 1941: Under no circumstances would Japan attack the United States of America, Great Britain or the Netherlands East Indies;
13. 8 July 1941: Japan had so far not considered the possibility of fighting the Union of Soviet Socialist Republics;
14. 10 July 1941: Japan contemplated no action against French Indo-China;
15. 5 December 1941: Troop movements in French Indo-China were precautionary measures.

Appendix D extracts some important provisions of international conventions on acts of warfare and Japan's assurances to comply with those provisions, which were used to support the counts in Group Three of the Indictment (Conventional War Crimes and Crimes against Humanity). Those conventional provisions include:

1. Convention No. 4 done at The Hague on 18 October 1907, concerning the Laws and Customs of War on Land, and Convention No. 10 done at the same time and place, concerning Maritime War. Japan was a party to both Conventions, together with about 40 other nations, and therefore was obliged to abide by them.
2. International Convention relative to the Treatment of Prisoners of War, done at Geneva on 27 July 1929. It was signed by 47 nations, and thus became strong evidence of the commonly recognized principles of international law which all nations ought to comply with. Although Japan did not ratify the said Convention, it was binding upon Japan because Japan was one of its original signatories, and

because by a communication to Switzerland dated 29 January 1942 and to Argentina dated 30 January 1942, Japan admitted to apply mutatis mutandis the provisions of this Convention.
3. International Convention for the Amelioration of the Condition of the Wounded and Sick in Armies in the Field, done at Geneva on 27 July 1929, also known as the 'Red Cross Convention'. Japan was a party to the said Convention, together with over 40 other nations. It also stated repeatedly during wartime (for instance, on 29 January and 13 February of 1942) that it would 'observe strictly' the Convention.

The above three Conventions were signed and ratified, or acceded to, by most countries in the world at that time, and thus correctly embodied and expressed the principles of international law. In the light of certain important articles, the latter part of this Appendix D enumerates and briefly describes 15 types of serious breaches of these Conventions by the Japanese armed forces, which constituted the background material and an overview of the charges under Group Three of the Indictment.

Appendix E records the respective positions held by the 28 defendants in the Japanese government from 1928 to 1945 (the period of prosecution in the Indictment), thereby demonstrating their individual responsibility during the Japanese war of aggression. This has been covered earlier in Sect. 3.3, 'Selection of and Bibliographic Information on the 28 Defendants' of this chapter, and so will not be repeated here.

A short Preamble, followed by 55 Counts and five Appendices, constituted the complete Indictment filed by the IPS to the Tokyo Tribunal for the prosecution of 28 Japanese major war criminals.

3.5 Characteristics and Defects of the Indictment

The Indictment filed by the IPS to the Tokyo Tribunal against Japanese major war criminals had one prominent feature, which was also its shortcoming—the charges against the defendants (a total of 55 counts) were complicated and narrowly categorized. They lacked in logical rigour and some counts overlapped or conflicted with each other, making the Indictment confusing for ordinary readers. The Tokyo Indictment was unlike the simple and clear indictment in the Nuremberg Trial against German major war criminals; this drawback will be explored later in this section.

Given below is a discussion on the two minor differences between the two indictments.

First, the accused defendants in the Tokyo Indictment were all prisoners detained in Tokyo and tried in person before the Tribunal, with no trial by default, like Martin Bormann in the Nuremberg Trial. This was only a practical difference since there was no express requirement in either of the two Charters about trial by default. The Nuremberg Tribunal listed a war criminal who had not been captured as a target of prosecution, which led to trial by default, but the Tokyo Tribunal did not do so. In Tokyo, all the accused war criminals were present in court from the very first day of the trial. During a long period following Japan's surrender, Mutō, Satō, Kimura and Itagaki were detained abroad by the Allies as prisoners of war because they were commanding troops in overseas battlefields at the time of the surrender; but they were all escorted to Tokyo before the official opening of the Tokyo Trial. Therefore, all the defendants in the Tokyo Tribunal (except for those who died or became mentally ill) stood trial in person for the entire court proceedings. In contrast, defendant Bormann in the Nuremberg Trial was absent when the judgement was given, so the Nuremberg Tribunal had to make a default judgement.[51]

The next difference was that the Nuremberg indictment, in addition to accusing the 22 leading German war criminals, also requested the Tribunal to examine a number of important Nazi organizations (groups, institutions) during the trial and to adjudicate and declare them as 'criminal organizations', whereas the Tokyo prosecution did not raise such a request. The Tokyo indictment did not prosecute any Japanese fascist organization or group unlike that at Nuremberg. Such a difference had

---

[51] Martin Bormann was one of the 22 German major war criminals sentenced by the Nuremberg Trial. There were originally 24 defendants accused by the prosecution at Nuremberg. However, Robert Ley committed suicide in prison and Gustav Krupp was diagnosed with psychosis, so only 22 defendants were finally sentenced on 30 September 1946. Bormann had absconded before the trial and was not captured by the police during the course of the proceedings, but the Nuremberg Tribunal did not stop his trial (his defence was carried out by a court-appointed lawyer), and sentenced him to death by hanging in his absence. Bormann's whereabouts are unknown to this day. According to an article in the *Time* magazine published on 25 December 1964, he may still be alive and living a fugitive's life.

little to do with the indictments themselves or the opinions of prosecutors but existed because of the different provisions in the two Charters.

Article 9 of the Nuremberg Charter provides: 'At the trial of any individual member of any group or organization, the Tribunal may declare (in connection with any act of which the individual may be convicted) that the group or organization of which the individual was a member was a criminal organization.' According to this rule, the Nuremberg Tribunal had the power to declare any group or organization involved in the crimes committed by defendants as a criminal group or criminal organization.

Regarding the procedures of the declaration, Article 9 of the Nuremberg Charter further provides:

> After receipt of the Indictment, the Tribunal shall give such notice as it thinks fit that the prosecution intends to ask the Tribunal to make such declaration and any member of the organization will be entitled to apply to the Tribunal for leave to be heard by the Tribunal upon the question of the criminal character of the organization. The Tribunal shall have power to allow or reject the application. If the application is allowed, the Tribunal may direct in what manner the applicants shall be represented and heard.

As to the nature of the declaration, the Nuremberg Charter further identified it as a decisive one, so that no one could raise any objection to it in any subsequent criminal proceedings against any member of the organization. Article 10 clearly provides:

> In cases where a group or organization is declared criminal by the Tribunal, the competent national authority of any Signatory shall have the right to bring individuals to trial for membership therein before national, military or occupation courts. In any such case the criminal nature of the group or organization is considered proved and shall not be questioned.

It can be inferred that at Nuremberg, the prosecution accused not only Göring and 21 other German major war criminals, but also a number of groups, organizations or institutions that were responsible for the planning and execution of aggression, such as the Leadership Corps of the Nazi Party, the Reich Cabinet, the General Staff, the High Command, the SS, the SA and the Gestapo.[52]

---

[52] In the Judgement of the Nuremberg Trial, the organizations, groups or institutions declared as 'criminal' were: The Leadership Corps of the Nazi Party, the Gestapo and SD,

The IPS in the Tokyo Trial, however, had no such task or power to prosecute organizations. Therefore, the accused in the Tokyo indictment were limited to individual defendants and not extended to those fascist militarist groups or organizations that they presided over or participated in. The task of the Tokyo Tribunal was only to determine the personal liabilities of the individual defendants; it was neither empowered nor required to declare any group or organization as a 'criminal group'.[53]

The foregoing has described two differences between the Tokyo indictment and the Nuremberg indictment: the former did not charge any defendant in absence or penalize any criminal organization.

In the Nuremberg Trial, the only four crimes charged by the prosecution against the defendants were: (a) participation in a common plan or conspiracy for the accomplishment of a crime against peace; (b) planning, initiating, and waging wars of aggression and other crimes against peace; (c) war crimes in violation of the laws or customs of war; and (d) crimes against humanity. Such a clear-demarcation of crimes made it easy for the prosecution to present evidence and enabled the Nuremberg Tribunal to focus on the vital issues for issuing judgement.[54]

---

the SS and the SA. Those declared as non-criminal were: the Reich Cabinet, the General Staff and the High Command. The judge from the Soviet Union had a different opinion; he believed that the Reich Cabinet, the General Staff and the High Command should also be announced as criminal organizations and groups. His opinion was not read out in court when the judgement was pronounced, but was attached to the judgement and made public as minority opinion. See *Judgment of the International Military Tribunal for the Trial of German Major War Criminals* (Chinese Translation), World Affairs Press, pp. 250–262.

[53] The Tokyo Tribunal was neither empowered nor required to declare any organization or group as a 'criminal organization' or 'criminal group', but the Tribunal in the course of the trial did review and research on some Japanese organizations and groups which had advocated fascist militarism and war of aggression, such as the Black Dragon Society, the Cherry Blossom Society, the National Foundation Society, the Great Japan Youth Party, the Great Japan Political Association, and the Imperial Rule Assistance Association. The prosecution provided many materials on the purposes, structures and activities of those organizations and groups, as well as the relationship of the individual defendants with them. However, the purpose of the Tribunal's review and research was not to determine or declare them as criminal organizations or criminal groups, but to ascertain the role of the defendants in those criminal organizations and groups, and how they used such organizations and groups to carry out their criminal activities.

[54] See the conviction of Göring as an example, *Judgment of the International Military Tribunal for the Trial of German Major War Criminals* (Chinese Translation), World Affairs Press, pp. 139–144.

On the other hand, the Tokyo indictment had as many as 55 counts; many of those counts conflicted with each other and lacked rigorous logic, hence causing confusion.

For example, 'Murder' ought to be considered as a Conventional War Crime because it was not defined as a separate category in the Tokyo Charter. It was, however, specified as a specific group with sixteen counts (Counts 37–52) in the Indictment. This was not only logically inconsistent with the provisions of the Charter, but also diminished the content and significance of the two crime categories: Conventional War Crimes and Crimes against Humanity—only a few counts (Counts 53–55) were included in these two main categories. Brutal massacres and some other specific types of manslaughter were meant to be prosecuted as Crimes against Humanity, but the Indictment had indiscriminately grouped all homicides under the single category, 'Murder'.

In addition, Crimes against Peace (the crime of aggression) in the Indictment had as many as 36 counts, which was nearly two-thirds of the total number of counts. There was a fixed number of counts for each step in the war of aggression: five counts of conspiracy to wage such wars (Counts 1–5), twelve counts of planning and preparing such wars against certain countries (Counts 6–17), nine counts of initiating such wars against those countries (Counts 18–26), and ten counts of waging such wars against those countries (Counts 27–36). Understandably, it was an arduous task for the IPS to enumerate and categorize all the steps of aggression—since aggression was the biggest crime committed by the defendants, the prosecution perhaps wished to provide as many details as possible to impress the court. However, this approach made it difficult to provide supportive evidence for these many charges, and the allegations could not be substantiated well in theory or logic.

Count 1 alleged that the defendants participated in the formulation of a big, ambitious common plan or conspiracy to dominate Asia and the Pacific region and eventually to conquer the world; then Counts 2, 3, 4 and 5 concerned common plans or conspiracy of aggression against specific countries. The last four counts appeared superfluous because they could easily be included in Count 1. Counts 6–17 charged the defendants with planning and preparing aggressive wars; Counts 18–26, with initiating aggressive wars; and Counts 27–36 with waging aggressive wars (i.e. engaging in actual armed attacks). Such a rigid demarcation was not required because the waging of war would necessarily include planning, preparation and initiation, especially in a war of aggression; historically, a war of aggression has never been waged without these preliminary steps. The Indictment accused the defendants both for common conspiracy of aggression and waging of the war (the armed attack); it also assigned separate counts for the pre-war procedures of planning, preparation and initiation of the war. Therefore, Counts 6–17 (planning and preparation of aggression) and Counts 18–26 (initiation of aggression) were redundant and Counts 27–36 (waging of wars of aggression) were sufficient by themselves.

Even among the last ten counts of the group (Counts 27–36) for waging of aggressive wars, there were three unnecessary counts. One of them concerned China; in Count 27, the defendants were charged with a war of aggression against China from 18 September 1931 to 2 September 1945 (for 14 years), whereas in Count 28, for the same offense, the period was between 7 July 1937 and 2 September 1945 (for 8 years). Excepting this difference, Count 28 was identical to Count 27. Logically, the war against China that commenced on 18 September 1931 must necessarily include the period between 7 July 1937 and 2 September 1945; so it was unnecessary and illogical to list them as two separate counts. Another example of redundancy can be seen in Count 29 and Count 30: the former charged the defendants with a war of aggression against the United States, and the latter, against the Philippines, for the same period from 7 December 1941 to Japan's surrender on 2 September 1945. It was illogical to treat them as two different counts, because the Philippines was not officially independent but was a part of the United States before Japan's surrender. Last, Count 34 was also problematic, where the defendants were charged of waging a war of aggression against Thailand (Siam). Thailand was always the ally of Japan in World War II. It was therefore unreasonable to allege that Japan invaded Thailand.[55]

---

[55] Immediately after the start of the Pacific War, Thailand signed an 'Alliance Treaty' with Japan in Bangkok on 21 December 1941, with effect from the same day. Article 2 of the treaty provides: 'In the event of an armed conflict between Japan or Thailand and one or several third countries, Thailand or Japan shall immediately stand on the side of the other as its ally and assist the other with all political, economic and military means.' Article 4 states: 'Japan and Thailand assure each other that, in the event of joint operations, no truce or conciliation shall be concluded by either party alone, unless a common agreement is reached.' Before Japan surrendered, Thailand had always been an alliance of Japan. Only on 11 September 1945, after Japan's surrender, did Thailand address a note to Japan and inform it to abolish the treaty as 'the treaty is not in accord with the status of world peace'. See *Collection of International Treaties (1934–1944)*, World Affairs Press, pp. 341–342.

Based on the above discussion, we can infer that most of the 55 counts in the Indictment were unnecessary. Perhaps the drafters of the Indictment from the IPS had strived to be ingenuous and meticulous; but the result was unsatisfactory.

The bench found it difficult to process the 55 counts listed in the Indictment. In the course of the trial, the evidence provided by the prosecution was not enough for each count. In general, there was sufficient evidentiary material, but it proved inadequate if it had to be divided to correspond with each individual count.

As the trial progressed, the problems in the Indictment were increasingly felt by the judges. However, the Indictment had been 'accepted' by the Tribunal and the trial was in progress, so it was not practical to ask the IPS to modify it midway during the trial. The Tribunal could only try to simplify these 55 cumbersome counts as far as possible, so that the accusation would not be complex and convoluted. It could, however, never be as simple as the Nuremberg indictment that had just four counts.

After considerable deliberation, the judges decided to compress the 55 counts by eliminating 45 of them and minimizing them to ten. They believed that the quality of the trial would not be adversely affected by this drastic deletion of counts. The Tribunal's intention to simplify the Indictment was at first only an internal decision of the judges to use a shorter list of counts to determine the defendants' conviction and punishment; they did not intend to disclose the list during trial.

In the final Judgement, however, the Tribunal declared the reduction of 55 counts to ten and mildly stated the reasons for eliminating the rest of the counts.

Following are the ten counts finally retained in the Judgement[56]:

1. COUNT 1 accuses all the Defendants of a common plan or conspiracy, the object of which was that Japan should secure the military, naval, political and economic domination of East Asia and of the Pacific and Indian Oceans, and of all countries and islands therein and bordering thereon and for that purpose should alone

---

[56] The full text of the ten counts can be found above in Sect. 3.4 of this chapter. We have repeated and summarized their key contents here, since they were the only counts recognized and maintained by the Tribunal, and played a very significant role in its proceedings and judgement.

or in combination with other countries having similar objects wage declared or undeclared war or wars of aggression.
2. COUNT 27 accuses that all the Defendants on and after the 18th September, 1931, waged a war of aggression against the Republic of China.
3. COUNT 29 accuses that all the Defendants on and after the 7th December, 1941, waged a war of aggression against the United States of America.
4. COUNT 31 accuses that all the Defendants on and after the 7th December, 1941, waged a war of aggression against the British Commonwealth of Nations (including the United Kingdom, Australia, Canada and New Zealand).
5. COUNT 32 accuses that all the Defendants on and after the 7th December, 1941, waged a war of aggression against the Kingdom of the Netherlands.
6. COUNT 33 accuses that the Defendants ARAKI, DOHIHARA, HIRANUMA, HIROTA, HOSHINO, ITAGAKI, KIDO, MATSUOKA, MUTO, NAGANO, SHIGEMITSU and TOJO (12 in total), on and after the 22nd September, 1940, waged a war of aggression against the Republic of France.
7. COUNT 35 accuses that the Defendants ARAKI, DOHIHARA, HATA, HIRANUMA, HIROTA, HOSHINO, ITAGAKI, KIDO, MATSUOKA, MATSUI, SHIGEMITSU, SUZUKI and TOGO (13 in total), during the summer of 1938, waged a war of aggression against the Union of Soviet Socialist Republics.
8. COUNT 36 accuses that the Defendants ARAKI, DOHIHARA, HATA, HIRANUMA, ITAGAKI, KIDO, KOISO, MATSUI, MATSUOKA, MUTO, SUZUKI, TOGO, TOJO and UMEZU (14 in total), during the summer of 1939, waged a war of aggression against the Mongolian People's Republic and the Union of Soviet Socialist Republics.
9. COUNT 54 accuses that the Defendants DOHIHARA, HATA, HOSHINO, ITAGAKI, KAYA, KIDO, KIMURA, KOISO, MUTO, NAGANO, OKA, OSHIMA, SATO, SHIGEMITSU, SHIMADA, SUZUKI, TOGO, TOJO and UMEZU (19 in total), on and after 7th December, 1941 (the launch of the Pacific War), ordered, authorized and permitted the Commanders-in-Chief of the several Japanese navel and military forces in each of the several

theatres of war in which Japan was then engaged, and the officials of the Japanese War Ministry, and the persons in charge of each of the camps and labour units for prisoners of war and civilian internees in territories of or occupied by Japan and the military and civil police of Japan, and their respective subordinates frequently and habitually to commit the breaches of the Laws and Customs of War, as contained in and proved by the international conventions, assurances and practices, against the armed forces of the Allied countries and against many thousands of prisoners of war and civilians then in the power of Japan belonging to the Allied countries, and thereby violated the laws of war. In the case of the Republic of China, the said orders, authorities and permissions were given in a period beginning on the 18th September, 1931 (the Mukden Incident), and the following Defendants were responsible for the same in addition to those named above: ARAKI, HASHIMOTO, HIRANUMA, HIROTA, MATSUI, MATSUOKA and MINAMI (7 in total).

10. COUNT 55 accuses that the Defendants DOHIHARA, HATA, HOSHINO, ITAGAKI, KAYA, KIDO, KIMURA, KOISO, MUTO, NAGANO, OKA, OSHIMA, SATO, SHIGEMITSU, SHIMADA, SUZUKI, TOGO, TOJO and UMEZU (19 in total), on and after the 7th December, 1941 (the launch of the Pacific War), being by virtue of their respective offices responsible for securing the observance of the international conventions and assurances and the Laws and Customs of War in respect of the armed forces in the Allied countries and in respect of many thousands of prisoners of war and civilians then in the power of Japan belonging to the Allied countries, deliberately and recklessly disregarded their legal duty to take adequate steps to secure the observance and prevent breaches thereof, and thereby violated the laws of war. In the case of the Republic of China, the said offence began on the 18th September, 1931 (the Mukden Incident), and the following Defendants were responsible for the same in addition to those named above: ARAKI, HASHIMOTO, HIRANUMA, HIROTA, MATSUI, MATSUOKA and MINAMI (7 in total).

The above 10 counts were retained by the Tribunal after careful consideration of the 55 counts in the Indictment. Eight of these 10 counts are Crimes against Peace (the crime of aggression), and the other two concern Conventional War Crimes (violations of the laws or customs of war) and Crimes against Humanity. In fact, the last two counts are both crimes violating the laws and customs of war, with one (Count 54) being the positive acts of the defendants in their duty, that is, they ordered, authorized or permitted their subordinates to commit crimes in breach of the laws and customs of war, and the other (Count 55) being the negative acts, or omissions, of the defendants in their duty, that is, despite their duty to secure the observance of the laws and customs of war, they deliberately disregarded that responsibility or obligation, and did not take adequate steps to stop or prevent their subordinates from committing crimes in breach of the laws and customs of war. As for the Crimes against Humanity, since it was not listed in the Indictment as an independent category, the Tribunal could not adopt an original approach to make it a separate charge. Thus, although the Tokyo Charter empowered the Tribunal to try Crimes against Humanity, in practice the Tribunal did not exercise that power; the IPS did not make any special accusation of such crimes against the defendants, although they often used the phrase 'against humanity' against the defendants when presenting evidence and debating in court.

The Tribunal held that it would be sufficient to retain only Count 54 (positive acts) and Count 55 (negative acts or omissions) as Conventional War Crimes. The Tribunal believed that all the 16 counts (Counts 37–52) grouped under 'Murder' in the Indictment could have been included in Counts 54 and 55; it was therefore unnecessary to individually enumerate the names, locations and dates of the homicides. It was also problematic to have that many counts because the Tribunal would risk omitting important details and it would be difficult to produce evidence for every murder charge.

For the accusation under Crime against Peace (the crime of aggression), the Indictment had listed as many as 36 counts, which was compressed by the Tribunal into eight counts: Count 1 charged an overall common plan or conspiracy of the Japanese aggression, and Counts 27, 29, 31, 32, 33, 35 and 36 (7 in total) dealt with the waging or execution of wars of aggression against China, the United States, the British Commonwealth of Nations, the Netherlands, France, the Soviet Union and Mongolia. The Tribunal considered that these eight counts summarized all 36 counts in the Indictment without omitting any detail because the main common plan or conspiracy necessarily included any partial schemes or individual plots; also, the waging (execution) of a war always included the preliminary steps of planning, preparation and initiation of the war. It was not only confusing to treat every step of a war against every country as a separate count for prosecution, but also challenging to procure adequate evidence for each. Consequently, the Tribunal concluded that the eight counts were sufficient for the defendants' crimes of aggression, and the rest of the 28 were superfluous.

The 55 counts enumerated in the Indictment were streamlined into only ten for the trial during all stages of the proceedings. They served as the basis for the formal conviction and sentencing of the defendants. As mentioned before, although the Indictment was still more complex than that of the Nuremberg Trial, it was simpler than before. It was easier to try the defendants with ten counts than with the original 55 of the Indictment.

It is worth reiterating that the Tribunal did not announce its decision to reduce the number of counts to ten until the final Judgement was rendered; however, the bench had always been uneasy about the complexity in the Indictment, and had desired to compress the counts for the smooth conduct of the trial. In the Judgement, the Tribunal cited the reasons for eliminating the 45 counts.[57] The Tribunal's justifications were moderately pronounced so as to not offend the IPS. It did not directly criticize the Indictment for being illogical or complicated, although those were its serious drawbacks.

---

[57] With regard to the Tribunal's reduction of the 55 counts to 10 and the specific reasons for the deletion of the 45 counts, see *Judgment of the International Military Tribunal for the Far East* (Chinese Translation), The 1950s Press, pp. 18–21.

CHAPTER 4

Trial Proceedings of the International Military Tribunal for the Far East

4.1 Basic Provisions on Trial Proceedings in the Tokyo Charter

An important reason for the delay of the Tokyo Trial was the complexity in its proceedings. Apart from the basic provisions of the Tokyo Charter, a number of specifications in the Rules of Procedure were drafted by the Tribunal. This section outlines the Charter's provisions for the course of the trial. The presentation and admission of evidence, the testimony and examination of witnesses and other procedures will be elaborated in the subsequent sections.

The 'Course of Trial Proceedings' under Article 15 of the Tokyo Charter specifies the following steps for the Trial:

(a) The indictment will be read in court, unless the reading is deemed unnecessary by all accused.[1]
(b) The Tribunal will ask each accused whether he pleads 'guilty' or 'not guilty'.
(c) The prosecution and each accused (by counsel only, if represented) may make a concise opening statement.

---

[1] In accordance with Article 1(a) of the Rules of Procedure formulated by the Tribunal to supplement the Charter, a copy of the Indictment should be delivered to the defendants, 14 days before it was openly read out in court, and it should be translated into the language understood by the defendants (Japanese).

(d) The prosecution and defence may offer evidence, and the admissibility of the same shall be determined by the Tribunal.
(e) The prosecution and each accused (by counsel only, if represented) may examine each witness and each accused who gives testimony.
(f) Accused (by counsel only, if represented) may address the Tribunal.
(g) The prosecution may address the Tribunal.
(h) The Tribunal will deliver judgement and pronounce sentence.

In accordance with these stipulations the trial was divided into eight stages, beginning with the reading of the Indictment and concluding with the pronouncement of the sentence.

The stages of the trial adopted by the Tokyo Tribunal were similar to those of the Nuremberg Tribunal. The only difference between the two was that in Nuremberg, any defendant could make the final statement or the 'closing statement', while in Tokyo the prosecutor, not the defendants, made the final statement. This means that in Tokyo, the final speaker at the end of the court hearing was from the prosecution, but in Nuremberg, it was from the defence.[2]

The Tokyo Trial slightly deviated from the trial structure suggested in the Tokyo Charter. The actual Trial had the following stages:

1. The prosecution read the Indictment in court.
2. The Tribunal asked each defendant to plead either 'guilty' or 'not guilty'.[3]
3. The prosecution made an opening statement.[4]
4. The prosecution offered evidence (documents and witnesses). (This was a long, cumbersome step which took more than six months. The evidence of the prosecution was presented in phases.

---

[2] See *Charter of the International Military Tribunal*, Article 24.

[3] This step is called 'arraignment' in the common law system and is the first and most important step in a criminal case. After the defendant hears the indictment read by the prosecutor, the court will ask him if he pleads guilty or not guilty. On pleading 'guilty' he gives up his right to defence. The court may terminate the proceedings at this juncture and render a judgement according to the crime charged in the indictment. If he pleads 'not guilty', the trial will proceed in accordance with regular procedures. All the 28 defendants tried in the Tokyo Tribunal had pleaded 'not guilty' at the arraignment.

[4] The 'opening statement' is when the prosecutor gives a general introduction to the purpose and the key points of the prosecution.

Before presenting a segment of the evidence, an associate or assistant prosecutor gave a brief introduction of the prosecution claims and the documents and witnesses presented for evidence. The defence could object to an evidentiary document being presented and cross-examine a witness of the prosecution after he testified.)

5. The defence offered evidence (documents and witnesses).
(This was also a lengthy procedure which extended beyond ten months. In phases, the defence presented suitable evidence to challenge the evidence of the prosecution and the charges made against the defendants. At first, a general summary of the case was presented by a defence lawyer and then, before presenting a segment of the evidence, a lawyer gave an introduction of the refutation and the relevant documents and witnesses for it. The prosecution could object to an evidentiary document being presented and cross-examine a witness from the defence.)
6. The prosecution rebutted the evidence presented by the defence (at this stage the prosecution might offer fresh evidence for rebuttal).
7. The defence rebutted the claims made by the prosecution (at this stage the defence could offer further evidence, but only that which was directed against the rebutting evidence submitted by the prosecution in the previous step).
8. The prosecution addressed the Tribunal.
9. The defence addressed the Tribunal.
10. The Chief Procurator made a closing statement.
11. The Tribunal delivered the judgement and pronounced the sentences.

The above-mentioned procedure, which was undertaken by the Tokyo Tribunal, mostly complied with the provisions of the Charter, except in some instances when it was slightly altered during the trial for the sake of convenience. Once the Chief Prosecutor made his closing statement, the defence counsel requested an opportunity to make a final defence statement, but the Tribunal declined it because it was neither necessary nor stipulated in the Charter. Therefore, it is apparent that the trial proceedings of the Tribunal predominantly conformed to the terms in the Charter.

The Tokyo Trial was influenced by the common law system because the drafters of the Tokyo Charter were trained in it and many members of the Tribunal were accustomed to its Anglo-American structure. For example, according to Article 12 'Conduct of Trial', 'The Tribunal shall: (a) Confine the trial strictly to an expeditious hearing of the issues raised by the charges; (b) Take strict measures to prevent any action which would cause any unreasonable delay and rule out irrelevant issues and statements of any kind whatsoever'. In practice, however, the Tribunal permitted the defence lawyers (mainly American lawyers) to take advantage of the discrepancies in the complex customary rules of procedure of common law system. This was particularly evident during the 'presentation and admission of evidence', and the 'testifying and examination of witnesses'. It is an established fact that the rules for evidence under common law system are more complex and rigid than any legal system in the world.

4.2 Procedures for the Presentation and Admission of Evidentiary Documents

4.2.1 Types and Nature of Evidentiary Documents

The Tokyo Tribunal practiced 'evidentialism' wherein the final judgement was based on evidence formally admitted by the Tribunal. Therefore, it was imperative that either party collected and submitted evidence in its own favour to be admitted at trial. This was an important but arduous task for both prosecutors and defence counsel.

The Tribunal spent 16 months, which was about two-thirds of trial time, for hearing and noting evidences (documents and witnesses). Some of the most intense arguments between the two parties took place during evidence presentations (Fig. 4.1).

Evidences were of two kinds: documents and witnesses.

The complex process of attendance, testification and examination of witnesses will be explained in the next section. The current section discusses the measures taken and rules applied by the Tribunal for the presentation and admission of evidentiary documents (often simply referred to as 'documents'). The Tokyo Tribunal admitted more than 4300 submitted documents of both parties (exclusive of those rejected), which was a record-breaking occurrence in the judicial history of the world.

Article 13 of the Tokyo Charter, under the title 'Evidence', explains the presentation and admission of documents as follows:

4 TRIAL PROCEEDINGS OF THE INTERNATIONAL MILITARY TRIBUNAL ...   223

Fig. 4.1 Prosecution and defence

(a) <u>Admissibility</u>. The Tribunal shall not be bound by technical rules of evidence. It shall adopt and apply to the greatest possible extent, expeditious and non-technical procedure, and shall admit any evidence which it deems to have probative value. All purported admissions or statements of the accused are admissible.

(b) <u>Relevance</u>. The Tribunal may require to be informed of the nature of any evidence before it is offered in order to rule upon the relevance.

(c) <u>Specific evidence admissible</u>. In particular, and without limiting in any way the scope of the forgoing general rules, the following evidence may be admitted:

   (1) A document, regardless of its security classification and without proof of its issuance or signature, which appears to the Tribunal

to have been signed or issued by any officer, department, agency or member of the armed forces of any government.
(2) A report which appears to the Tribunal to have been signed or issued by the International Red Cross or a member thereof, or by a doctor of medicine or any medical service personnel, or by an investigator or intelligence officer, or by any other person who appears to the Tribunal to have personal knowledge of the matters contained in the report.
(3) An affidavit, deposition or other signed statement.
(4) A diary, letter or other document, including sworn or unsworn statements, which appear to the Tribunal to contain information relating to the charge.
(5) A copy of a document or other secondary evidence of its contents, if the original is not immediately available.

(d) Judicial Notice. The Tribunal shall neither require proof of facts of common knowledge, nor of the authenticity of official government documents and reports of any nation or of the proceedings, records and findings of military or other agencies of any of the United Nations.

(e) Records, Exhibits and Documents. The transcript of the proceedings, and exhibits and documents submitted to the Tribunal, will be filed with the General Secretary of the Tribunal and will constitute part of the Record.

This article deals with the adoption of documents as evidence. Items (a) and (b) require that the taking of evidence should be simple, without the formalism of common law tradition. Despite this provision, the Tribunal permitted sophistry and formalistic argumentation by both parties during trial, thus delaying the proceedings.

Item (d) acknowledges that the probative value of known facts is guaranteed. This is a common provision in general procedural law.

Item (e) stipulates the procedures for the adoption, registration and filing of the evidentiary documents.

Item (c) is the most important provision which specifies the content, type and admissible mode of submission of evidentiary documents. Apart from the written statements of witnesses,[5] this provision permits the Tribunal to admit the following documents as evidence:

1. Government documents and any documents signed or issued by state agencies or officials (including military personnel);
2. Reports of the Red Cross and its members, and reports of individuals such as doctors, investigators or other persons who had knowledge of the facts described in the reports;
3. Private diaries, letters or any other documents considered relevant to the case by the Tribunal;
4. Copies of any of the above documents (along with the reason for non-availability of their originals).

A majority of the 4300 admitted written exhibits were sourced from government archives and were thus closely scrutinized by the Tribunal. Some of them were from the governments of Allied Powers and others from the Japanese government. As mentioned before, some secretly buried files of the Japanese were discovered by the occupation force and restored to the Archives Office on the third floor of the Tribunal. Both the prosecution and the defence were licenced to scour the material for favourable evidences and present them to the Tribunal as documentary evidence.[6] On the other hand, most of the documents of Allied governments belonged to the prosecuting countries, it was more convenient for the prosecution to procure and utilize them. Moreover, all the major Allies had sent their own associate and assistant prosecutors who knew how to access their nation's archives, to work at the IPS. Theoretically, the defence counsel had an equal right to the files of the Allied government, and the Tribunal was obliged to help them exercise the right. Section III of the Tokyo Charter is subtitled as 'Fair Trial for Accused' and under it, an item of Article 9, 'Procedure for Fair Trial' states:

(e) <u>Production of Evidence for the Defence</u>. An accused may apply in writing to the Tribunal for the production of witnesses or of documents. The application shall state where the witness or document

---

[5] The written statement or written testimony ('affidavit') of the witnesses (present or absent from court) will be discussed in Sect. 4.3 of this chapter.

[6] See Chapter 2, Sect. 2.6 of this book.

is thought to be located. It shall also state the facts proposed to be proved by the witness or the document and the relevancy of such facts to the defence. If the Tribunal grants the application, the Tribunal shall be given such aid in obtaining production of the evidence as the circumstances require.

On account of this provision, the defence was allowed to obtain evidentiary documents from the government archives of the Allied countries. If the defence chose to apply for such a privilege, the Tribunal was obliged to assist the defence in this regard after the latter had completed the necessary application procedure. The Tribunal also had to facilitate the summoning of witnesses and procurement of other documents for the defence.[7]

Apart from government documents (including those signed by department heads), Red Cross reports and records of doctors, intelligence officers and investigators were also admitted by the Tribunal. The prosecution presented many such documents during the hearing of alleged atrocities by the defendants ('Conventional War Crimes' and 'Crimes against Humanity').

The Tribunal also admitted excerpts from diaries, letters and other private documents which were related to the cases presented by both parties. Some of the prominent records include Kōichi Kido's diary spanning for more than a decade (*The Diary of Marquis Kido*, 18 volumes in total) and memoirs dictated by Kinmochi Saionji and recorded by Kumao Harada (*The Saionji-Harada Memoirs*). These two records portrayed a detailed history of Japan's policies and activities of the defendants in the then political scenarios of Japan. Both parties extracted relevant materials from these records and submitted them as evidence. The parties did not present many private letters or personal documents. An exception was a long letter from Puyi (of the puppet state 'Manchukuo') to defendant

---

[7] Governments of the Allied countries differed in their responses towards the defence counsel's request for evidence. Some governments were perfunctory, indifferent or uncooperative. Some other governments, such as the United States, were more helpful. It granted almost all requests of the accused war criminals for evidence in their defence. Not only were the US government archives used by the defence counsel, but even some American high-ranking persons (such as George Marshall, the US Secretary of State, and Joseph Grew, former US ambassador to Japan) provided written testimonies to the Tribunal in favour of the defendants.

Jirō Minami, requesting assistance. The authenticity of this document was challenged in court (this will be discussed later in more detail).

Both parties had to endeavour to present the originals of the above-mentioned documents to the Tribunal for registration and filing. If the original could not be presented for a valid reason approved by the Tribunal, a transcript or photocopy could be submitted instead. Many important documents from the Allied governments were submitted as transcripts or photocopies.

The Tokyo Charter did not expressly permit the presentation of films, photographs or weapons as evidences. However, owing to the clause, 'the Tribunal shall not be bound by technical rules of evidence', the Tribunal relaxed the criterion and accepted non-documentary evidences. For example, to illustrate Japan's preparation for the aggressive war and the dominant role of defendant Sadao Araki (a typical warlord) therein, the prosecution had submitted a film entitled *Critical Period of Japan* (or *Japan in Time of Emergency*) as evidence. The Tribunal accepted the film and ordered it to be shown in court. The movie which exposed Japan's aggressive ambitions was watched with bated breath by the audience.[8] The prosecution submitted a film named *Bright Life of the Captives* (or *Nippon Presents*) as a proof of Japan's hypocritical and deceptive propaganda, for the hearing on Japanese army atrocities. This film was also accepted as an exhibit and shown in court. Furthermore, photographs of captive camps (taken secretly by prisoners) presented by the prosecution during the hearing on Japanese maltreatment of Australian prisoners of war as evidence of the miserable living conditions there, were admitted by the Tribunal. The lawyer of defendant Iwane Matsui, the principal criminal in the Nanking Massacre, presented a picture of an altar set in the defendant's family residence as proof of his remorse. The altar was believed to be built on the soil from Yuhuatai (the site of the largest massacre committed by the Japanese army in Nanking). It had a memorial tablet bearing the inscription: 'To the Chinese officers and soldiers killed in action'. Matsui had tried to ease his conscience by praying every

---

[8] Since the Japanese Emperor was known to make an appearance in that film, Araki came to court dressed in formal attire to watch the film that day. This was proof of his ardent loyalty to the Emperor. It should be noted that the Tribunal took a laissez-faire attitude towards the defendants' clothing and did not insist that they wear prison clothes. During trial, they were dressed in Western-style jackets or old Japanese undress uniforms. Hardly anyone wore the traditional kimono and clogs.

morning and evening for those who had died in the massacre.[9] This strange evidence was accepted by the Tribunal, but the picture was not sufficient to subdue the death sentence on Matsui.

However, most of the evidences adopted by the Tribunal were written documents and conformed to the Charter's requisite for 'documents' instead of 'material/physical evidence'.

This completes the discussion of the admissible types of evidentiary documents in the Tokyo Tribunal. Given below are the formalities involved in the presentation and admission of evidentiary documents.

4.2.2 Steps and Formalities for the Presentation and Admission of Evidentiary Documents

This is the prerequisite procedure which either party had to undergo before presenting a document to an open session of the Tribunal[10]:

1. The document had to be translated into English or Japanese if the original was in either of these languages. If the document was in a third language (such as Chinese, Russian, German or French), it had to be translated into English as well as Japanese. If only a part or some parts of the document were to be used as evidence, such a part or parts had to be highlighted in the original document and translated into English and/or Japanese.
2. After the document was translated, the party who offered it in evidence had to prepare about 150 copies of it (by printing, stereotyping, mimeographing or photocopying).
3. A copy of the document to be presented as evidence had to be given to the accused or his counsel by the prosecution, or to the prosecution by the defence, a minimum of 24 hours before it was to be submitted as evidence. A copy also had to be given to the officer in charge of the Language Section under the Secretariat of the Tribunal.

---

[9] The photograph showed the two memorial tablets installed by Matsui, one read: 'To the Chinese officers and soldiers killed in action', and the other: 'To the Japanese officers and soldiers killed in action'. It was absurd to treat the aggressor and the victims of aggression on an equal footing.

[10] See *Rules of Procedure of the International Military Tribunal for the Far East*, Rule 6.

A copy of the evidentiary document had to be given to the other party at least 24 hours before it was submitted to the Tribunal, so that the opposite party had sufficient time to go through it. The opponents checked for translation errors and unfavourable points and considered whether to raise objection and apply for the rejection of such documents on some valid basis. This was a daunting task for either party. The scrutiny of evidentiary documents was a main subject in the 'battle of wits' between the parties. A copy of the evidentiary document had to be also given to the head of the Language Section at least 24 hours before evidence submission to give the department sufficient time to examine the document for translation errors. In case of any such errors, the officer could either advise the party producing it to voluntarily declare the correction or apply to the Tribunal for making the correction in its open session.

As mentioned earlier, the parties and the Language Section of the Tribunal had much work to do before a document was presented in the court hearing. They were involved in translating, printing, perusing and considering the evidentiary document that was to be presented at court. As the Tribunal admitted more than 4300 evidentiary documents during the trial (exclusive of those rejected), their processing demanded extensive human and material resources.

After completing the above-mentioned three formalities, the concerned party would name and enumerate the evidentiary document; for example, 'Prosecution Document No. X' or 'Defence Document No. Y'. Thereafter, when the document had to be presented at an appropriate stage of the trial, the concerned party could introduce it to the Tribunal.

On behalf of the party producing the evidence, the prosecutor or the defence counsel stood at the podium facing the bench and stated: 'I now present (or produce, introduce, offer in evidence) Prosecution Document No. X (or Defence Document No. Y).' Under special circumstances, a few words about the document and its relevance to the case were also mentioned, but in most cases it was not, because these particulars were already mentioned by the concerned party at the beginning of each phase of the trial.

After the statement was made, if there was no objection from the opposite party, the President declared the admission of the evidence. The Clerk loudly announced, 'Prosecution Document No. X (or Defence Document No. Y) is admitted and will be marked (or given) Exhibit No. Z.'

The exhibits were numbered according to their time of admission and irrespective of whether they belonged to the prosecution or the defence.

After the Clerk made the announcement, the person presenting the evidence could read aloud the contents of the exhibit. After reading, the document was officially included in the dossier and placed on file. The portion of the document that was read out was also taped and transcribed to be aggregated in the Tribunal's repository. This is when a document submitted by one party was duly accepted by the Tribunal as evidence. However, the situations could be more complicated. Given below are other possibilities:

After the request for admission of a document was made, a representative of the Language Section could call to attention some errors in the translation and ask permission for making modifications. As the Language Section was a unit of the Tribunal itself, its requests were often approved by the Tribunal. Moreover, the Language Section was an unbiased unit which would object only if there was a valid translation error, unlike the opposite party who might deliberately attack the other party's evidence. Therefore, this rarely occurred during the trial.

In another scenario, the representative of the opposite party (a prosecutor or a defence lawyer) objects to the evidentiary document soon after the request for its admission is made and asks the Tribunal to take corresponding action. Their requests could be one of the following three types:

1. Having found errors or shortcomings in the translation of the document submitted by the other party, it is requested that certain changes be made to the translation of the document. In such a case, the Tribunal asks the 'Language Arbitration Board' comprising three persons to study and review the document.[11] The Tribunal decides based on the analysis made by the Board and then announces its acceptance or rejection of the party's request.
2. A party claims to have found defects in the document presented by the other party (e.g. papers not issued by the competent authorities,

---

[11] All the three members of the Language Arbitration Board had to be always seated in court to settle any disputes arising from the language translation at any instant during the court hearing. The Board was the authority on language issues and its decisions were final. See Chapter 2, Sect. 2.6 of this book.

flawed seals or signatures, questionable dates or places) and therefore requests the Tribunal to reject the document or to instruct the other party to retrieve it for amendment. In order to avoid delays, the Tribunal usually denied such a request by citing the provisions of Article 13(a) of the Tokyo Charter.[12] However, if the opposite party alleged that the document was forged or fabricated, the Tribunal had to consider it. For instance, when the defence presented a letter written by Puyi of Manchukuo to the Japanese War Minister Minami, the prosecution considered it to be a forged document and objected to its being presented. At this juncture, the Tribunal could not simply deny the prosecution's request because it challenged the validity and not merely the format of the document.[13]

3. A party argues that the document submitted by the other party is not relevant or significant to the case and requests the Tribunal to reject it. This was the most frequent objection made by both parties, and especially by the defence counsel who often used this method to trigger disputes and protract the trial.

The relevance or significance of a document to a case depends upon its content, and determining them was a bigger task than resolving translational errors and formational defects of the document.

First, after objecting to the document and requesting for its rejection, the representative of the opposite party (a prosecutor or a defence lawyer) had to succinctly state his reason for devaluing it. His statement had to be brief, forceful and precise because lengthy explanations may prompt the judges to pass a ruling against him. Therefore, when a party received a document from their opponent, 24 hours prior to the hearing, they

---

[12] Article 13(a) of the Tokyo Charter provided that the Tribunal 'shall admit any evidence which it deems to have probative value'. It was a liberal rule which gave much discretionary power to the Tribunal. The Tribunal took advantage of this provision sometimes; however, it often refused to utilize this provision due to the influences of the formalistic rules of evidence in the common law system. During the 16 months of evidence collection from both parties, the Tribunal had adopted a wavery and self-contradictory stance.

[13] The Tribunal tested the validity of the document by entrusting a panel of experts to perform handwriting authentication. On the recommendation of the Chinese judge, Zhang Fengju, professor of Chinese at Peking University, was invited to be a member of the panel. However, since the experts' opinions differed, the matter was not pursued further and was left unresolved by the Tribunal.

would first examine whether to object to the admission of the document. If so, they would determine the reasons for which it can be challenged and the manner in which the reasons can be effectively presented. This was one of the topics of contention in the 'battle of wits' between the two parties. Each party would strive to find fault with the documents of the opposite party and contest over the smallest concerns.

After the objector made his statement, the party presenting the document could refute the grounds of objection and insist on the admission of the document. The objector could then make another statement and the first party could again refute it. The Tribunal ended this reiterative process after one or two rounds of debate. The President would declare, 'We have heard enough. We will now make a decision on this.'

As the trial progressed, the ruling procedures adopted by the bench lessened in complexity.[14]

At the beginning of the trial, every time a party objected to an evidentiary document, the President would announce a short recess after listening to the arguments of both parties. The judges would go to the meeting room to discuss the problem and then return to the courtroom to announce their decision. It took at least 20 minutes to handle one objection. The judges began to feel that the arguments were much ado over nothing.

The objections became more frequent and tiresome because the defence lawyers were using this as a method to delay the trial. They identified loopholes and objected to all documents submitted by the prosecution.

The Tribunal soon adopted a new strategy to deal with the deliberate protraction by the defence. It cancelled the recess for the judges' discussion and instead instructed the judges to vote in court to make a decision. A judges' conference was held only if the President considered it necessary, or one of the judges particularly wished to hold a meeting.

The method of voting was simple. The judges had small notepads on their desks. After the President terminated the debate of the two parties, each judge penned his support or opposition to the objection on a sheet of paper and handed it to the President. The President counted the number of votes in favour of and against the objection and announced the majority opinion as the ruling of the Tribunal. If the adopted ruling

---

[14] See Chapter 2, Sect. 2.3 of this book.

overruled the objection, the Clerk announced that the document had been admitted and marked as Exhibit No. Z (as opposed to Prosecution Document No. X or Defence Document No. Y). The contents of the document were then read aloud by the person presenting it. If the Tribunal sustained the objection, the person presenting the document had to withdraw it and step down from the podium.

The Tribunal's new method of ruling saved much time, but it did not dissuade the defence counsel from passing objections to the prosecution's documents. Their primary motive of delaying the trial proceedings was still accomplished because of the steps involved: their grounds of objection, the prosecution's reply, and interpretation of the statements of both parties. Therefore, the defence counsel spared no effort to make objections throughout the trial.

This encapsulates the entire journey of an evidentiary document from preparation (translation, printing and delivery to those concerned) to admission. Although most of the submitted documents were uncontested, the few (more than 10 per cent) that were challenged from among the 4300 evidentiary documents presented to the Tribunal substantially delayed the proceedings.

Furthermore, many presented documents (also estimated at more than 10 per cent) that were objected to by the other party were rejected by the Tribunal after debate. The rejected documents were not among the 4300 accepted exhibits, but their scrutinization consumed much of the Tribunal's time.

Thus, it can be inferred that the presentation and admission of evidentiary documents were cumbersome and difficult activities for both the parties as well as the bench, and were time-consuming processes in the Tokyo Trial.

4.3 Procedures for the Attendance and Testifying of Witnesses

4.3.1 Summons of Witnesses and Rules Before Appearing in Court

As discussed earlier, there were fierce debates between the opposing parties on the validity of an evidentiary document because of the complexity involved in the procedures for its presentation and admission. However, the procedures for the attendance and testifying of witnesses were even more complex and triggered intense arguments between the two parties. As the Tribunal had permitted 419 witnesses presented by both parties to testify in court, the process of testification consumed the greatest amount of time during the Tokyo Trial.[15]

The provisions regarding witnesses in the Tokyo Charter and the Rules of Procedure are relatively simple and as follows:

In Article 9 of the Charter, 'Procedure for Fair Trial', Item (d) gives a defendant the right to examine any witness—'An accused shall have the right, through himself or through his counsel (but not through both), to conduct his defence, including the right to examine any witness, subject to such reasonable restrictions as the Tribunal may determine.' Item (e) requires the Tribunal to assist the defendant in summoning witnesses—'An accused may apply in writing to the Tribunal for the production of witnesses.... The application shall state where the witness ... is thought to be located. It shall also state the facts proposed to be proved by the witness ... and the relevancy of such facts to the defence. If the Tribunal grants the application, the Tribunal shall be given such aid in obtaining production of the evidence as the circumstances require.'

Article 11 of the Charter 'Powers' provides in Items (a) and (d) that the Tribunal shall have the power 'a. To summon witnesses to the trial, to require them to attend and testify, and to question them' and 'd. To require of each witness an oath, affirmation, or such declaration as is customary in the country of the witness, and to administer oaths'.

In Rule 4 of the Rules of Procedure on 'Witnesses', Item (a) states: 'Prior to testifying before the Tribunal, each witness shall make such oath or declaration or affirmation as is customary in his own country.' Item (b) provides: 'Witnesses, while not giving evidence, shall not be present in court without the permission of the Tribunal. The President shall direct, as circumstances demand, that witnesses shall not confer among themselves before giving evidence.'

---

[15] Of the 419 witnesses, 109 were provided by the prosecution ('prosecution witnesses'), and 310 by the defendants ('defence witnesses'). Testification took much of the trial time. For example, the testifying and examinations of Emperor Puyi of the puppet Manchukuo took eight complete days. Other important witnesses included John Liebert, an American expert on Japan; Cyril Wilde, a British colonel from Southeast Asia; James Richardson, a US admiral; Ryukichi Tanaka, a former Japanese major general; Chin Teh-Chun, the mayor of Peking during the Marco Polo Bridge Incident; and Wang Len-Chai, the Wanping County commissioner and magistrate. The testification of each took several days during the trial.

The above items only specify the obligations of the witnesses towards the Tribunal and the defence's right to summon and examine witnesses; they do not explain the procedure for testimony and examination. Therefore, the Tribunal adopted the customary rules for witnesses followed in courts of the common law system. However, the customary rules of the common law system are known to be more complicated than any legal system, owing to which, Article 13(a) of the Tokyo Charter provided: 'The Tribunal shall not be bound by technical rules of evidence. It shall adopt and apply to the greatest possible extent expeditious and non-technical procedure, and shall admit any evidence which it deems to have probative value.' In practice, the Tribunal followed the common law system for procedures concerning witnesses and evidentiary documents, and made mild modifications for complex procedures.

Given below is the procedure for summoning a witness and the rules to be followed by the witness before he appears in court.

Before any trial phase, each party had to submit to the Tribunal for review and approval, the list of witnesses invited to appear at that phase and the reasons for inviting them. The Tribunal sent notices to the approved witnesses informing them of the trial phase and tentative date on which they had to appear in court. The Tribunal was lenient in its scrutiny of the proposed witnesses and rarely rejected any of them. The Tribunal paid special attention to the requests of the defence, to ensure a fair trial. It also tried to persuade witnesses to testify for the accused.

Most of the defence witnesses were Japanese, many of whom lived in Tokyo, and hence could promptly attend the trial on the designated date and time. They had no problems of transportation or accommodation and their waiting period in Tokyo was brief. The expenses for their reception were paid by the defence, who were recompensed by the Japanese government.

On the contrary, the prosecution witnesses had more complex backgrounds; they comprised Japanese residents in Tokyo or other places in Japan, Japanese war criminals detained at Sugamo Prison, Americans working in the GHQ in Tokyo, members of the Allied missions in Japan, and special foreign invitees called to testify at the Tribunal. The first four types were easily received and quickly disposed, but it was difficult to ensure the attendance of overseas witnesses at the trial.

Except under special circumstances, the GHQ was responsible for the reception, accommodation and transportation of witnesses in Tokyo. Additionally, each witness was given a daily allowance of $1 during their stay in Tokyo. Some individuals, such as the senior officials or celebrities from the Allied Powers, gave up this privilege and were instead attended to by their countries' missions in Japan.

A few witnesses were also summoned from prisons of the Allied Powers. Each nation's representative mission in Tokyo held custody of its witnesses because the mission was responsible for escorting them back to their home countries after their testification. For example, Puyi, Emperor of the puppet state Manchukuo, was summoned from the Harbarovsk Prison of the Soviet Union to testify in court. He was monitored during his court attendance in Tokyo and thereafter, escorted back to Harbarovsk by the Soviet mission.

The arrangements made for the witnesses in Tokyo were simple, but it was a difficult task to persuade them to wait to testify.

As the trial process of the Tribunal had many unforeseen complications, it was difficult to estimate the time duration for each trial phase. Consequently, the date on which a witness had to appear in court could not be ascertained. This was not a problem for the witnesses residing in Tokyo or even elsewhere in Japan, but it was a problem for the overseas witnesses from the Allied Powers who had come to Japan especially for this purpose. Witnesses grew impatient when they were made to wait in Tokyo for an unspecified number of days. Those who had to attend to some work in their own countries were restless to leave Tokyo. If they could not be convinced to stay, they were allowed to temporarily go home and return to Tokyo. Alternatively, they were allowed to testify before time. However, as doing so could alter the sequence of the proceedings and cause confusion, the Tribunal did not always allow it. The only time the Tribunal resorted to this alternative was when a group of Chinese and foreign witnesses from China had to testify for the Nanking Massacre in 1937. These witnesses were invited by the IPS and comprised officers, businessmen, professors, priests, and heads of charities. The hearing on the Japanese occupation of Nanking could not take place for a long time after they arrived in Tokyo. After many days of wait, they requested sanction to return to China. Therefore, the prosecution made a special request to the Tribunal to permit those witnesses to testify in advance. The Tribunal approved it and the witnesses were allowed to testify in court in sequential order. They underwent the process of direct examinations by the prosecutors and cross-examinations by the defence lawyers for many days.

Based on the common law system, witnesses in court are strictly categorized into two types: 'prosecution witnesses' summoned at the request of the prosecution and 'defence witnesses' summoned at the request of the defence.

Once identified as either a 'prosecution witness' or a 'defence witness', the witness is forbidden to communicate with the opposite party or its representative. Therefore, a witness identified by the Tribunal as a 'prosecution witness' was barred from even socializing with anyone from the defence. Similarly, the 'defence witness' was strictly prohibited from communicating with the prosecutors or their representatives. This being the case, both parties at the Tokyo Trial had to strictly avoid communicating with the other party's witnesses.

If a prosecutor or a defence lawyer was reported to have contacted the other party's witnesses, it was declared as a case of 'tempting the witness' and the Tribunal could disqualify him from appearing in court.[16] The concerned witness could also be suspended or his testimony be invalidated.

Another rule that the witnesses had to observe was that, before testifying, they could not be present in court without the permission of the Tribunal (Rule 4[b] of the Rules of Procedure of the Tribunal). This rule ensured that the witness was naïve about the state of affairs in court with respect to that case, and that he was 'simple-minded' when he had to testify. This rule, however, was not effective because the witness could still gather details of the real situation in court from the party inviting him. Before giving testimony, the witness frequently discussed with the lawyers of his party (prosecution or defence, as the case may be) about his stance, testimony, and manner in which he should respond to the cross-examination. The Tribunal sanctioned such an interaction but forbade the witness's unnecessary presence in court as an observer; it believed that the witnesses could infer much from observing the court proceedings and those 'external influences' could influence their otherwise 'simple-minded' testimony. This unreasonable rule denigrated a witness to a mercenary who only abided by his master's words. Nevertheless, this rule was exercised on both parties and their witnesses during the trial.

---

[16] As explained under Chapter 3, Sect. 3.2 above, the offense 'tempting the witness' in the common law tradition, meant to confuse, soften, entice or bribe the other party's witness, making him less capable of testifying for his party.

Some witnesses at the Tokyo Tribunal and in the common law courts were undoubtedly 'mercenary' because a witness from one party was allowed to testify for the other party at a different trial stage. This could be compared to the mercenaries who, during the Spanish Civil War in the 1930s, fought sometimes for the Republican Army against the Nationalists and at other times for the Nationalist Army against the Republicans. For example, witness Ryukichi Tanaka (a Japanese Major General) testified in court a few times, both as a prosecution witness and a defence witness. Another example is of Tomokatsu Matsumura (a Japanese Major General) who was a prosecution witness to claim that the defendant Yishijirō Umezu had participated and presided over the plan of aggression against the Soviet Union but later testified as a defence witness for Umezu, vouching for his congenial attitude towards the Soviet Union.

The Tokyo Tribunal did not deter the practice of 'serving one party on one day and the other party on another day'. The witness was free to testify for the other party after his testimony for the first party was completed.

Another rule in the Tokyo Trial was that the witness should attend court only voluntarily to testify. A case in point was when the defence counsel ushered in a Japanese man named Konichi Hatano to testify for the defendant, but Hatano refused to testify for him. This greatly embarrassed the defence and the President immediately ordered that Hatano should be sent away. Further, he rebuked the defence counsel for compelling a witness to testify against his will.[17]

The above-mentioned rules were to be followed by the witnesses before taking the stand. Next is a discussion on the procedure to be followed by the witnesses during their examinations at court and the rules regarding their attendance.

4.3.2 *The Oath, Affirmation or Declaration of Witnesses*

When a party (prosecution or defence) had to produce evidence during the trial, it could ask the Tribunal to summon a witness to court after stating the facts it intended to prove through that witness. The Tribunal would usually grant the request.

---

[17] See *Transcripts of Proceedings and Documents of the International Military Tribunal for the Far East* (29 April 1947), pp. 21062–21063.

The witness would be escorted to the witness box by the Marshal of the Court and asked to take his oath. In the common law system, the witness's oath is very important; all testimonies had to be given under oath. If a witness refused to take an oath, his testimony would be considered as null and void, and the court would not use his testimony as evidence. However, exceptions could be made if the witness states that the oath challenged his theistic or atheistic principles. The oath would then be changed to a solemn, secular affirmation or declaration.

The Tokyo Tribunal adopted a more flexible approach to oath-taking by witnesses. Owing to the different nationalities of the witnesses, the Tribunal's oath was not as rigid as that in common law courts. It only required the oath to be in conformity with the law and customs of the witness's own country. Article 11(d) of the Charter stipulates that the Tribunal has the power 'to require of each witness an oath, affirmation, or such declaration as is customary in the country of the witness'. Rule 4(a) of the Rules of Procedure provides: 'Prior to testifying before the Tribunal, each witness shall make such oath or declaration or affirmation as is customary in his own country.' Thus, there were variations in the oaths taken by witnesses.

If a witness was British or American, he could take an oath administered by the Marshal of the Court in the typical procedure of the common law courts. The Marshal and the witness each raised his right hand. The Marshal read each sentence, and the witness repeated it. The last sentence was the exclamation 'So help me God!' If the witness was not from the common law countries, he could sign, seal or provide a fingerprint on a prepared written affirmation or declaration in accordance with the domestic law of his country. In such a case, the declaration was: 'I solemnly affirm and declare according to my conscience that I will tell the truth, under the pains and penalties of perjury....' After signing or sealing, the sheet was handed over to the Marshal of the Court and the oath-taking process thus completed. The steps for testimony were as follows: 'direct examination', 'cross-examination' and sometimes 're-direct examination' and 're-cross-examination'. This procedure was in the convention of the common law system. It is a known fact that the rules of procedure for witness testification in common law courts are complex. Therefore, it was not an easy task for a witness to testify in the Tokyo Tribunal. Some of them underwent three or four of the steps, for days together, before leaving the witness box. During the two-year open sessions of the

Tribunal, the time spent on the testification of about 400 witnesses was more than half of the total trial period.

4.3.3 Four Steps of Testifying and Examinations of Witnesses

We will now discuss the four steps of the witness's testimony and examination: 'direct examination', 'cross-examination', 're-direct examination' and 're-cross-examination'. However, not all of the 400 witnesses in the Tokyo Trial underwent these four steps; many witnesses left the stand after one or two steps. As the four stipulated steps were undertaken by the majority of witnesses, it is necessary to explore the nature and significance of each step and the rules that the parties and their witnesses had to abide by at each step. This can also help one understand the testifying process in the Tribunal, which is one of the main reasons for the protraction of the Tokyo Trial.

4.3.3.1 First Step: Direct Examination

'Direct examination' is also called examination-in-chief, which means the direct or chief inquiry of the witness. An equivalent phrase in Chinese translates to 'original examination'. This is the first inquiry of the witness, based on which the cross-examination, re-direct examination and re-cross-examination are performed.

Direct examination is undoubtedly the primary step of the witness examination because the facts required to be verified through the witness, the data seen and heard by the witness, and the opinions and feelings of the witness are disclosed at this step.

In civil law countries, direct examination is usually performed by the judge; the judge asks questions and the witness answers them. In principle, both parties can raise questions to the witness only through the judge.

On the contrary, in the common law system, direct examination is not performed by the judge, but by the representative of the party providing the witness. The direct examination of a prosecution witness is carried out by the prosecutor and that of a defence witness by the defence counsel. The Tokyo Tribunal unsurprisingly adopted this common law practice.

In the Tokyo Tribunal, the direct examination of a witness started immediately after he was brought to the witness stand and had taken his oath.

The examiner usually began his direct examination by asking the witness's name, age, place of origin and career experience, and eventually proceeded to the concerned case. The witness's responses to the examiner's questions were recorded in the Tribunal's records; this constituted the most important part or 'core' of the witness's testimony. The subsequent cross-examination, re-direct examination and re-cross-examination would be structured around this core.

Since the witnesses were invited by the party conducting the direct examination, there was naturally a cordial relationship between the examiner and the witness, and consequently, the question-answer session proceeded smoothly. As a matter of fact, the questions to be asked and their responses were rehearsed in advance. The examiner was the 'director' of the process who could extract all necessary details from the witness's responses. The professional competence of a prosecutor or a defence counsel was demonstrated in the direct examination. A good counsel extracted a testimony unfavourable to the opposite party in a few questions, while a mediocre counsel wasted time questioning the witness, without gathering any favourable evidence. Such an interrogation by an incompetent counsel could bore the audience and prove advantageous to the other party, and at times, provoke a reprimand from the bench.

There were certain rules that had to be observed during direct examination. Most of these rules were derived from the traditional practices of common law courts and were not expressly provided in the Tokyo Charter or the Rules of Procedure of the Tribunal.

First, the questions and answers between the examiner and the witness should be confined to facts within the scope of the trial, that is, they had to be directly related to the case. The Tribunal had the power to stop any transgression, and the opposite party could ask the Tribunal to direct the examiner to withdraw his question or instruct the witness to not reply on the grounds of 'no relevance to the case' or 'no importance to the case'. The bench would immediately make a ruling to that effect.

Second, the witness should entirely depend upon his memory to respond, and he was forbidden from carrying written notes or any other references without the consent of the Tribunal. This rule was founded on the assumption that recalled words were authentic and reliable, whereas referenced words may have been contrived. Therefore, a witness could not reference any written material while giving testimony, unless he had already stated its necessity and received permission from the bench to use it.[18]

Third, when the witness answered questions, he could not recount anything from hearsay. In the common law system, prohibition against 'hearsay evidence' is very strict.[19] In the words of Edward Coke, a famous British jurist, a witness 'can state the facts experienced by his five senses. He should relate what his eyes have seen, ears heard, tongue tasted, nose smelled, or skin touched, but he cannot say what he has heard from a third person'. In order to consider the words spoken by a third person, it was necessary to summon that person to testify in court. In the early days of the Tokyo Trial, the Tribunal had tried to strictly enforce this rule. However, this rule was relaxed from September 1946 onwards because of practical difficulties in enforcing it. Therefore, a witness in the Tokyo Tribunal was allowed, within certain limits, to report the facts that he had heard from others. The probative value of such 'hearsay evidences' was determined by the discretion of the judges. The Tribunal, however, did not accept any rumours.

Fourth, the examiner should not ask the witness facts or opinions beyond his knowledge capacity, and the witness should not answer such questions, failing which the Tribunal would automatically stop the examination or the opposing party would object to it and request the Tribunal to stop it. For example, a Chinese or Japanese soldier would not be asked the total number of Chinese or Japanese army men engaged in the Sino-Japanese War, because that was beyond his knowledge capacity. Such questions could be asked to a war minister, a chief of staff, or a senior officer of China or Japan. Although his answers may be biased,

---

[18] Puyi, Emperor of the puppet state Manchukuo, glanced at a small notebook hidden in his hands while giving testimony. Upon noticing this, the defence counsel immediately asked the bench to stop the interrogation and retrieve the notebook for review. Puyi argued, 'My notebook is written in Chinese characters.' The president said, 'That does not matter. One of our colleagues is a Chinese judge who is proficient in Chinese, and he can read what you've written.' After receiving it, the Chinese judge found that only a dozen dates were scribbled in the shabby little note book in sentences such as 'I was born in 1906...', 'My first enthronement in 1909...', 'the Revolution of 1911...', 'The First World War began in 1914...' and 'The First World War ended in 1918'. Puyi appeared to have carried that notebook to aid his memory and avoid panicking while being questioned, and not to intentionally violate the rule.

[19] 'Hearsay evidence' refers to the things reported by a witness in court which he has not personally experienced, but has heard from others. Hearsay evidences were generally inadmissible in common law courts.

he was qualified to answer them on account of his status and knowledge capacity. The probative value of his answers was determined by the Tribunal. According to the strict rules of common law system, all others, excepting an 'expert witness', could only objectively relate what he has seen, experienced, or are familiar with. However, the Tokyo Tribunal relaxed this rule and sometimes allowed a witness to express their opinion or estimate within the scope of their knowledge capacity.

There was yet another important rule concerning evidences in the common law system, which was not rigidly observed by Tokyo Tribunal—The non-permissibility of a 'leading' or 'suggestive' question in the examination of witnesses.[20] A leading or suggestive question was to a question which in itself contained hints to the answer. It prompted a required response from the witness. Such questions are strictly forbidden in the common law courts because they can confuse the witness and compromise his free will as a witness. Initially, this rule was adhered to in the Tokyo Trial, but later the Tribunal found it difficult to enforce it, as such a close scrutiny of the questions asked would delay the trial process. Eventually, the Tribunal abandoned this rule. As the Tribunal had not adopted the jury system, the non-application of this rule did not affect the quality of the interrogation.

The above discussion summarizes the rules which had to be observed by the examiner and the witness in a direct examination. The witnesses also had to answer the questions raised by the Tribunal. Any judge who needed some clarification from the witness could raise a question to the

---

[20] It means that in the question itself there are factors that 'lead' or prompt the witness to answer it in a particular manner, thus limiting his response to the question. For example, the witness is abruptly asked, 'Did you see A kill B with a knife or a gun?' This will be considered a leading or suggestive question because the witness has to restrict his answer to 'with a gun' or 'with a knife'. The examiner ought to have first asked the witness, 'Did you see A kill B?' Only then he should ask him with what weapon he saw A kill B. This logical manner of questioning removes the suspicion of manipulating the witness's answers. However, this common law rule is not all that reasonable because the witness was always free to assert, 'I did not see A kill B', or 'A did not kill B with a knife or a gun, but with a....' Unless the witness was foolish or simple-minded, his freedom of answering the question was not restricted. On the other hand, it was necessary because of practice of jury system in common law courts. The jurors were usually ordinary, simple-minded residents who were likely to be confused and trapped by such questions. The Tokyo Tribunal, however, did not adopt the jury system and all judgements on facts and other legal issues were made by the judges themselves; therefore, there was no need to rigidly enforce the prohibitions.

witness through the President. However, it was rare for the bench to directly question the witnesses. The bench was generally detached from the process of direct examination and apart from delivering its final judgement on the case, mainly concerned itself with making impartial rulings on disputes, protests and applications of the two parties during the trial.

Since the testification of a witness is conducted through questions and answers—a method used in common law courts, his testimony was composed of responses to all questions. The advantages of this method of interrogation are that the witness's responses to specific questions were precise and authentic; moreover, under the scrutiny and surveillance of the other party, his attitude was measured and conscientious. However, this is only a formalistic understanding of the process. As mentioned before, the questions and answers in a direct examination were essentially arranged by the examiner and the witness in advance.

The greatest disadvantage of an interrogative testimony is the time wastage because the process was unfocused and fragmentary. The testimony of a witness at the Tokyo Trial which was completed in an hour when conducted with his uninterrupted statement, lasted for more than five hours in the interrogation method, with many interruptions from the opposite party and the difficulties of interpretation. It was inferred that the two methods greatly differed in their time duration.

Initially, the Tokyo Tribunal practiced only the question-and-answer method of direct examination. Within two months, however, the Tribunal found that this time-consuming method could prolong the trial indefinitely. Since the cases were complex, witnesses were numerous, and the speeches of the Japanese lawyers and witnesses were lengthy, the Tribunal decided to change the approach for direct examination of witnesses.

After several judges' conferences and discussions with both parties, the Tribunal exercised its power to modify technical rules of evidence when necessary. On 18 June 1946, the Tribunal declared its intention to replace the method of interrogation in the direct examination of a witness by a reading of his testimony. The new process was as follows: The witness prepared his testimony as an affidavit, and the prosecution or the defence (depending on which party provided the witness) translated his affidavit into the language used in court (either from Japanese to English or vice versa) and served it to the other party before the hearing commenced. The other party was given an affidavit well in advance so that it had enough time to decide whether to object, and plan the cross-examination. After the witness took his oath, the counsel of the witness's party would ask the witness, 'Is this the affidavit you made for the court?' When the witness said 'yes', the examiner would ask, 'Do you believe that the statements set forth in this affidavit are true?' When the witness answered 'yes' again, the examiner would request the Tribunal to admit the affidavit. Upon the Tribunal's agreement, the Clerk would announce its admission and assign it an exhibit number and the examiner read out the affidavit. The affidavit was simultaneously translated in the headphone as it was being read out, thereby saving much time.

If the opposite party had any objection to the affidavit, it had to raise it and cite the reasons for objecting to it, before its admission by the Tribunal. In such a case, registration and reading would not take place until the Tribunal's ruling on it.

The direct examination concluded after the examiner read out the affidavit. He could raise further questions for the witness, if he had any. Only a few supplementary questions were raised because the affidavit had been rehearsed already.

The change in the method of direct examination from interrogation to reading out the affidavits was a revolutionary step in the trial procedure of the Tokyo Tribunal. Had the Tribunal continued with the conventional common law practice of interrogation for direct examination of witnesses, the Tokyo Trial would have been protracted indefinitely. Among various measures taken by the Tribunal to hasten the trial, this was undoubtedly the best.

4.3.3.2 Second Step: Cross-Examination

Cross-examination is an important step in testification, although not compulsory for every witness. If the other party does not wish to cross-examine the witness after his direct examination, the process of testification terminates and the witness can leave the stand.

The other party can give up its right to cross-examine the witness for the following reasons: The facts stated by the witness are simple and clear with no loopholes; the witness is firm and his testimony is reasonable, so the opposite party cannot extract any favourable details from him; or the facts stated by the witness have no probative value and, in the opposite party's opinion, will not be taken seriously by the court. For instance, the defence invited many former colleagues, comrade-in-arms or subordinates of the defendants to testify in the Tokyo Trial. The witnesses vouched for the honesty, peaceable nature and willingness for international cooperation of the defendants. The prosecution usually refrained from cross-examining such witnesses as an expression of their contempt.

The rest of the witnesses were inevitably cross-examined. It is estimated that about half of the 400 witnesses who appeared in the Tokyo Trial were cross-examined.

Cross-examination is carried out by the lawyer or representative of the opposing party. For the Tokyo Trial, the prosecution witnesses were cross-examined by the defence counsel, and the defence witnesses, by the IPS, i.e. the Chief Prosecutor and the associate and assistant prosecutors from the different Allied countries. A defence witness was cross-examined by only one prosecutor because the IPS was a single unit, while a prosecution witness could be cross-examined by one or several defence lawyers. The defence lawyers did not comprise a unit, but were a group of counsel representing the different interests of different defendants. Therefore, if a witness's testimony was made against several defendants, he could be cross-examined by a counsel of each of those defendants. For example, Puyi, the emperor of the puppet state, attacked the defendants Itagaki, Doihara, Minami, Hoshino, Kaya and a few others in his testimony. Therefore, he was tediously cross-examined by the counsel of each of those defendants; Puyi's testimony lasted for eight days. Other witnesses, such as Chin Teh-Chun, Cyril Wilde, John Liebert, Joseph Ballantine and Ryukichi Tanaka, were also at the witness stand being cross-examined for days together.

The main objective of the cross-examination was to question the witness in such a manner that his testimony appeared incorrect, false, inconsistent, illogical or nonsensical, thus reducing its probative value. The second objective was to attack the credibility of the witness so that the court doubts the testimony. The third objective was to raise new questions (questions on subjects not dealt with during the direct examination) to exact favourable responses.

A competent prosecutor or defence counsel effectively performs the above-mentioned objectives. Since the conflict between the two parties culminates at the point of cross-examination, the examiner exerts his best efforts to find fault with the witness and his testimony.[21]

---

[21] In the Tokyo Tribunal, Arthur Comyns-Carr, the associate prosecutor from the UK, was considered the best examiner of cross-examinations. His questions were sharp, penetrative and precise, and frightened the defence witnesses and lawyers. On the other hand,

The cross-examination is the most difficult step for the witness. In the direct examination, rehearsed questions are asked amiably by a representative of his own party, whereas in the cross-examination, the witness is harshly interrogated by an opponent. The questions in the cross-examination can be unpredictable, strange, or even irrelevant. Therefore, the witness has to be vigilant while answering and not allow the examiner to take advantage of his responses. The British jurist Harris once compared the cross-examination of witnesses to the anatomical examination of the dead. He wrote: 'It is somewhat like anatomy in forensic medicine; what is different is that the witness is alive, and he is very sensitive to torture.'[22]

The Tokyo Tribunal always disputed over the scope of questioning witnesses in the cross-examination. Ideally, the cross-examination must be confined to the content of the witness's testimony, that is, the facts related and the opinions expressed in the direct examination. If left unchecked, the cross-examination procedure would become an endless battle of words, and the witness would get confused. Unfortunately, the Tribunal did not make the right choice in the early days of the trial but modelled it on the British precedents, which adopted a liberal stance towards variety of questions asked in the cross-examination. Except for

many of the American defence counsel were mediocre; they were often rebuked for their stupid questions by the President. For example, Japanese witness Tamon Meada testified for the prosecution that the Japanese warlords had tried to limit the education and influence the ideology of young people to subject them to aggressive war policies. The American counsel Kleiman asked the witness in his cross-examination, 'Among the courses that were taught in the elementary school, was not Japanese language taught?' The President interrupted by saying, 'That is utterly impossible. Was not the Japanese language taught in the Japanese schools?' He instructed the witness not to answer. Kleiman proceeded to ask, 'Was arithmetic taught to those students?' The President said sternly, 'Well, that is impossible. This is a serious case. You are before the International Military Tribunal for the Far East trying former leaders of Japan of the greatest series of crimes ever committed against men.' He then again instructed the witness not to answer. Kleiman tried to justify his question and continued, 'Was music, penmanship, drawing, Japanese history, needle work, taught in the schools?' The President was furious with these stupid questions and said, 'The witness need not answer.' Only after this third setback did Kleiman pick up his briefcase and said in a low voice, 'No further questions.' This was a striking example of the foolery of the American defence counsel. See *Transcript of Proceedings and Documents of the International Military Tribunal for the Far East* (2 August 1946), and Chapter 2, Sect. 2.5 of this book.

[22] *Experience in the Legal Profession*, p. 38. Cited from М. Ю. Рагинский and С. Я. Розенблит, *International Trial of the Japanese Major War Criminals*, p. 123.

some irrelevant questions, none of the questions raised in the cross-examination were stopped by the Tribunal. This encouraged the examiner to question the witness on subjects uncovered during the direct examination to exact responses that are useful for future debates and summaries by the opposite party.

This proved to be a bad idea because it created ramifications and ambiguity and wasted time. Consequently, on 25 June 1946, the IPS applied to the Tribunal for a change in practice, but it was denied by the President without consultation with the other judges.[23]

The indiscriminate refusal by the President caused dissatisfaction among some judges. They believed that it was necessary to restrict the scope of cross-examination to prevent the protraction of the trial. After several rounds of discussions among the judges, a resolution to that effect was passed at the judges' conference and announced in court on 25 July 1946.[24]

The resolution stated: 'The Tribunal has decided that in the future all cross-examinations shall be limited to matters arising in the examination in chief.' Therefore, when questioning a witness in the cross-examination, the examiner could only ask questions related to subjects that were mentioned in the witness's testimony, namely the facts stated or opinions expressed in the direct examination. Additionally, those questions also had to be on important, case-related subjects and not on trivial, incidental issues.

After defining the scope of cross-examination, the questioning of witnesses was restricted. Although there was no clear demarcation between the main and trivial subjects, the Tribunal could forbid the witness from answering certain questions raised by the examiner during cross-examination. If the examiner continued to ask irrelevant questions, the Tribunal could reprimand him or stop his cross-examination. Additionally, the party providing the witness (i.e. the party conducting the direct examination) could also request withdrawal of irrelevant questions or prohibition of response, from the Tribunal.[25]

---

[23] *Transcripts of Proceedings and Documents of the International Military Tribunal for the Far East*, p. 1358.

[24] *Transcripts of Proceedings and Documents of the International Military Tribunal for the Far East*, p. 2512.

[25] In the cross-examination, the examiner stood at the podium and asked many questions to the witness sitting in the witness box. A representative of the party providing the

Since the scope of cross-examination was restricted by the Tribunal, the time consumed in this intense verbal combat between the parties was greatly reduced. With regard to speeding the trial procedures, this modification was revolutionary and significant.

Although the cross-examination was meant to be restricted to the subjects mentioned in the testimony, a question attacking the credibility of a witness was allowed to be posed. Such an attack was not expressly permitted in the Tokyo Charter, the Rules of Procedure or the resolution of the judges' conference, but owing to the influence of the common law system, the Tribunal adopted a tolerant attitude towards such questions.

An attack on the disposition or credibility of a witness was beyond the permitted limits of cross-examination, but during the Tokyo Trial, the cross-examiner often freely questioned the witness's credibility, without any objection from the Tribunal. For instance, when the former Japanese major general Ryukichi Tanaka testified for the prosecution, an American defence counsel asked him in the cross-examination, 'Were you mentally sick?' He also asked Tanaka, 'Have you been promised any immunity that you will not be indicted as war criminal by giving your testimony here?' Furthermore, in the cross-examination of the prosecution witness John Goette, the American defence counsel asked, 'What pay are you receiving during the period that you are in attendance upon this Tribunal?' He explained that 'in our practice in the United States we feel that there is no more important method of impeaching a witness than to show his (pecuniary) interest in the matter'. In another instance, towards the end of his lengthy testification, Puyi, Emperor of the puppet state Manchukuo, was asked by the Japanese defence counsel, 'Do you know that the Chinese government proposes to try you as a criminal for collaboration with Japan?'

Although the Tribunal did not encourage attacks on the witness's disposition and credibility, it took no measures to thwart them. This was undoubtedly because of the influence of common law system in which tarnishing a witness's reputation to make the court doubt his credibility and reduce the probative value of his testimony was permitted in cross-examination.

---

witness (usually the examiner of the direct examination) sat near the cross-examiner. When the latter asked an inappropriate question, he could immediately go to the podium and raise an objection to the bench. In that situation, he acted like the witness's 'protector' or 'guardian'.

Furthermore, the cross-examiner in the Tokyo Tribunal could refer a document while questioning the witness and have it filed as a numbered exhibit after interrogation. For example, the Japanese defence counsel presented a letter requesting assistance, from Puyi to defendant Minami (the then Japan's War Minister), to refute Puyi's claim that only Japanese warlords were involved in the establishment of Manchukuo and he himself had been in a state of abject passivity. The letter was immediately submitted to the Tribunal as an evidentiary document and was accepted and filed. However, its authenticity was questioned by many, inside and outside court.

Among the 4300 written exhibits formally admitted and registered by the Tribunal, several hundred of them were submitted during cross-examination.

According to common law tradition, cross-examination in the testification process is crucial, to testing or effectively enhancing the probative value of the witness's testimony. If a witness makes irresponsible remarks or fabricates tales in the direct examination, he is bound to be 'beaten black and blue' by the other party during the cross-examination. On the contrary, if a witness speaks the factual truth of his experience, then he is more prepared to face the cross-examination with confidence. His answers are bound to be clear, without discrepancies which can be taken advantage of by the other party. As the Chinese proverb goes: 'True gold does not fear fire.' Most of the Chinese and Western witnesses in the hearing of the Nanking Massacre were credible. Their testimonies were true and their attitudes resolute. The Japanese and American defence lawyers tried their best to unsettle them during the cross-examinations, but the witnesses efficiently countered each of their questions. Finally, the defence had to accept defeat.

Theoretically, the process of cross-examination cannot be criticized. However, in practice, it often demands much time and resources. Especially in a court such as the Tokyo Tribunal which dealt with several hundred complex cases and witnesses, the practice proved to be labour-intensive and expensive, and greatly prolonged the trial.

The cross-examination could not be conducted through written statements, nor was it (or could be) discussed between the parties in advance. It had to be conducted only by interrogation and the answers to all questions had to be translated (from Japanese to English or vice versa, or to both English and Japanese if the witness spoke a third language). The translation itself often took more time than the interrogation. Moreover, the prosecution and the defence had time-consuming arguments about whether a raised question was within the scope of the testimony. For example, during the testification of Chin Teh-Chun, former Vice Minister of Defence of the Chinese government, the reading of his affidavit in the direct examination took about two hours, but the interrogation in the cross-examination lasted for more than four days. In the case of Puyi, Emperor of the puppet state Manchukuo, nearly seven out of eight days of his testification was spent in cross-examination. It is estimated that in the nearly two years of the open sessions of the Tokyo Trial, almost half of the trial time was spent in cross-examining hundreds of witnesses.

4.3.3.3 Third Step: Re-direct Examination

Re-direct examination is a direct examination of the witness for the second time. Like the first direct examination, the re-direct examination is conducted by a representative of the party inviting the witness (a prosecutor or a defence counsel). It is usually performed by the examiner of the first direct examination himself.

The re-direct examination, like the cross-examination, is not always necessary. After the direct examination, the opposite party can disclaim its right to cross-examine the witness, and the testification process thus completes. Similarly, after the cross-examination, the examiner of the direct examination can choose not to perform the re-direct examination and therefore, the witness's testification comes to a close.

However, if the party performing the direct examination wishes to re-examine the witness, it can perform a re-direct examination and the court must permit it.

The Tokyo Trial had strictly limited the scope of re-direct examination. The examiner could only ask the witness to confirm or clarify topics covered in the cross-examination. Any other question would be prevented by the Tribunal or opposed by the opposite other party.

Nevertheless, if the examiner wished to question the witness on a topic that had not been covered in the direct examination or cross-examination, he could do so in the re-direct examination with prior permission from the Tribunal. This was, however, a rare occurrence because the main objective of the re-direct examination was to clarify the issues that were raised in the direct examination but distorted in the cross-examination. Therefore, the Tribunal would allow such a special request only when it was absolutely necessary.

4.3.3.4 Fourth Step: Re-Cross-Examination

Re-cross-examination is also not imperative to the testification process. After the re-direct examination of the witness, the opposite party can choose not to re-cross-examine the witness, and the court will release the witness from his role of testifying before the court.

Re-cross-examination is conducted by the party which has done the cross-examination. Usually, it is carried out by the same examiner as in the first cross-examination.

The Tokyo Tribunal imposed a strict restriction on the scope of re-cross-examination. Here, the examiner could only question the witness about new facts or opinions mentioned in the re-direct examination with the Tribunal's special permission. If the witness did not make any new comments in the re-direct examination, the re-cross-examination would be inconsequential.

This completes the discussion of the four steps of the testification process that a witness attending the Tokyo Tribunal undergoes, and their associated rules.

It is evident that the first step was mandatory for every witness. Many witnesses underwent the second step. Only a small number of witnesses were involved in the third step, and very few underwent all four steps.[26] Out of the total 419 witnesses, only about 30 underwent the entire round of testification.

The first and second steps of the testification process were most important. The first step was the foundation for the whole process. The second step was intense and illustrated the fierce conflict between the parties. It was a ruthless ordeal for a witness to undergo the second step of testification. Meanwhile, it placed heavy demands on the Tribunal because it was the most time-consuming and controversial step of testification.

---

[26] Among the 419 witnesses, 16 defendants (including Tōjō and Araki) took the witness stand in the Tribunal. According to Article 9(d) of the Tokyo Charter, the defendant could conduct his defence either through himself or through his counsel but not through both. Since all the defendants in the Tribunal hired lawyers to defend themselves, the 16 defendants were interrogated as 'witnesses' rather than defendants. Under the criterion that the testification should be voluntary, nine defendants refused to testify; they were: Hiranuma, Hirota, Doihara, Umezu, Kimura, Satō, Shigemitsu, Hoshino and Hata. Although they appeared in court every day, for the entire trial, they only sat quietly in the dock. It was believed that those nine defendants were cunning enough not to expose themselves and 'ask for trouble'.

Disputes over language translation or the scope of questions broke out easily, necessitating a quick decision by the bench.

The testification of witnesses proved to be a more interesting spectacle than legal debates or the reading of evidentiary documents for spectators and journalists. When those 'special guests' came to testify in the Tribunal, the public gallery became crowded and the news reporters became more alert. Some such 'special guests' were Puyi, Emperor of the puppet state Manchukuo; Chin Teh-Chun, Mayor of Peiping (Peking) during the Marco Polo Bridge Incident; Wang Len-Chai, the then head of Wanping County; John Powell, editorial writer of *Millard's Review*; James Richardson, US Admiral; Cyril Wilde, British Colonel; Ryukichi Tanaka, nicknamed as 'The Monster'; and the once-powerful defendants: Tōjō, Koiso, Araki, Kido, Minami, Shimada, Itagaki, Hashimoto and Matsui. It was said that a ticket to the courtroom sometimes costed more than a thousand Japanese yen on the black market. During the long Tokyo Trial, news reporters across the world flocked mainly to the testimonies and cross-examinations of witnesses. The journalists were less interest in the evidentiary documents and legal debates in court.

Testifying and examination of the witnesses consumed most of the time during the Tokyo Trial; it is estimated that more than 50 per cent of the open hearing time was spent on witness testification, out of which about 80 per cent of the time was spent on the second step, i.e. the cross-examination (Fig. 4.2).

4.4 Affidavits from Non-attending Witnesses and the Defendants' Confessions

During the course of the entire trial, the Tokyo Tribunal admitted 4336 evidentiary documents, out of which 2734 were provided by the prosecution and 1602 by the defence.

Four hundred and nineteen witnesses were summoned to testify in court: 109 'prosecution witnesses' and 310 'defence witnesses'. All of them attended court for oral or written testimony in the direct examination, many were cross-examined by the opposite party, and some underwent the re-direct examination and the re-cross-examination procedures. Owing to such extensive tests in court, the Tribunal easily accepted their testimonies as evidence.

There were some witnesses who were unable to testify in court because of health problems or career obligations, but who were willing to provide

Fig. 4.2 Puyi's testimony

written testimonies for the prosecution or the defence. The written testimonies were treated differently from ordinary evidentiary documents. They were either presented with a solemn oath in court or in the presence of a judicial officer and signed or sealed by the witness. This kind of written testimony under oath is called an 'affidavit' in common law courts, which means that the honesty and accuracy of its content are guaranteed by the oath of the witness; if there is any false or deceptive statement, the witness would be severely punished for breaching his oath.

Article 13(c)(3) of the Tokyo Charter stipulates that the Tribunal should admit 'an affidavit, deposition or other signed statement'. This broad provision permits a solemnly written testimony in the form of an affidavit to be unquestioningly accepted by the Tribunal. Since the President and many other judges exhibited a typical prejudice of the common law system against affidavits, and the defence counsel were opposed to it, the admissibility of an affidavit was debated for several days before finalizing it.

According to the common law tradition, a witness should testify in open court and, if required, be cross-examined by the opposite party before the court accepts his testimony as evidence. Therefore, the party providing the witness must ensure that the court can summon him to attend court in person; otherwise, he will lose his status as a witness. A written testimony cannot replace a witness's physical presence in court.

There are a few exceptions to this established rule. For example, when a witness giving written testimony promises to appear in court but dies or takes ill suddenly, the court can admit his written testimony.[27] Another exception is when the written testimony has been obtained and certified by the judge himself, or if it was made in the presence of the other party or its lawyer and the witness has promised to be cross-examined in court when necessary. Only such written testimonies were meant to be accepted by the court; the rest had to be rejected. This depicts a preconceived notion of the common law courts that cross-examination was the best manner of examining a witness and a written testimony presented in his absence could not bear the same probative value.

The tradition of the common law courts, however, was broken during World War II itself. The 'rules of procedure' promulgated by the United Kingdom in 1940 clearly allowed the prosecutors to use the written statements of witnesses as evidences and written testimonies were largely accepted in the US military courts. However, in the Tokyo Tribunal, several judges who came from common law countries could not extricate themselves from the influence of the common law system. This caused heated debates between the judges of divided loyalties. The judges who were against the common law procedures won the dispute because their stance was backed by the Tokyo Charter itself. Article 13 of the Charter has a general provision: 'The Tribunal shall not be bound by technical rules of evidence. It shall adopt and apply to the greatest possible extent, expeditious and non-technical procedure, and shall admit any evidence which it deems to have probative value.' Moreover, Item (c)(3) of this

---

[27] For a witness who cannot appear in court because of serious illness or other valid reasons, the court may send a 'commissioned judge', along with a clerk, a stenographer and lawyers of both parties, to the witness's residence for a small-scale court session. This can be called a 'bedside court hearing', similar to an open court hearing in which there is direct examination, cross-examination (if necessary) and questions by the judge. The details of the hearing are recorded and added to the official transcripts of court proceedings. This method is permitted by all courts including those based in the common law system. The Nuremberg Tribunal used it many times. However, the Tokyo Tribunal used it only once—Judge Northcroft from New Zealand conducted a 'bedside court hearing' for bedridden witness Kanji Ishihara. See *Transcripts of Proceedings and Documents of the International Military Tribunal for the Far East* (4 April 1947), pp. 19384–19390.

Article further specifies that the Tribunal should admit 'an affidavit, deposition or other signed statement'.

Although this problem was resolved among the judges, the American defence lawyers still posed objections in the open hearings. Consequently, there were arguments between the President and the American counsel.

For instance, on 3 July 1946, barely two months after the commencement of the open sessions, Alan Mansfield, the Australian associate prosecutor, requested the Tribunal to accept as evidence several abstracts of the affidavits made by witnesses who personally experienced the brutal atrocities of Japanese army across the Pacific battlefields. He explained to the Tribunal, 'Most persons making the affidavits and statements are not in Japan but in various countries, and it is not intended to call them before the Tribunal. The prosecution is relying on the provision in the Charter in Article 13(c)(3), allowing affidavits, depositions or other signed statements to be produced in evidence.'

Soon after Mansfield had spoken, William Logan and a few other American lawyers rushed to the podium and loudly protested. They said that the introduction of affidavits as evidence without summoning the deponents 'involves a right which has long been recognized in the Anglo-Saxon law, and a right which is almost inalienable and recognized by this Tribunal, that the right to cross-examination is one which cannot be done away with'.

President Webb immediately refuted the criticism with the words, 'That is the usual rule. But we are operating under a Charter which does not preserve the right in itself.' 'We are not bound by the rules of evidence or the rules of procedure. The Charter prevents that.'

The President had made an immediate ruling because it had already been approved by the majority of the judges. This problem had been discussed many times at the judges' conferences and a decision had been made. Despite the President's retort, the American lawyers continued to object. The President then said sternly, 'I do not know of any court, or of any authority, that can review us....'

However, owing to technical reasons, the large number of affidavits regarding the Japanese army atrocities presented by Mansfield on behalf of the prosecution were not admitted as evidence in the court session of that day. It was only on 29 August 1946 that the Tribunal formally accepted affidavits or written statements from persons who did not appear in court and were not cross-examined.[28] From then onwards, both parties submitted many affidavits instead of presenting witnesses in court. Nearly 775 affidavits were submitted during the Tokyo Trial and were part of the 4336 exhibits accepted by the Tribunal. Each was assigned a uniform exhibit number according to their time of admission, and the admission procedure was the same as that for other evidentiary documents (as described in Sect. 4.2 of this chapter).

President Webb was a senior Australian judge educated under the common law system. Therefore, under the influence of common law, Webb was sceptical about the testimony of an un-cross-examined witness. However, since he represented the Tribunal, and the Tokyo Charter and the resolution of the judges' conference permitted the admission of such a testimony, he had to defend its admissibility in the open sessions. In actuality, he did not endorse the probative value of the affidavits of absent witnesses. Consequently, while accepting an evidence of this kind, he added 'we accept it for whatever probative value it may have', or 'it is admitted, subject to the usual terms', which meant that its probative value had to be determined in the future. Those unnecessary 'provisos' were proofs of the President's scepticism, but were harmless, unassailable statements which could not be censured by other judges.

Another noteworthy point about the affidavits was its difference from other evidentiary documents. Among the thousands of documents produced in evidence during the Tokyo Trial, some were archives from government agencies or social institutions, others were reports and correspondences of officials, and some others were private diaries, letters, memoirs and other writings. All documents shared a common feature: they were all pre-existing documents and not created specifically for the Tokyo Trial. This meant that the documents were strongly objective and thus had a good probative value. Although the affidavits bore the oath of the deponent, they bore traces of subjectivity because they were created for the benefit of the deponent's party and presented to the court by that party's representative on behalf of the deponent. In case of an affidavit, the opportunity to test a witness's testimony by aggressive cross-examinations is lost. Therefore, many judges, especially those from countries following common law procedures who recognize the

---

[28] Regarding admission of the affidavits of non-attending witnesses, see *Transcripts of Proceedings and Documents of the International Military Tribunal for the Far East* (3 July and 29 August 1946).

'inalienable right to cross-examination', found the probative value of a non-attending deponent's affidavit to be limited. They felt that it could not be compared with other documentary evidences or testimonies of the witnesses appearing in court. Therefore, the President was always reluctant to accept such affidavits as evidence in the Tokyo Trial.

This completes the discussion about the conditions for making the affidavit, the manner in which it was admitted by the Tribunal, and its probative value. The next discussion is on another kind of document: the statement of the accused war criminals in the interrogations.

As mentioned earlier in Chapter 3, Sect. 3.2 'Investigation and Preparation for Prosecution by the IPS', after the arrest of four batches of alleged major war criminals by the GHQ, more than 100 Japanese suspects were detained at Sugamo Prison, and the IPS (which had been designated as the prosecuting organ for the future international trial) conducted a preliminary investigation on them in late 1945. The investigation procedures by the IPS became intense after the promulgation of the Tokyo Charter on 19 January 1946 and the announcement of the list of judges on 14th February. This was because the Tokyo Tribunal was soon to be established, and the trial of Japanese Class-A war criminals would begin. The IPS limited their investigation to the more than 20 war criminals selected from the arrestees as defendants to be tried in the first case. The IPS performed detailed interrogations of the selected defendants; some of them were interrogated for five or six times and their interrogations resulted in pages of written records.

All but four (Itagaki, Kimura, Shigemitsu and Umezu) of the 28 Class-A war criminals prosecuted in the Tokyo Tribunal had interrogation records made by the IPS during its long investigation. Itagaki and Kimura were commanding troops overseas (in Singapore and Burma, respectively) and were arrested by the local military authorities when Japan surrendered. They were not escorted to Tokyo until the Tribunal officially opened, and therefore the IPS did not have an opportunity to interrogate them and record their statements. In the case of Shigemitsu and Umezu, there was no time for interrogation because the IPS had omitted to include them in the list of defendants until the last minute.[29]

---

[29] From the time when a prisoner was formally identified as a defendant in the Tokyo Trial, he was considered to be on the opposing side of the prosecution and, unlike in the previous period when he was detained but not yet indicted, he could no longer be contacted by the prosecution except in the open court. This was a rule particular to the

The IPS had thus made an interrogation report for each of the other 24 defendants. The report was a word-for-word record of the questions and answers between the interrogator and the defendant in the interrogation. At the Tokyo Trial, the two parties had disagreements about the manner in which those 24 interrogation reports should be used, and whether they could be used as evidentiary documents and admitted by the Tribunal.

During the trial, the IPS tried presenting the interrogation records and requested the Tribunal to accept them as exhibits. The defence objected for the following reasons: (a) The record had not been signed by the concerned defendant or shown to him for his review and correction. (b) The record was a result of a unilateral effort by the prosecution without a representative from the Tribunal or defence. (c) Such an interrogation had been conducted only with some and not all (Itagaki and three others omitted) of the defendants. Therefore, those without records had an advantage over the rest. On the basis of these shortcomings, the defence urged the Tribunal to refuse admitting the interrogation records as evidence.

The problem was also discussed among the judges. Most of the judges without a common law background considered it acceptable to admit interrogation records as evidence. This was because the decision was in accord with the explicit provision of the Tokyo Charter: 'The Tribunal shall not be bound by technical rules of evidence. It shall adopt ... non-technical procedure, and shall admit any evidence which it deems to have probative value.'[30] As the interrogation records were a result of arduous efforts of the IPS, they definitely had probative value. However, the common law judges were in favour of the conventional rules of evidence in the common law system. They believed that the unconditional admission of interrogation records was inappropriate because these records were disjunct with mainstream affidavits and did not sufficiently safeguard the interests of the defendants.

Owing to the difference in ideas among judges, the Tribunal adopted an intermediary approach: (a) The interrogation record of any one defendant could not be submitted to the Tribunal as a whole for admission as evidence. (b) If the defendant took the witness stand, he could voluntarily

---

common law system, which was followed by the Tokyo Tribunal. Since Itagaki, Kimura, Shigemitsu and Umezu had not been arrested before the indictment, the IPS could not interrogate them and take their statements. See Chapter 3, Sect. 3.2 of this book.

[30] *Charter of the International Military Tribunal for the Far East*, Article 13(a).

acknowledge the entire content of his interrogation record to be correct, so that it would become a part of his testimony. (c) If the defendant took the stand but did not acknowledge the entire content of his interrogation record, then the prosecutor could take as much advantage of the unacknowledged content and urge him to admit certain facts or else be proven self-contradictory. In this way, the Tribunal efficiently dealt with the defendants' interrogation records.

However, it was solely the choice of the individual defendant to decide whether he would testify as a witness. This was because the Tribunal had no powers to compel anyone to testify at court; its powers were limited to approving the witness lists prepared by both parties and assisting the parties in summoning the persons thereon. Konichi Hatano's example was a case in point.[31]

The defendants did not speak in defence of themselves (they were defended by their counsel), and some of them (nine, including Doihara, Hirota, Hiranuma, Umezu, Shigemitsu, Kimura, Satō, Hata and Hoshino) refused to take the witness stand to testify. They sat mutely in the dock, day after day, without giving the prosecution a chance to cross-examine or use the content of their interrogation records for cross-examination during the entire trial. Those nine defendants were thought to have slyly evaded testification because their cases were complex and they had confessed much during investigation. If they had testified, they would have been aggressively cross-examined by the prosecution. Therefore, they preferred to be silent. The prosecution thus lost the opportunity to use their interrogation records.

In a bid to lessen their guilt, some of the 16 defendants who volunteered to testify as 'defence witnesses' (Tōjō, Koiso, Araki, Itagaki, Minami, Mutō, Oka, Shimada, Ōshima, Shiratori, Tōgō, Kaya, Suzuki, Hashimoto, Kido and Matsui), tried justifying their crimes. Hideki Tōjō and some others even exalted themselves as 'national heroes' by glorifying their crimes. Before his direct examination, Tōjō had slyly managed to add the statement, 'This is a historic document' to his written testimony. When the Tribunal uncovered his ploy, he was immediately rebuked for his action by the President.

The prosecution aggressively cross-examined defendants who were willing to testify and forced them to confess and acknowledge facts

---

[31] See Sect. 4.3.1 of this chapter.

formerly stated during investigation. If they denied or modified their previous statements, the prosecutors accused them of self-contradiction and inconsistency and put them in a disadvantageous position.

Thus, most of the interrogation records prepared by the IPS were well utilized during the trial, except for a few that belonged to defendants who did not testify. It was a pity that those painstakingly prepared interrogation records were defective (were not read out to the interrogated persons or signed by them) and therefore were not completely adopted as evidences by the Tribunal. Since the Tokyo Tribunal practiced 'evidentialism', any document that was not officially admitted or any testimony that was not a part of the trial records could not be referenced by the parties in their debates and summaries or by the Tribunal in its final judgement.

4.5 Criticism of the Trial Proceedings

The Tokyo Trial took place for a long time mainly because of the complexity and multifariousness of the trial procedures.

Some contradictions can be seen in the provisions of the Tokyo Charter.

In accordance with the Charter's suggestion of a 'prompt trial' for Japanese war criminals, Article 12 ('Conduct of Trial') provides: 'The Tribunal shall: (a) Confine the trial strictly to an expeditious hearing of the issues raised by the charges. (b) Take strict measures to prevent any action which would cause any unreasonable delay and rule out irrelevant issues and statements of any kind whatsoever', and Article 13 ('Evidence') stipulates: 'The Tribunal shall not be bound by technical rules of evidence. It shall adopt and apply to the greatest possible extent expeditious and non-technical procedure, and shall admit any evidence which it deems to have probative value.' Undoubtedly, these articles aimed to lessen the trial period.

However, in an attempt to make the trial 'fair', the Charter also stipulates many complicated rules which hinder the possibility of an expeditious trial. Those rules were not necessarily an integral part of a fair trial, but peculiar aspects of the common law system. For example, the meticulous procedure of direct examination and cross-examination given in Article 15 of the Charter, reflects cumbersome common law traditions.

Experts from common law countries drafted the Tokyo Charter and the Rules of Procedure of the Tribunal. Moreover, most members of the

Tribunal had a common law background. Consequently, the provisions as well as the implementation of trial proceedings, directly or indirectly, bore the influence of Anglo-American law. As mentioned before, the common law system is a historical legal system with a formalistic pattern, a high degree of subjectivity and complicated procedures.

Therefore, there was a contradiction between purpose and methodology in the trial proceedings of the Tokyo Tribunal. In summary, although the Tokyo Charter had empowered the Tribunal to make decisions for an expeditious trial, the complex rules adopted by the Tribunal, and the customary prejudices held by the common law judges towards trial proceedings, prevented the occurrence of an expeditious trial.

The Tribunal tried to minimize this problem by using written testimonies (affidavits) instead of conducting interrogations during the direct examination. It also limited the scope of questions in the cross-examination to the content of the witness's testimony during direct examination. These two measures taken at an early period of the trial by the Tribunal made 'revolutionary' changes to the trial procedures of the Tribunal. Since the Tribunal received more than 400 witnesses, without these timely changes the Tokyo Trial may have extended a year longer.

The Tribunal's efforts to achieve a 'prompt trial' were not enough because it failed to effectively exercise the powers granted to it by Articles 12 and 13 of the Tokyo Charter.

Given below is a discussion of some shortcomings of the trial proceedings in the Tokyo Tribunal. If they had been rectified during the trial, the Tokyo Trial would have been shorter and more politically influential.

First of all, the court was too lenient towards the defence. It was necessary to take measures to make the trial fair for the defendants; however, when this privilege was misused by the defendants, the Tribunal did not take any remedial action. For example, the Tokyo Charter provided that 'each accused shall have the right to be represented by counsel of his own selection' but did not specify how many lawyers each defendant could have and whether he could have lawyers of different nationalities. In practice, the Tribunal allowed each defendant to engage one American lawyer and an unlimited number of Japanese lawyers. Some defendants, such as Shigetarō Shimada, had as many as eight lawyers, while many others had at least five each. Consequently, each defendant had a small defence group and those groups combined to form a large, strong team. The lawyers in those groups frequently diverted the attention of the Tribunal from the main issues. They exploited the leniency of the Tribunal and tried to delay the trial. The American lawyers, especially, wasted time pestering the Tribunal about minor common law procedures. A number of American lawyers, such as Ben Bruce Blakeney, misbehaved in court and passed offensive remarks against the Soviet Union and their own country, the United States. They foresaw a third world war because of the tense relationship between the Soviet Union and the United States. Therefore, they hoped to protract the trial so that the Tokyo Tribunal may be dissolved and they could escape judgement.

The Tribunal hardly took any steps for the disturbances caused by the defence counsel. However, the Tribunal once disqualified two American lawyers from appearing in court, which made the defence counsel less aggressive.[32] Nevertheless, the Tribunal's measures were unable to adequately address the situation. In order to give the impression of a 'fair trial', it allowed the defence counsel to delay the trial with numerous interruptions. It imposed no sanction when they used the trial sessions as a forum to preach the fallacy of the accused and defame the Allied countries. This illustrates the leniency of the Tribunal towards the accused.

The Tribunal's leniency is also seen in the absence of a stipulation for defendants to take the stand and be interrogated in court. According to the Tokyo Charter, a defendant could not stand in his own defence if he had engaged a lawyer to do it for him.[33] Apparently, this provision limited the defendant's right to defence, but actually it provided him with an opportunity to escape direct interrogation. They could, however, volunteer to testify as 'defence witnesses', but the scope of their testimonies was limited. Therefore, cleverer defendants did not sign up as witnesses to avoid direct confrontation with the bench and the prosecution. Even the defendants who were willing to be cross-examined were questioned by the bench and the prosecution on only the topics covered in the direct examination, instead of being interrogated thoroughly on their crimes.

---

[32] In accordance with the provisions of Article 12(c) of the Tokyo Charter, the Tribunal stopped the service of two American defence counsel, David Smith and Owen Cunningham. For the reasons and processes of their dismissal, see Chapter 2, Sect. 2.5 of this book.

[33] *Charter of the International Military Tribunal for the Far East*, Article 9(d).

A defendant's refusal to speak in the Tribunal was permitted based on a traditional rule in the common law system against self-incrimination.[34] According to this rule, a criminal defendant could refuse to answer a compromising question or even opt to be completely silent during a trial. The motive of this rule is to protect the accused from making any statement against himself out of ignorance or fear of the court or prosecutor. Since the accused is entitled to remain silent, the barbaric practices of 'forced confession' and torture were averted.

This rule of protecting the accused against self-incrimination is peculiar to the common law system and does not exist in many other countries of the world as it does not conform to the concept of a 'fair trial'. It may be reasonable to apply this policy for simple, domestic criminal cases, but it was inappropriate for application in complex international cases as that handled by the Tokyo Tribunal. Some of the facts could not be determined without directly questioning the concerned defendant. Therefore, as described by the Chinese, the rule against self-incrimination created a context of 'getting half the result with twice the effort'. The accused could not be threatened or oppressed in any way at the Tokyo Tribunal. However, the Tribunal's strict adherence to this traditional rule of the common law system against self-incrimination, foiled its hope for a 'just and prompt trial'. The strict application of this rule could only be attributed to an allegiance to the common law system and an excessive leniency towards the accused.

A second drawback of the trial proceedings was the imperfect scrutiny of declared witnesses. Although the parties themselves decided whom to invite and made a list of witnesses to be approved and summoned by the Tribunal, the Tribunal was expected to instruct the concerned party to furnish 'the facts proposed to be proved by the witness ... and the relevancy of such facts to the defence', apart from providing details about their background.[35] If the Tribunal was dissatisfied with those statements, it had the right to refuse to summon certain witnesses. However, it rarely

---

[34] The rule against self-incrimination means that a criminal defendant has the right to refuse to make any confession or statement in court that may portray him as guilty. Therefore, he can remain silent during the trial, without answering any questions raised by the prosecution. This is a very important rule in the common law system for the protection of human rights. The United States has included this rule in the Fifth Amendment to the Constitution and considers it a sacred and inviolable right of all citizens.

[35] *Charter of the International Military Tribunal for the Far East*, Article 9(e).

scrutinized the lists and usually approved all the witnesses proposed by the parties. During the course of the trial, witnesses walking in and out of the courtroom was a common feature and their testification consumed most of the trial time. There were a total of 419 witnesses: 109 'prosecution witnesses' and 310 'defence witnesses'—a record-breaking occurrence in the judicial history of the world.

It is worth mentioning that the number of the defence witnesses received by the Tribunal was nearly thrice as many as prosecution witnesses. This is another demonstration of the Tribunal's clemency towards the accused. However, the testimonies of many of those defence witnesses were irrelevant and ambiguous. Many of them were the defendants' relatives, friends, former colleagues or subordinates, who were nominated by the defence to speak in their favour. They were unaware of the facts of the case. When they faced the prosecution's cross-examination, they either rambled or stared mutely. Hence, their testimonies had no probative value. The Tribunal finally admitted: 'In the experience of this Tribunal, most of the witnesses for the Defence have not attempted to face up to their difficulties. They have met them with prolix equivocations and evasions, which only arouse distrust.'[36]

If the Tribunal had carefully checked the details of the witnesses (such as the relationship between the witness and the defendant, the witness's qualification and experience, the facts he could prove, and the relevance of such facts to the case), at least one-third of the proposed defence witnesses could have been rejected. This would have saved much time and averted the difficulties involved in the subsequent evaluation of the evidence. Moreover, the reputation, quality of proceedings and political influence of the Tribunal would have increased.

The formalistic and laissez-faire approach adopted by the Tribunal was a major setback to the Trial.

The third drawback of the trial proceedings was the failure to fully utilize the provision of a 'commissioned judge' and 'hearing outside the courtroom' (or 'bedside court hearing').

According to the Tokyo Charter, 'The Tribunal shall have the power: ... to appoint officers for the carrying out of any task designated by the Tribunal, including the power to have evidence taken on commission.'[37] The practice of appointing officers to collect evidence outside

---

[36] *Judgment of the International Military Tribunal for the Far East* (Chinese Translation), Part A, Chap. 1, The 1950s Press, pp. 9–10.

[37] *Charter of the International Military Tribunal for the Far East*, Article 11(e).

the courtroom is used in the judicial systems of many countries. Usually, the court sends a judge called the 'commissioned judge', along with a clerk, a stenographer and other court staff and the legal representatives of both parties, to the location of the witness or any other place designated by the court to obtain the witness's testimony. This saves the time lost in public hearings. The procedures of the 'hearing outside the courtroom' are simpler than a formal court hearing, but still achieves the purposes of examining the witness and recording his testimony.

In the Nuremberg Tribunal for German major war criminals, the practice of gathering evidence outside the courtroom by a judge on commission was frequently employed and saved much of the trial time. This was probably one of the reasons why the Nuremberg Trial was completed in a short span of ten months. Unfortunately, the Tokyo Tribunal adopted this provision of the Tokyo Charter only once during the entire trial, that is, in 1947, for a witness (former Lieutenant General Kanji Ishihara) who was bedridden in his hometown Sakata City, Yamagata Prefecture.

Rest of the witnesses (exceeding 400) testified in court and were examined in the formal open sessions of the Tribunal.

As mentioned before, the defence witnesses who constituted three-fourths of the total witnesses, gave testimonies of little value. Even if the Tribunal had omitted to exercise its power to reject witnesses, it could have used commissioned judges to gather evidence outside the courtroom for some cases, to save trial time. Its failure to do so was a further setback to its trial proceedings.

Yet another shortcoming in the trial proceedings was that the Tribunal permitted many counsel to cross-examine witnesses.

Cross-examination was the most challenging and time-consuming step of the trial proceedings. Unlike direct examination, cross-examination could not be replaced by a written alternative, but had to be conducted through interrogations in court. The questions and answers between the examiner and the witness had to be translated to English or Japanese, or to both from a third language. This consumed time and triggered disputes about the fidelity of translation. The disputes were deferred to the Language Arbitration Board for arbitration. In addition, the scope of the cross-examination (e.g. whether a question to the witness was related to his main testimony) also instigated frequent arguments between the two parties and required a court ruling.

The Tribunal ought to have imposed limitations on cross-examination. However, the majority of the judges from common law countries had an implicit faith in cross-examination and an impractical understanding of 'fair trial'. Therefore, the Tribunal did not take any measures to limit the excessive cross-examination. Although it had restricted the scope of questioning to the main issues mentioned in the witness's testimony under direct examination, any breach against this directive was not stopped immediately or taken seriously.

As the Tribunal had not limited the number of cross-examiners, a witness could be cross-examined by several counsel and for several times after his direct examination. This was an unreasonable practice of 'bombing in waves' which enervated the witnesses. The discussion turned from the salient points of the witness's testimony to side-line topics and triggered unnecessary arguments. Thus, much of the trial time was wasted in the lengthy cross-examinations.

The IPS usually assigned only one prosecutor for the cross-examination of a defence witness. The questions drafted beforehand were asked by the designated examiner. In rare circumstances, the witness was additionally questioned by another prosecutor.

However, in the case of a prosecution witness, each of the defence counsel (both American and Japanese) could cross-examine him after his direct examination. This created much confusion, caused unnecessary stress to the witness and wasted much trial time. For example, when Puyi, Emperor of the puppet state Manchukuo, testified in court for the prosecution, the direct examination took only half a day, while the cross-examinations lasted for more than a week, with seven or eight defence counsel as cross-examiners. A similar situation occurred in the cross-examination of many other prosecution witnesses including Chin Teh-Chun, John Liebert, Cyril Wilde, James Richardson and Ryukichi Tanaka. If the cross-examination of Puyi had been conducted by only one defence counsel with consolidated questions, it would have saved at least half of the trial time and improved the quality of the cross-examination.

Since there was no limit on the number of cross-examiners, the defence lawyers would take turns to interrogate the same prosecution witness for some reason or the other. Although most of their questions were repetitive or senseless and frequently objected to, they helped achieve the defence's objective of wasting time and protracting the trial.

The Tokyo Charter ensured that each accused or their counsel examined each witness who testified[38] but that did not mean that the defendants enjoyed unrestricted right to cross-examination. The Tribunal had the power to stipulate in its Rules of Procedure or court order that

---

[38] *Charter of the International Military Tribunal for the Far East*, Article 15(e).

any witness provided by either party could be cross-examined by only one representative of the other party (a prosecutor or a defence counsel), and that all the questions to be addressed to the witness should be consolidated and coherently asked by that representative. If the Tribunal had stipulated this, both of the parties would have been treated equally, much time could have been saved, and the confusion caused by repetitive cross-examinations could have been avoided. The failure of the Tribunal to make such a stipulation was also one of the trial's shortcomings.

The above-mentioned points are a few major drawbacks in the trial proceedings of the Tokyo Tribunal; the minor ones have been omitted.

These problems were mainly due to the influence of the common law procedural rules. The Tokyo Charter suggested 'prompt trial and punishment of the major war criminals' and 'to adopt and apply to the greatest possible extent expeditious and non-technical procedure' but paradoxically adopted some complicated procedures of the common law system that countered its objective. During the trial, those complicated procedures were further influenced by common law prejudices of the Tribunal members with a common law background. Therefore, the Tokyo Trial could not be conducted expeditiously, and it protracted for two and a half years.

INDEX

A

Act of State, 21, 27
Administration Department, 103–107, 115
Admission, admissibility of evidence, 40, 90, 109, 110, 219, 222, 228–230, 232, 233, 245, 257, 259
Affidavit, 97, 224, 225, 244, 245, 251, 254, 256–259, 262
Allied and Associated Powers (or the Allied Powers) in World War I, 2, 3, 31
Allied Powers (or the Allies, or the Allied countries) in World War II, 4, 35, 120
Araki, Sadao, 68, 149, 151, 153, 157, 158, 162, 171, 180, 182, 187, 192, 193, 195, 199, 200, 202, 203, 215, 216, 227, 252, 253, 260
Archives of the Tokyo Tribunal, 115, 118
Arraignment ('guilty' or 'not guilty'), 43, 68, 219, 220

Arrest warrants, 40, 121–128, 132, 133, 136, 137, 152, 176
Assistant prosecutors, 48, 50, 81, 83–85, 113, 147, 221, 225, 246
Associate prosecutors (or Associate Counsel), 41, 48, 80, 81, 83–85, 139, 141, 147, 148, 150, 154, 195, 246, 256
Axis Powers, 1, 4, 5, 24, 153, 163, 172, 176, 179

B

Bataan Death March, 56, 147
Bernard, Henri, judge from France (or the French judge), 55
Blakeney, Ben Bruce, 97, 263
Blewett, George, 95, 96

C

Charter of the International Military Tribunal for the Far East (or the Tokyo Charter), 10, 39, 60, 101, 139, 187, 259, 263–265, 267

Charter of the International Military Tribunal (or the Nuremberg Charter), 6
Chief of Staff of the GHQ, 100
Chief Prosecutor (Chief of Counsel) of the Tokyo Tribunal, 41, 79, 85, 139, 185, 187
China Group of the prosecution, 84
Chin, Teh-Chun, 104, 234, 246, 251, 253, 267
Civil law, 59, 67, 70, 86, 90, 105, 185, 240
Class-A war criminals, 1, 2, 8, 20, 35–37, 40, 45, 59, 77, 78, 87, 119, 121, 122, 124, 126, 128, 133, 137, 138, 140, 149, 152, 154, 155, 176, 183, 184, 258
Class-B and Class-C war criminals, 36, 37, 76, 111
Clerk, 107–110, 113, 185, 186, 229, 230, 233, 245
Closing statement, 43, 78, 220, 221
Coleman, Beverly, 95, 96
Collegiate system, 79, 80, 139
Commissioned judge, and bedside court hearing, 46, 255, 265
Common law, 42, 59, 63, 65, 67, 69, 86, 89, 90, 98, 105, 141–144, 184, 220, 222, 224, 231, 235, 237–245, 249, 250, 254, 255, 257, 259, 261–264, 268
Comyns-Carr, Arthur S., 81, 83–85, 246
Conspiracy, 11, 12, 117, 158, 178, 182, 188–191, 195–198, 201–203, 211–214, 217
Conventional War Crimes, 12, 13, 15, 17–20, 26, 33–36, 68, 77, 189, 195, 201, 203, 207, 212, 217, 226
Cramer, Myron, judge from the USA (or the US judge), 55
Crimes against Humanity, 12, 13, 17–20, 26, 33, 35, 36, 188, 189, 201, 203, 207, 211, 212, 217, 226
Crimes against Peace (or Crime of Aggression), 9, 11–13, 17, 18, 20, 26, 34–37, 146, 188, 189, 195, 203, 211, 212, 216
Cross-examination, 50, 69, 70, 83–85, 87, 88, 95, 145, 236, 237, 239–241, 244–253, 255–257, 260, 261, 265–268
Cunningham, Owen, 68, 69, 89, 100, 263

D

Death penalty, capital punishment, 43, 77
Defence, 16, 21, 22, 26, 29, 32, 33, 41, 43, 46, 50, 56, 57, 68–70, 72, 78, 81, 83–85, 87, 88, 90, 93–96, 98–101, 103, 105, 109, 114, 116, 117, 143–145, 167, 170, 178, 185, 209, 220, 221, 223, 225, 226, 228–232, 234, 235, 237, 238, 240, 244–246, 250–254, 259, 260, 262–267
  defence counsel, 50, 55, 68, 70, 72, 87, 88, 90, 94, 221, 225, 226, 229, 233, 238, 240, 246, 247, 263, 267
  defence lawyers, 11, 17, 20, 21, 50, 123, 146, 221, 232, 236, 237, 246, 250, 267
Defendants (the accused), 21, 26, 28–33, 44, 48, 49, 58, 68, 70, 73, 77–79, 84, 86–90, 93, 94, 96, 99, 100, 104, 106, 111–113, 117, 120, 128, 133, 139–146, 149–154, 157, 159, 167, 171–173, 182, 184, 186–203, 206, 208–220, 226, 227, 234,

238, 245, 246, 252, 258–260, 262–265, 267
Direct examination, 70, 83, 88, 236, 239–241, 243–251, 255, 260–263, 266, 267
Doihara (or Dohihara), Kenji, 77, 84, 117, 121, 125, 145, 151, 153, 158–160, 164, 165, 180, 192–196, 200–202, 215, 216, 246, 252, 260

E
Emperor of Japan, 7, 152, 205
Evidence, 10, 17, 18, 25, 26, 37, 42, 43, 45, 70, 77–79, 83–85, 87, 90, 94, 95, 101, 105, 109, 110, 116–118, 137, 139, 140, 142–149, 152, 167, 175, 184, 194, 207, 211, 212, 214, 217, 218, 220–231, 234, 235, 239, 243, 244, 253–259, 261, 265, 266
Evidentialism, 105, 222, 261
Evidentiary document, 42, 109, 114, 116, 118, 148, 221, 222, 224, 226, 228–230, 232, 233, 235, 250, 253, 254, 257, 259
Exhibits, 109, 110, 224, 225, 227, 230, 233, 245, 250, 257, 259

F
Fair trial, 41, 58, 87–89, 96, 99, 100, 234, 235, 261, 263, 264, 266
Finance of the Tokyo Tribunal, 113

G
General Headquarter (GHQ), 10, 40, 46, 48, 53, 58, 65, 67, 74–78, 83, 90, 94–96, 99–102, 110–118, 119–123, 125, 128, 132, 133, 136–139, 147, 167, 175, 176, 187, 235, 258
General Secretary, 41, 48, 62, 72–76, 86, 88, 100–102, 105, 107, 108, 113, 130, 185, 224
Geneva Conventions, 14–16, 29
Goko, Kiyoshi, 137, 138, 140, 151
Golunsky, Sergei Alexandrovich, 81, 84, 154
Göring, Hermann, 6, 20, 31, 32, 112, 210, 211

H
Hague Conventions, 14–18, 24, 29, 196, 199, 204
Hashimoto, Kingorō, 94, 121, 125, 151, 153, 157, 158, 160, 161, 174, 192, 193, 199, 202, 203, 216, 253, 260
Hata, Shuroku, 132, 151, 153, 161, 168, 180, 182, 193, 194, 199–202, 215, 216, 252, 260
Hearsay evidence, 242
Higgins, John P., judge from the USA (or the US judge), 55, 58
Hiranuma, Kiichirō, 128, 129, 132, 142, 151, 153, 157, 162–164, 166, 168, 192–196, 199, 200, 202, 203, 215, 216, 252, 260
Hirota, Kōki, 51, 128, 129, 151, 153, 162, 163, 173, 182, 193, 195, 196, 199, 200, 202, 203, 215, 216, 252, 260
Homma, Masaharu, 121, 125, 137, 138, 172
Honjo, Shigeru, 123, 125–127, 136, 137, 164
Hoshino, Naoki, 129, 151, 153, 163, 164, 193, 195, 196, 200–202, 215, 216, 246, 252, 260
Hsiang, Che-Chun (Xiang Zhejun), 81, 84

Huanggutun Incident, 117, 150, 159

I
Indictment, 6, 10, 28, 41, 43, 77–79, 86, 87, 97, 140, 141, 143–145, 148, 149, 152, 154, 184–187, 189, 191, 192, 194, 195, 201, 203, 204, 206–212, 214, 217–220, 259
Individual responsibility, 3, 11, 21, 26, 27, 30, 33, 208
Instruments of Surrender, 6, 7, 9, 39, 53, 61–65, 76, 80, 119, 121, 124, 152, 177, 183, 189
International law, 11, 12, 15–18, 20–24, 26–30, 37, 38, 41, 77, 95, 103, 117, 188, 190, 191, 193, 194, 199, 207, 208
International Military Tribunal for the Far East (or the Tokyo Tribunal, or the Tokyo Trial): passim, 1
International Military Tribunal (or the Nuremberg Tribunal, or the Nuremberg Trial), 1
International Prosecution Section (IPS), 10, 76, 78–81, 83, 85–87, 96, 97, 138–141, 143–150, 152, 154, 159, 185–187, 208, 211, 212, 214, 218, 225, 236, 246, 248, 258, 259, 261, 267
Ishihara, Kanji, 46, 129, 255, 266
Itagaki, Seishirō, 77, 84, 144, 145, 151, 152, 159, 164, 165, 180, 193–195, 199–202, 209, 215, 216, 246, 253, 258–260

J
Jaranilla, Delfin, judge from the Philippines, 55, 56
Judgement of the Nuremberg Trial, 210

Judgement of the Tokyo Trial, 22, 33, 45
Judges' conference, 41, 55, 58–60, 62, 65, 69, 71–74, 96, 102, 109, 185, 186, 232, 244, 248, 249, 256, 257
Judges (Members) of the Tokyo Tribunal, 22, 185
Jurisdiction, 6, 9–12, 17, 20, 21, 26, 38, 40–42, 68, 80, 184

K
Kaya, Okinori, 121, 125, 151, 153, 165, 246, 260
Keenan, Joseph B., 68, 79–81, 83–87, 95, 137–139, 141, 147–151, 185, 186, 195. *See also* Chief Prosecutor (Chief of Counsel) of the Tokyo Tribunal
Kido, Kōichi, and Kido's diaries, 116–118, 133, 134, 146, 151, 153, 154, 166, 167, 193–196, 199–202, 215, 216, 226, 253, 260
Kimura, Heitarō, 144, 151–153, 167, 168, 193, 196, 201, 202, 209, 215, 216, 252, 258–260
Kiyose, Ichiro, 93–95
Kleiman, Samuel J., 96–98, 247
Kodama, Yoshio, 130, 133
Koiso, Kuniaki, 94, 125, 130, 151, 153, 168, 173, 177, 180, 182, 192, 194, 200–202, 215, 216, 253, 260
Konoe, Fumimaro, 122, 127, 133–137, 157, 162–167, 170, 175, 179–182

L
Ladybird, British HMS, and Panay, American USS, 126, 160, 161

INDEX 273

Language Arbitration Board, 50, 51, 104, 230, 266
Laws and customs of war, 12, 14, 16, 18, 29, 31, 201, 202, 207, 216, 217
League of Nations, 25, 127, 128, 157, 170, 179, 180, 191, 199, 204, 205
Legal Affairs Section of the GHQ, 96
Leipzig Trials, 4, 17, 31
Liebert, John, 234, 246, 267
Logan, William, 256

M

MacArthur, Douglas, 7, 8, 9, 45, 66, 67, 79, 85–87, 138. *See also* Supreme Commander for the Allied Powers
Manchukuo, 129, 157, 159, 163–165, 171, 182, 183, 250
Mansfield, Alan, 81, 256
Marco Polo Bridge Incident, 104, 129, 134, 148, 150, 159, 194, 234, 253
Marshal of the Court, 52, 107, 108, 110, 111, 113, 239
Matsui, Iwane, 77, 126, 147, 151, 153, 169, 170, 180, 182, 193, 194, 199, 200, 202, 203, 215, 216, 227, 228, 253, 260
Matsuoka, Yōsuke, 93, 126–128, 151, 153, 170, 179, 184, 193–197, 200, 202, 203, 215, 216
McDougall, E. Stuart, judge from Canada (or the Canadian judge), 55, 67
Meada, Tamon, 247
Mei, Ju-ao, judge from China (or the Chinese judge), 38, 55, 63–65, 81
Mens rea ('guilty mind'), 27, 29

Minami, Jirō, 126, 151, 153, 171, 180, 182, 192, 202, 203, 216, 227, 231, 246, 250, 253, 260
Ministry of War (or War Ministry) of Japan, 46, 47, 116, 126, 131, 171, 176, 177, 179–181, 201, 216
Moscow Conference of Foreign Ministers in 1945, 6, 8
Mukden Incident, 125–127, 135, 150, 157–159, 171, 174, 175, 179, 180, 194, 216
Mutō, Akira, 151, 153, 171–173, 180, 209, 260

N

Nagano, Osami, 93, 117, 127, 151, 153, 172–174, 184, 193, 195, 196, 201, 202, 215, 216
Nanking Massacre, 56, 77, 126, 147, 148, 160, 169, 170, 227, 236, 250
Northcroft, E. Harvey, judge from New Zealand, 46, 55, 67, 255
Nyi, Judson T.Y. (Ni Zhengyu), 84, 145

O

Official position, 30, 188
Oka, Takazumi, 151, 153, 173, 174, 260
Ōkawa, Shūmei, 93, 130, 151, 153, 157, 158, 160, 174, 175, 179, 184
Opening statement, 43, 68, 86, 219, 220
Orders of the superior, 30
Ōshima, Hiroshi, 134, 151, 153, 175, 176, 179, 260

P

Pacific War, 47, 57, 67, 121, 123, 124, 127, 134, 135, 153, 164–166, 168, 172, 173, 177, 178, 180–182, 213, 215, 216
Pact of Paris (or the Kellogg-Briand Pact), 23–26, 197, 199, 205
Pal, Radhabinod, judge from India (or the Indian judge), 21, 22, 43, 55
Patrick, Lord William Donald, judge from the UK (or the UK judge), 55, 61, 67
Peace Treaty with Japan in San Francisco, 115, 120
Pearl Harbour attack, 8
Potsdam Declaration, 6–8, 39, 78, 119, 124, 138, 189
President of the Tokyo Tribunal, 55, 61, 65–67, 80, 100
Prosecution, 3, 35, 40, 43, 45, 46, 50, 67, 69, 70, 72, 76, 78, 79, 81, 83–86, 95, 98, 101, 103–105, 109, 114, 117, 138, 139, 143–147, 152, 153, 167, 184, 185, 187, 189, 208–211, 220, 221, 225, 227, 228, 230, 231, 233–238, 240, 246, 247, 249, 254, 256, 258–260, 263–265, 267
Provost Marshal, 107, 110–113
Puyi, Emperor of the puppet Manchukuo, 50, 104, 226, 231, 234, 236, 242, 246, 249–251, 253, 267

Q

Quorum, 41, 60

R

Raginsky, M.Ю., 60, 84, 185, 186
Re-cross-examination, 50, 239–241, 252, 253
Re-direct examination, 50, 239–241, 251–253
Review of the judgement, 10, 44, 105
Richardson, James, 234, 253, 267
Röling, B.V.A., judge from the Netherlands (or the Dutch judge), 55
Rozenblit, С.Я., 60, 84, 185, 186
Rules of Procedure, 41, 42, 67, 88, 89, 99, 144, 219, 222, 234, 237, 239, 241, 249, 255, 256, 261, 267

S

Saionji-Harada Memoirs, 226
Saionji, Kinmochi, 134, 135, 146, 226
Satō, Kenryō, 131, 151, 153, 176, 180, 209, 252, 260
Seating arrangement of the bench, 61, 66
Secretariat, 41, 47, 101–103, 107, 108, 228
Shidehara, Kijurō, 68, 135
Shigemitsu, Mamoru, 7, 144, 145, 151–153, 177, 183, 192, 193, 195, 200–202, 215, 216, 252, 258–260
Shimada, Shigetarō, 121, 124, 136, 151, 153, 174, 178, 193, 196, 202, 215, 216, 253, 260, 262
Shiratori, Toshio, 126, 151, 153, 176, 178, 179, 260
Single-head system, 79–81, 86, 139
Smith, David F., 33, 68, 69, 89, 100, 263
Soviet Union Group of the prosecution, 81, 83

Special Proclamation for the Establishment of the Tokyo Tribunal, 36
Sugamo Prison, 45, 110–113, 125, 127, 132, 133, 136, 137, 140–142, 152, 154, 235, 258
Supreme Commander for the Allied Powers, 6, 8–10, 36, 39, 40, 44, 45, 48, 53, 55, 56, 59, 63, 67, 74–76, 79, 119, 139
Suzuki, Teiichi, 68, 95, 121, 125, 151, 153, 179–181, 193, 194, 196, 197, 199–202, 215, 216, 260

T
Takayanagi, Kenzo, 68, 95
Tanaka, Ryukichi, 126, 234, 238, 246, 249, 253, 267
Tani, Hisao, 77
Tavenner, Frank, 81, 83, 85
Tempting the witness, 143, 237
Tōgō, Shigenori, 51, 121, 125, 151, 153, 180, 181, 260
Tōjō, Hideki, 93, 94, 106, 117, 122–124, 126, 130, 135, 136, 150, 151, 153, 164, 165, 168, 169, 173–175, 177–182, 252, 253, 260
Translation work, and the Translation Section, 103–105
Treaty of Versailles, 2, 3, 26, 31

U
Umezu, Yoshijirō, 7, 94, 144, 145, 151–153, 177, 180, 182, 183, 192–194, 199–202, 215, 216, 238, 252, 258–260
Uzawa, Somei, 93

V
Vasiliev, Nicolai, 81, 84
Voting by the judges, 41, 72, 109

W
Wang Len-Chai, 104, 234, 253
War of aggression (or aggressive war), 11, 12, 21–27, 29, 30, 35, 36, 46, 117, 120, 134, 136–138, 145, 146, 149, 150, 153, 160, 164, 165, 167, 169, 170, 173, 174, 180, 188, 191–195, 208, 211–213, 215, 227, 247
Webb, Sir William, 44, 55, 57, 63–69, 86, 95, 185, 256, 257. *See also* President of the Tokyo Tribunal
Wilde, Cyril, 234, 246, 253, 267
Witnesses, 40–43, 48, 68–70, 72, 78, 83–85, 88, 94, 95, 103, 104, 107, 108, 114, 139, 143, 145–148, 184, 219–222, 225, 226, 233–241, 243–248, 250–253, 255–258, 260, 262–267
World War I, 2, 4, 26, 37, 57, 173
World War II, 1, 2, 4, 11, 12, 15, 17–19, 28, 31, 35, 37, 38, 46, 56, 57, 99, 136, 147, 149, 213, 255

Y
Yamaoka, George C., 95
Yamashita, Tomoyuki, 112, 121, 125, 172
Yokohama Trials, 77
Yokota, Kisaburo, 103

Z
Zaryanov, Ivan Michyevich, judge from the Soviet Union (or the Soviet Union judge, the Soviet judge), 55, 57, 73

Printed in the United States
by Baker & Taylor Publisher Services